MINDTRAPS
Unlocking the Key to Investment Success

Roland Barach, Ph.D.

with Foreword by:

Van K. Tharp, Ph.D.

Van K. Tharp Associates
8303 Belgium Street
Raleigh, NC 27606

Production Manager: Donald J. Ryan
Jacket Design: Sprecher Design House
Layout and design: Craig Conley
Typeface: Cloister
Printer: BookCrafters

Publisher: Van K. Tharp Associates
           International Institute of Trading Mastery, Inc.
           8308 Belgium Street
           Raleigh, NC 27606
           Phone: 919-362-5591   FAX: 919-362-6020
           Internet: http://www.prosperity-club.com/iitm

ISBN 0-935219-07-2

Dedicated to the memory of my parents who would have been proud, to my wife who is, and to my children whom I hope will be.

Acknowledgments

Without the help of many people, this book would have remained merely an idea. I gratefully acknowledge their assistance. Susie Anschell provided excellent editorial help and advice. Barry Alberstein helped with all computer issues and made many helpful comments, and when he reads the entire book, I am sure he will make many more. Le Roy Beach kept me from making egregious errors by reviewing the cognitive chapters, and any errors that remain in those chapters are of course mine. Most important, I want to acknowledge the assistance of my wife, Decky Fiedler, for her valuable ideas and editorial assistance and for her encouragement, for the writing time she gave me by taking care of our children, and for her willingness to reread chapters ad nauseam and beyond. Last, the examples and stories come from my personal experiences, the experiences of friends and acquaintances, and clinical cases. For heuristic purposes and to highlight psychology principles, the first-name stories combine the experiences of different people; even though the people are fictitious, the principles, however, are true and applicable.

Roland Barach, Ph.D.

Foreword

by
Van K. Tharp, Ph.D.

If you're reading this book, chances are you've begun the road to real success in the markets. My own research and consulting work with traders and investors has proven that the "mind" is the key factor in investment performance. People could go to hundreds of seminars about the market and still have little or no chance for real success. It was only when they started to work on themselves – to assume that their financial performance had something to do with their beliefs, emotions, and decision making skills – that they saw a real and permanent change in their performance.

I have always said that investors must go through three phases before they can become successful. In the first phase, they are typically looking for someone to tell them what to do. What should I buy in the market now? Should I sell this stock now? At cocktail parties, I'm frequently asked what I think the market is going to do and when it might be time to sell or buy. These are trivial questions, but they are what the average person wants to know. Your chances of making money are much greater if you make your own decisions. But, in order to do that, you must have rules for making those decisions.

Phase two is when a person takes the next step and decides to look for the magic system for making money in the market. In most market circles, phase two is called the search for the "Holy Grail." Most people never find it because of a psychological bias people have to think that the perfect system is one that will signal the perfect entry to the markets.

However, this search can last forever. Software companies now cater to this bias, because current market software gives the investor a lot of indicators that basically answer the question of when to enter the market.

If you apply enough indicators to a set of data, you can perfectly predict the market – at least the historical data to which you applied the indicators. Unfortunately, when you attempt to make decisions with the same indicators on today's markets, you'll find that your ability to predict future prices is dismally inadequate. Suddenly, you're back to square one.

Our research has shown that you can enter the market randomly, letting a coin flip determine whether you are long or short, and still make money. The "Holy Grail" has nothing to do with indicators that tell you when to enter the market. It has to do with 1) how you get out of the market; 2) your money management or asset allocation; and most importantly, 3) your behavior and psychological make-up.

Notice that both phase one and phase two of an investor's progress involve looking outside of oneself for the answers. Phase one looks to another person for information. Phase two looks for the magic system. Both assume that the answer is elsewhere – anywhere but within us.

Interestingly enough, the mythical search for the "Holy Grail" is all about a search for answers that lie within oneself. And, at some point in time, all successful traders and investors eventually realize that their financial rewards are a function of their performance in the market. In other words, whether or not you make money in the market is directly attributable to you. As a result, in phase three they start looking inside themselves for answers on how to be more successful. Hopefully, if you're reading this, you've started the search for the real secrets of investment success. If you are looking inside of yourself, I'm sure you will find the journey most profitable. This book is all about that journey.

The psychology of trading and investing may seem like an obscure topic, but at least one book has appeared on the topic every few years since the 1920s. Most of them have been written by market experts who have just happened to notice that behavior has something to do with market performance. Few of them discuss "psychology" from the perspective of "how to improve your performance" in the markets. Instead, most of them simply talk about how psychology influences markets. And just about all of these books disappear into obscurity in just a few years.

As a result, I was surprised and delighted when Dr. Roland Barach wrote *Mindtraps* in 1988. Psychological researchers had been studying how people made financial decisions for about five years, and Dr. Barach was the first to make that information available to the public.

When *Mindtraps* came out, my response was "This is the best book I've seen to date on the psychology of trading." Several great traders and investors, whom I've coached, also made similar comments. It was that good. But what happened to it? You would occasionally stumble upon a copy in a bookstore for the next year or so, and then it totally disappeared.

In 1992 my firm started selling the books that I recommend to traders and investors who wanted to work on themselves to improve their performance. *Mindtraps* was one of the books I wanted to carry. However, I was informed that it was out of print and that the copyright had reverted back to the author. I self-publish my own books to make sure that they are constantly available, so I thought that the obvious step with *Mindtraps* was to acquire the rights to it and republish it myself. You are reading that new edition now – *Mindtraps: Unlocking the Key to Investment Success*.

Mindtraps refer to psychological obstacles to successful performance.

Dr. Barach lists 88 of them in this marvelous book. These 88 mindtraps include emotional biases, personality flaws, beliefs and attitudes that make winning difficult, and decision making biases that erode the pocket book.

Dr. Barach not only explains the many problems that investors face in dealing with the market, he also offers real, workable solutions. It is a superb book and I am happy to be a part of it.

Some of Dr. Barach's mindtraps are quite situation specific. For example, Mindtrap #16 (Wanting To Hold On To A Stock For Too Long A Time), in the right context, is the perfect frame of mind for a good trend-follower. When a trend-follower opens a position in the market, he or she hopes to hang onto that position forever. If you are such a trend-follower, you simply let the market tell you when the move is over, so you must, by definition, give back some of your profits. However, you must have specific rules to tell you when to get out of the market.

This brings up an important point – how can you best use this book. To begin with, you need a specific methodology for playing the market, including 1) entry rules; 2) rules about when to get out of the market to preserve capital; 3) rules to take profits; and 4) money management or asset allocation rules. If you don't have these four sets of rules, then you are probably the victim of all of Dr. Barach's mindtraps. If this applies to you, Chapter 8 covers goals and action plans and thus will give you a good start.

Unfortunately, most people don't have an adequate system to guide their behavior because of various mindtraps. That's why this book is so important for your progress. Chapters 9 through 14 give excellent information that you should be aware of when you develop a system.

In addition, I've recommended some material at the end of this book that will also help you with system development. Once you have developed a specific system for investing, you need to simply notice what keeps you from following that system. Which mindtraps seem most pertinent? Study them and follow the suggestions that Dr. Barach gives for overcoming them. Self-awareness is a major step in overcoming mindtraps. Once you realize how you are producing your own losses, you can then take the necessary steps to turn your financial future around.

However, I recommend one word of caution. Notice the parts of the book that you most want to skip, saying to yourself, "This area doesn't pertain to me. I don't want to do this now." Those areas may be the most deadly *Mindtraps* for you – the areas about which you are still in denial (See Mindtrap #20 on Denial).

You are starting an exciting journey into the inner world of investing. I am delighted to play a small part in pointing the way for you. If I can be of any assistance to you on your journey, please don't hesitate to give my firm a call. We'd be happy to show you how to get more information or just answer your questions.

Van K. Tharp, Ph.D.
International Institute of Trading Mastery, Inc.
919-362-5591 (phone)
919-362-6020 (fax)
Raleigh, North Carolina

"We Have Met the Enemy and He Is Us" – Pogo

On August 25, 1987 the Dow Jones Industrial Average closed at an all time high of 2,722; on October 2, 1987 the market closed near a respectable 2,640; seventeen days later the market stood at 1,738. This 1,000 point drop wiped out a trillion dollars of investor equity even though no fundamental economic changes occurred or major news stories broke. The economic problems used to explain the crash, and the huge budget and trade deficits, were known for years. In spite of these problems, prior to the crash there was a widely held *perception* that the market would go to 3,000 or 3,600 by the next year and this helped drive the market to its heights. After the crash, it was "obvious" to everyone that the market had been greatly overvalued and was at unsustainable levels. Obviously, economic factors (the outer world) are important for understanding the stock market; however, if the market reacted only to economic information, it would be less volatile and more predictable, but it does not. What produces both the complexity and the challenge of the market is its human elements – perception, emotion and judgment – the inner world. These psychological factors are too often obstacles to stock market success, and investors need to learn ways of overcoming them.

I call these psychological obstacles to stock market success *mindtraps* because they are not due to a lack of intelligence, smart investors are just as susceptible to them as anyone else. Mindtraps are inherent in how we experience emotions, approach life, process information, and make decisions. This fact has generally not been understood by market writers. For example, stock market investors have been warned many times about the dangers of following "the crowd." However, the crowd is not a "them"; it is you and I, and its actions are *typical* of the way people behave. If the crowd is susceptible to misperceptions, makes consistent errors in judgments, or goes to emotional extremes, then these are ways that you and I are inclined to react – and simply willing ourselves not to do so will not be effective. Being a clinical psychologist, I am only too well aware that merely telling someone how to act is not sufficient. For example, most people know what they need to do to improve their lives (go on a diet, exercise more, or stop smoking), but this is not enough to get them to do it. The way to overcome the psychological and emotional mindtraps that prevent success in the stock market is to learn how and why people are prey to such mindtraps and then to practice ways of overcoming them.

That is the basic approach of this book. First, a group of mindtraps are examined, and then ways of overcoming them are covered. Emotions are examined first, since fear and greed are considered the driving forces in the market. They both cause distortions of reality – fear blinds us to opportunity; greed blinds us to danger. At times they operate on us separately, but usually they pull at us simultaneously, and this interaction affects us in ways that are quite troublesome but not intuitively obvious. Other emotions, such as hope, depression, and regret, can take investors on an emotional roller coaster ride that leaves them not only poorer but also emotionally worn out. These emotions, along with the operation of such psychological principles as reinforcement, punishment, vicarious reinforcement, and vicarious punishment, can lead investors to make wrong decisions that seemed all too reasonable at the time they were made.

Idiosyncratic attitudes and actions abound when it comes to money and the stock market. The same person who compares the prices of brands of soup at the grocery store, who would never put down $2 at the race track, borrows money (buys stocks on margin) and invests in the most speculative of stocks. Your neighbor spends months researching stereos, cameras, or even toaster ovens, yet he will put down thousands of hard earned dollars to purchase a stock on the basis of the sketchiest of tips, an item read in the morning paper, or a "feeling" about a company. Making maximum profits is not even the top priority of some investors; they may be more concerned with proving their intelligence or self-worth. No wonder it has been suggested that understanding the market may be the province not only of fundamental and technical analysis but also of psychoanalysis.

The middle section of the book examines irrational attitudes and personality characteristics that often prevent people from taking the actions required for success in the market. For example, some investors block themselves from making sensible market moves by setting impossible expectations for success. Other investors will pressure themselves into rash decisions, while still others are excessively cautious irrespective of market conditions. To avoid such pitfalls, investors must be aware of misleading attitudes and know how to replace them with attitudes that promote success.

We are aware that personality and emotional factors cause problems because we feel them throwing us off-course or see their effects on the actions of others. There are also mistakes from sources that are much different because they are "invincible." They do not interfere with our perceptions or our judgment but instead are inherent in how we make decisions and perceive the world. That is, they are "design flaws." When we make mistakes because of them, we are not doing anything *wrong*. We are operating the way we are supposed to, but our decisions still cause us to lose money. The only way we have come to know about these mindtraps is through psychological research into the decision-making process. Researchers have found that we are "preprogrammed" to make mistakes by unconsciously using rules of thumb which are typically helpful but occasionally very misleading. Knowledge about the design flaws in our decision making cannot only make our otherwise incomprehensible mistakes in the stock market understandable but also prevent us from making them. These mindtraps, along with those involved in prediction, information processing, and risk assessment, are covered in the last section of the book.

It is astonishing how little time and attention we dedicate to actually predicting market outcomes and how often we make decisions in a vague or impulsive manner. We will see how people do very well with certain types of decisions but have great difficulty with the types of decisions needed in the stock market. The way we deal with risk is not rational; we are cautious when we should be daring and are risk-seeking when we should be conservative. The context in which we place investment gains and losses can turn us into reckless plungers, tightfisted Scrooges or nervous Nellies, rather than the rational decision makers that success requires. Once again, these problem areas are not just described; the book also presents ways of overcoming them, including a "probability-making machine" that you can construct and suggestions for developing your own stock market system.

Learning that often we need to act contrary to our "reasonable" impulses is one of the most important and difficult lessons for success in the market. One premise of this book is that the stock market confounds investors because doing the "right thing" often leads to the wrong outcome. Attitudes, actions, and decision-making abilities that typically lead to success in other avenues of life too frequently lead to failure in the market because the market functions according to different rules than those that govern normal life. This is why the market can be so confusing to investors. For example, we are scared when we sense that a situation is dangerous, and it is usually sensible to avoid such situations. But when we are scared is often the right time to buy stocks, because the market *anticipates* the future and looks beyond today's bad news.

This book is the one I wish I had read when I started to invest. It aims at expanding your knowledge of yourself, psychology, and the stock market. It does not offer surefire techniques that will make you rich overnight; these do not exist. But it will make you money by saving you from costly mistakes. Most people learn from their mistakes, but if you are wise, you will learn from the mistakes of others. I hope my readers will use this book wisely.

R. B.

Contents

FEAR ON WALL STREET:

or, "The Sky Is Falling, the Sky Is Falling" – Chicken Little

Look back to the summer of 1982. The economy is in a recession. Such segments as construction are particularly hard hit, and many small businesses are failing. Unemployment is rising. There is serious concern about the survivability of the world banking system. Respected economists are discussing the possibility of a depression. Most financial advisers anticipate continued weakness in the stock market and recommend against investing there. A reasonable person would be cautious at such a worrisome time, concerned with protecting his or her assets, and not risk money in the stock market. Yet it was in this environment that one of the greatest bull markets in history began. Is it any wonder that the stock market confounds reasonable people?

Wall Street wisdom has it that fear and greed rule the markets. Fear and greed do greatly influence investors' decisions; they are mindtraps that repeatedly produce disastrous choices and financial losses. Even though most investors know this, that knowledge rarely protects them. Investors need to learn specific techniques for overcoming emotional obstacles to stock market success. Psychologists regularly study and treat emotional problems such as fear and anxiety. Methods of controlling fears and reining in desires have been developed; but those methods have not been applied to the emotional aspects of investing. Let us see what fear can do to a stock market investor, why people have this troublesome reaction, and how to deal with it.

John Q. Investor has just heard some bad news about the major stock in his portfolio. The stock is in a health care company that has been a favorite of investors. He bought it last week at his broker's recommendation. John Q. bought it at 35 because it had come down from its recent high of 45. The company had an excellent growth record, then it reported flat quarterly earnings. The stock dropped from 35 to 29 in one day as big institutions unloaded it.

John Q. feels terrible about losing his hard-earned money. As he sits in his chair looking over *The Wall Street Journal,* his heart is pounding, his blood pressure is rising, and his muscles are tense. He feels so agitated that he cannot sit still, and he begins pacing back and forth. He is terrified that the stock's price will fall further and more of his money will disappear. He focuses solely on the thought of falling prices, and he can envision nothing but continuing catastrophe ahead. His mind is racing so fast that he cannot rationally evaluate the problem. In fact, he does not want to think about it – he just wishes he had never bought the stock. His fear is so overwhelming that he is driven to act; he tells his broker to sell before the price drops even further. Within a week, the stock bounces back by three points as the sharp drop comes to be viewed as an over-reaction.

Clearly, John Q. overreacted emotionally and this interfered with his ability to rationally assess the situation. In the stock market we have to acquire, evaluate, and integrate a great deal of information. When our adrenaline is flowing and our hearts are pounding, it is difficult to gather, focus on, and then evaluate all of the potentially relevant facts. So why do investors react this way and block themselves from being more successful? To understand this, let us look at a different example of a very frightening situation.

You are on a camping trip in bear country. After swapping scary bear stories around the campfire, you snuggle up in your sleeping bag inside your tent. Suddenly you hear some strange noises out in the woods. Thoughts of huge grizzly bears prowling outside immediately spring to mind. You become alert to sounds that might signal impending danger. Your body mobilizes for action. Adrenaline is pumping, your heart pounds, and perspiration soaks your clothes. Your muscles tense so that you will be able to spring into action at the first sight or sound of an approaching bear.

In both situations a person's body and mind have responded as they typically do to anticipated danger.

1. The person only thinks about the danger and the dangerous aspects of the situation – bears or a stock taking a further nosedive.

2. The person searches the environment for any signs indicating danger – which means that other information is filtered out.

3. The person's body is gearing up so that it can respond to danger the moment it occurs – by fighting or fleeing.

If you are face-to-face with a giant grizzly, reacting this way is very helpful, but when you are facing financial losses, it is not. If a bear is closing in, you act immediately because it would be a fatal mistake to hesitate, but not taking a few minutes to calmly think through a decision may be a fatal financial mistake in the market. There is no survival advantage to dividing our attention and getting a "complete" picture of a physically dangerous situation. Knowing that deer, rabbits, and moose are out there along with the bear does not increase our ability to make it out alive. But taking time to evaluate a company's problems, to determine their consequences for the company's future, to look at the pluses as well as the minuses is required to survive on Wall Street. There is always a tomorrow in the stock market no matter how "bearish" today has been. It is important to take a long-range perspective (measured by months and years), but this is very difficult to do when your body is "screaming" for you to "run for your life."

People's bodies respond to frightening situations in the way they do because we are all born with a set of physiological reactions that occur together to help us cope with physically dangerous situations – by fighting or fleeing. But the fears people experience today are rarely provoked by life-threatening situations. The "dangers" we face tend to be *symbolic* dangers, such as fear of failure, bankruptcy, ridicule, or loss of money. Mankind has not evolved to deal with these "dangers," so our bodies automatically react to them as if a physical danger were present, and this interferes with our ability to think. It is hard to be clear-headed and process complex information rationally when your heart is thumping and you feel blood pounding in your head. In my clinical practice I see too many clients who suffer from such stress-related problems as headaches, ulcers, and hypertension because their bodies keep reacting with the fight or flight response to situations where they can neither fight nor flee. Consequently, they keep their reactions bottled up inside and wear their bodies down. Both on and off Wall Street it is important to perceive situations of minor importance (e.g., losing money on a stock) or of symbolic danger (e.g., embarrassment) for what they are and not to react to them as if they were dangerous and needlessly evoke the fight or flight response.

MINDTRAP #1:
THE STOCK MARKET ORIENTS TO THE FUTURE, WHILE PEOPLE ORIENT TO THE PRESENT; OR, WHY INVESTORS MISS THE MARK ON WALL STREET

It is important to control our fears because the time when we feel most afraid to invest is often the precise time that we should be buying; stock market professionals refer to this as "climbing the wall of worry." This is difficult to do since it runs counter to normal functioning. Ordinarily it is something occurring at present that is dangerous to us, not events that may occur in the future. Thus we avoid a dark, deserted downtown street late at night even though it may become safe the following day. The first rule for understanding the stock market, however, is that it anticipates the future and moves accordingly. The general market is said to anticipate the economy by six to nine months. It does this so well that the Commerce Department uses it as one of the leading economic indicators for predicting future economic growth – and in fact it may be the best of these imperfect indicators.

When we hear the worst news about the economy or a company, it is reasonable for us to feel fearful, expect worse things to follow, and want to avoid the situation; however, the market anticipates the future, so it will respond differently. While this may seem paradoxical, the market often rises when very bad news about the economy is reported because it assumes that the worst news is "out" and it anticipates better times ahead. Unfortunately, the poor individual investor is frightened by the bad news, avoids the market, and misses out. There can be clear financial advantages to purchasing at these times (Dreman, 1982). (This subject will be discussed further in Chapter 4, "Buy High, Sell Low.") Conversely, when long-awaited good news about profits or new products is announced, a stock may actually go down. The anticipated event has happened, and there is nothing else good to expect – hence the stock market adage "Buy on rumor, sell on the news."

Investors are often whipsawed because they are prisoners of their emotional reactions to current events and have difficulty in projecting a different future. In times of prosperity we expect continued prosperity; when inflation is high, we expect it to remain high. Since most people's investments follow their misleading emotions, some market writers advocate a basic strategy of generally investing contrary to the general consensus (Dreman, 1982). This means acting counter to the body's demands and not fleeing – avoiding – the situation but instead calmly assessing it. Since most investors are prisoners of their emotions, they avoid frightening markets and miss out on the best opportunities.

Responding to expectations about the future is in sharp contrast to how people function in most other aspects of life. In fact, it is considered neurotic to always anticipate the future and not live in the present. Psychologists see clients every day who are miserable and stressed out because they are so worried about the future ("what if I lose my job? What if I get sick? What if business turns down?") that they do not enjoy the present. Such clients are reprimanded and told to "stop and smell the roses" instead of being so concerned about the future. This is good advice because there is not much we can do about the "what ifs," about the things that *might* happen in the future. These are events that have not occurred and in all likelihood will not occur, and generally there is nothing that can be done about them until they occur. We can only deal with situations that are occurring now; there is little or nothing we can do about "What if I get sick... get laid off..." six months from now. But to function successfully in the stock market, you have to focus on that uncertain future and be aware that every one else is focusing on it too.

Fear can hinder your ability to make your best decisions through three basic mindtraps. You sell stocks after they have gone down because you fear further declines. You miss buying opportunities because when prices are low you are afraid, and although tempted to buy, you rationalize not acting. You sell early because you are afraid gains in price will disappear. Let us look at some examples of these mindtraps.

MINDTRAP #2:
OVERREACTING TO LOSSES; OR, THE STORIES OF MY STOCK'S DEATH HAVE BEEN GREATLY EXAGGERATED

AC&C is touted as a great opportunity. The company dominates its market and is now geared to move into new, profitable high-tech lines. You buy the stock at $20. It then drops to $16. During this time you read that the company's competitors are eating into its established base. The company doesn't seem to be getting a foothold in new areas, as other companies continue to develop new products and use their reputations to keep AC&C out. You hear that management is having difficulty in adapting to the competition the company is now facing.

Some analysts say the stock could go down to $10. You have already lost 20 percent of your investment; if the analysts are right you will lose half of your money. You feel terrible about buying the stock. You no longer have confidence in this company, and you are scared of even greater losses. You compute the amount you have already lost and how much more you could lose if your stock goes down to $10. Then one day it suddenly drops by 1 1/4. Now you feel really frightened. You see nothing ahead but disaster for this stock. So, angry about the losses you have already suffered and frightened of further ones, you sell the stock.

In time the stock begins edging up. The company is working hard to maintain its old business. Eventually some of its efforts in the new high-tech area begin paying off and start to look good for the future. Your original judgments about the company are turning out to be correct, and the analysts are revising their estimates. The price of AC&C's stock continues to increase since it is now being perceived more positively by money managers who have underinvested in the company. As the stock goes up, people who sold the stock short have to cover their positions and the stock climbs even higher. Eight months later the stock is selling for $24 a share, and some analysts say it may go to 30 within a year.

What caused you to lose money in this situation? When frightened, we are not able to evaluate a situation realistically; instead, *we tend to focus solely on the dangerous aspects* (because if the bear is near, we want to keep our eyes riveted on it). So we do not see the entire situation with both its negatives and positives. When we focus just on the discouraging news about a stock, we perceive the immediate situation as being more dangerous than it is, and the more dangerous it appears to be, the more frightened we feel. We act "reasonably" given our perception of the situation; however, fear has distorted that perception. When your stocks are going down quickly, you may feel that your money is being ripped away from you and that unless you act immediately, nothing will be left. Therefore, instead of taking the time to think about how things might be different in the future, you act immediately to save "what little" if you have left. Even a bearish stock market is like a roller coaster, whose downs we know will be followed by ups; it's not an airplane plummeting straight down. When stocks are falling, it is hard to remember that there is a floor, a price that people see as so cheap that they "have to" buy.

When frightened, we tend to see the present situation as being permanent; however, companies are *dynamic* and not static entities. They respond and adapt to changing business environments (though at times very slowly) in order to maintain and increase profitability. When filled with fear, we find it difficult to remember this and maintain the long-range perspective and patience that successful investing generally requires. When one of your stocks is going down quickly, it is useful to ask yourself whether the assumptions underlying your predictions for the company's future are still valid. If so, then you should maintain your basic long-term projections (even though they may take longer than anticipated to come to fruition).

MINDTRAP #3:
PASSING UP PROFITABLE OPPORTUNITIES WHEN FEELING FRIGHTENED; OR, LEARNING TO CLIMB THE WALL OF WORRY

Trans United is an airline company that has been having problems for many years. It has steadily lost money. Historically, it has had labor problems that have resulted in frequent strikes. It is selling near its yearly low of 10, after dropping from a high of 17. The general expectations for this company are poor. The news about the company is all bad: one of its unions is about to go on strike, the company is heavily in debt, and the strike may cost it a great deal of money. The airline industry is becoming more competitive, resulting in lower fares and profits.

Your own analysis of the situation is that oil prices will soon go down, producing increased profits for Trans United; that peak summer traffic will be greater than expected, because last year was particularly bad for tourism; and that any strike will be short-lived because Trans United's employees have seen the company use strikes as an excuse to bring in new, lower-paid workers. But all you hear about the company is negative. This fans your fear of further decreases in the price of its stock. You wonder why your thoughts on the situation are being ignored. When you think about buying, you feel fear build. You deal with your ambivalence by waiting, and you rationalize your decision by thinking that "the price may go down even further" and then you will buy. During the strike the price shows no further declines. The strike is soon settled, with employees making wage concessions, after which it slowly starts climbing up. Oil prices then drop, which you had expected, and this drives the price up very quickly. The stock goes up $2 in three days, and your chance for a quick 20 percent increase has vanished. You may then forget about the stock, while over the next few months it slowly inches up to $16 a share. You have missed a nice opportunity for profits because of fear and rationalizations.

In this example your fear inhibits you from acting and you rationalize your failure to act by arguing that you will buy "later" at a lower price. This is only fooling yourself, because you have not made a conscious judgment that the price will go lower but instead have come up with this "reason" as a way of avoiding acting. You feel better because you pretend that you have maintained your view, while your rationalization relieves your anxiety. In the future, weed out rationalizations by simply asking yourself, "Is it true that I believe _____ [e.g., the price will go down further], or am I *afraid* that this will happen?"

MINDTRAP #4:
TRACKING YOUR PROFITS INSTEAD OF YOUR STOCKS; OR, NOT KEEPING YOUR EYE ON THE BALL

Hewing & Packing is widely regarded as a well-run high-tech company. Its stock has declined from a high of 46 to 34 as the entire high-technology sector has been in a slump. Difficult times ahead have been forecast for the industry as a whole. You want to buy this stock because it may be cheap, but you are afraid. The economy could continue to decline, and if so, the stock would drop even further. This uncertainty has scared off other investors, resulting in the price drop. This time you take a chance and buy 200 shares of the stock. It drops to 32 and hangs around this price for a while. In time it begins going up as investors start feeling slightly more confident about the economy. The stock goes up to 38 1/4. Sentiment is beginning to change about the company and the economy. The market then goes up in what is described as a "technical adjustment." Hewing & Packing goes up to 39 3/4. The next day it drops one-fourth point, and the day after that it drops one-half point. You own 200 shares of the stock, and you see yourself with a neat $1,000 profit.

You feel great about having made a thousand dollars in a short period of time, and you do not want to lose that profit. You believe that the stock still has considerable potential, but you feel a little shaky about it now because it has gone down in the last couple of days. So to protect your $1,000 profit, you sell. "Nobody ever went broke taking a profit," you tell yourself after the sale. The stock drops a little further over the next couple of weeks, and you congratulate yourself on your stock market acumen. But then the entire market shoots up. The rally is led by the high-tech companies, with Hewing & Packing ahead of the rest. Eventually it goes to over $50 a share.

Your sale of this stock is an example of an arbitrary fear leading to a costly illogical decision. *You produced your own fearful situation* by thinking about a potential lowering of profits below the *arbitrary* figure of $1,000. Because $1,000 is a round amount, we may ascribe greater significance to it than it possesses and thus lose, perspective. That amount seems much more significant than $950 or $989. We would not necessarily sell at those amounts, but we are more likely to sell if the $1,000 figure is threatened.

Moreover, it is a major mistake to relate the amount of our profit, and a fear of loss, to the decision to sell. There is no logical relationship between the amount of our profit or loss in a stock and whether or not this is a good time to sell it. The market forces controlling the price of the stock are not aware of when we bought it, how much we paid for it, and how much profit we stand to make on it. The potential for gain in a stock may continue to exist even if we have made great profits in it already, and there may be no potential in a stock on which we have made a small profit or even sustained a loss. It is a dangerous mindtrap to make a connection between the decision to sell and the fear of a loss or the amount of a profit. This example again points to the importance of calmly examining both the positives and negatives of a situation and basing our decision on these. We should always avoid becoming distracted or excessively upset by irrelevant issues or excessive fears.

The examples given should not imply that every time we are fearful we are wrong. We may be rightfully afraid. There is no way to ensure success in investing, but I can guarantee that you will do the best you are capable of when you minimize your fear so that it does not interfere with your reasoning. The ability to do this is a quality we expect from experts in their fields. Airline pilots earn high salaries, not because their day-to-day work is so difficult, but because years of experience allow them to remain calm when facing frightening situations. This is the goal for all of us – to be able to keep our emotions in check while facing potentially dangerous situations. Ways to do this will be covered next.

GAINING CONTROL OVER YOUR EMOTIONS

So far, we have discussed fear and how it affects us both in life and in the stock market. Now let us move to the topic that *really* interests you: How can this help you make money?

Here are a number of steps that will lessen the impact of your emotions on your judgment. (Some of these steps have already been mentioned in the mindtraps covered but will now be discussed at greater length.)

1. Writing down your thoughts and feelings.

2. Focusing on facts and ferreting out rationalizations.

3. Writing down a description of the situation.

4. Compiling a list of the pros and cons of the situation.

5. Developing perspective on the situation.

6. Trying to anticipate how the future could be different from the present.

Writing Down Your Thoughts and Feelings

To control your emotions, you must first know what they are. The first step in this process is to *write down* as best you can how you think and feel about the situation. This does not have to be more than a quick line or two. "I am afraid the stock will go even lower." "I am afraid the market is headed for a tumble." "I am afraid of losing even more money on this stock." "I am afraid of what my wife will do when she hears about how much money I have lost so far." Put down what you really feel, since your feelings do influence you and writing them down will allow you to get a grip on them. Write, for example, that you feel that "all of my money will be gone" or that "I will look like a fool because the experts recommend the opposite of what I think" or that "the stock will keep going down and I will never get my money back."

Throughout this book I will urge you to write things down. Doing this is important. Years of clinical experience have shown that when things get said "out loud" (which includes writing), they do not seem as bad or feel as terrible as when they are rattling around in our minds. We perceive situations more realistically when they are articulated, and this is why articulating them makes them seem less terrible – because we find out that in reality they are not as terrible as we thought they were. For example, ruminating about money lost can be emotionally devastating until the situation is brought out into the open. Then you can realistically appraise the situation, see that it is not the end of the world to lose money in the stock market, that you are neither the first nor the last to have done it, and that you are reacting as if you had lost a limb or a loved one instead of just money.

You may think, "Writing things down makes sense, but I do not have to do that. It takes time, and I know how I feel." Or, "Writing things down makes sense for other people, but I do not have to do it." If this is so, you are falling into another mindtrap, namely *arrogance*. It is easy for us to believe we are more capable and competent than is the case. This subject is covered in later chapters on intellectual limitations and how people tend to overestimate their abilities, so for the time being I urge you to give the suggestions a try and to see whether they benefit you.

Focusing on Facts

Whenever we are making any decision, it is important to base it on the facts of the situation, as best we know them. In life it is easy to be misled by our rationalizations, hopes, or fears. If a stock is down, we want to believe that it will go back up; however, by basing our decision on the facts, we may be able to save ourselves from worse losses. A simple technique for honing in on the facts of a situation is to ask yourself questions like these:

> "What precisely has occurred?"
> "Is there any evidence that ... will happen?"
> "How do I know ...?"

It is on the basis of your answers to such questions that your decision should be made.

Writing Down a Description of the Situation

Write a brief "objective" statement of what is going on with the stock. This statement can be as simple or elaborate as you feel like making it. "The stock has dropped 15 percent in the last week after reports of huge second-quarter losses. . . . It is not a highly recommended stock. . . . Sentiment is against the stock. . . . The company is an average performer in its industry group. . . . It is financially sound. It has been consolidating its market for the last few years Management has been in a state of transition, bringing in new executives from other companies. . . . The company is in a highly competitive industry. . . . A quicker turnaround was expected for this company than has occurred. . . . The company has been well regarded in the past. . . . Poor decisions by previous management contributed to the problems it is now facing…"

With a descriptive statement in front of you, you have a body of information to review and think about. A written statement will provide you with a base of information from which to make judgments that is more consistent and larger than the jumble of ideas that pop into and out of your mind.

Compiling a list of the Pros and Cons of the Situation

From your description of the situation, make up a list of the positive and negative factors. Remember that when you feel scared, your emotions will always be pushing you to immediately get away from the "dangerous" situation. Your thoughts will be gravitating toward the negatives of the situation. You will therefore want to focus your thinking as much as possible on emphasizing the positive elements of the situation. Two columns labeled "positives" and "negatives" on the same sheet of paper can serve this purpose very well.

Positives	Negatives
Economy will continue to grow	Competitors very strong
New management in place	Company has not proven itself
Stable company	More bad news may emerge
Changes could pay off soon	Experts expect bad results
New efficiencies in place	Interest rates could go up
Bad news already accounted for	
Good dividend	

Review what you have written. Look at all the aspects of the situation. Then put the material down for a while and review it again later. A few minutes of thoughtful consideration will not cost you very much, but a rash decision could be very expensive.

Developing Perspective on the Situation

Whenever we are too close to a situation, we lose perspective on it. Since we are inherently close to daily events, it is easy to make mountains out of such molehills as today's stock market fluctuations. Fear leads us to narrow our focus even further. In order to overcome this mindtrap, we need to force ourselves to always broaden our perspective. This involves (1) enlarging our time perspective and (2) thinking in a larger economic and financial framework.

Almost all the things we usually get upset about, we have forgotten a week later. I use this fact clinically to help people reduce their stress. When they are feeling upset about an incident, they are supposed to ask themselves whether they will even remember the incident, let alone be concerned about it, a month later. If the answer is no then why be so upset about it now? If you are investing for the long haul, then you need to remember that you plan to hold your stock or mutual fund for a few years. During those years you have to expect occasional and at times extensive reverses. Every road up a mountain has some downturns, and the market does not go up in a straight line either. To maintain your perspective, you need to keep your eye on the mountain top, see how far you have come, and appreciate the ups and downs that you still have to traverse in order to get there.

It is important to have some expectations about market trends, including a time frame and price potentials on a stock or the overall market because these may follow not only a circuitous route but a torturous route. Stock market advisers state that corrections of 8-10 percent may not indicate a change in an overall upward trend. Even larger corrections can occur within the context of a long-term bull market. If you believe that it may take a couple of years for a stock or the general market to show good appreciation, then you won't be as upset by short-term declines because you can place them within the context of a larger picture.

Without a long-term perspective you cannot assess whether a stock is cheap, expensive, or reasonably priced. If you think that a bear market has started and you expect it to continue, a stock selling at $50 that previously sold for as high as $75 may appear cheap but is expensive, because, if your long-range perspective is correct, it will sell for only $25 in time. Conversely, a stock that has gone from $60 to $80, but that you expect to continue to rise for a few years, may appear expensive but is cheap compared to a future price of, say, $150.

In the stock market you always need a yardstick to understand what is going on. A 100-point drop in the Dow may seem like a lot by itself, but compared to the total value of the market it may be only a 2 percent decrease. To maintain perspective, we need to place the amount of change in some larger framework. If you believe that the market is in for a large bull move soon, a 2 percent change is unimportant; however, if you are investing in short-term options, then a 2 percent move can be very significant. In summary, in order to cope with fear, you must keep in mind a broad perspective on market trends and you must see changes as percentages of total amounts and not as absolute values (more on this in Chapter 13, "Assessing Risk and Reward").

Anticipating a Different Future

We can all describe and react to what is happening in front of us. You know a recession is occurring when corporate profits are coming down, the market is heading lower, and unemployment is rising. The difficult task is to anticipate what will happen in the future and to see that in time the economy will improve, profits will increase, and the stock market will head higher. This sounds easy to do, but investors have difficulty in doing it. What could help expand your awareness is to write down different scenarios for the future – both positive and negative. In the middle of a recession, for example, you might jot this scenario down: "The economy continues to get worse, but in time interest rates will come down and pent-up demand will build to spark a recovery." Another scenario might be: "The economy continues to get worse because of governmental policies and we will head into a depression." What is important is to identify a different future and the factors that could bring it about. Once you have a list of those factors, you want to be on watch for clues to their occurrence. Then, based on all the information you have, evaluate the likelihood of a scenario's occurrence. We all know what we should have done; in this way you can anticipate what to do. To do well in the market, you need to see things that others do not see, and that requires effort.

If you follow through on the above steps, you will not always be right in your judgment. But focusing on the facts, writing them down, evaluating both sides of the issue, keeping a broad perspective, and learning to anticipate the future will help control your fears. This will lead to more rational, and therefore better, decisions. More rational decisions will always enhance your performance, and they will allow you to feel more in control of your financial destiny.

CONTROLLING YOUR BODY'S REACTIONS

If you are feeling so frightened that you can't follow through with the recommended steps, then it is necessary to calm yourself down sufficiently to start thinking clearly.

Try the following one-minute relaxation exercise to calm down so that you can get to the task at hand. Feel free to make any adjustments in the exercise that fit your personal situation and increase the amount of relaxation you experience.

1. Shake the tension out of your body. You may have seen professional athletes shake their hands, arms, or legs before they compete. Do the same thing and shake what feels tense to you – arms, legs, neck, head, or shoulders.

2. Take five slow, deep breaths, and as you inhale, say to yourself, "I am..." and as you exhale, say, "...relaxing."

3. For the next three breaths, concentrate on your breathing. Feel the coolness of your breath as you inhale and its warmth as you exhale. Notice the warmth and relaxation in your body as you exhale – particularly how your stomach muscles relax with each and every breath.

4. Smile, even inwardly to yourself, and think about how silly it is for your body to get so excited about this situation. There are no actions that it can take, and it is only harming you to get so agitated. Smiling at a situation will usually allow you to get a quick perspective on it, and this is almost always reassuring. Things are not as bad as they feel.

5. Last, in your mind's eye picture yourself sitting down and calmly evaluating the situation you are facing. See yourself handling the situation in the best, most constructive way. For some people it is helpful to first imagine how someone they admire would handle the situation and then to picture themselves handling it in the same way.

This exercise might be helpful anytime you are under stress, not just when you are making stock market decisions. The more you use it, the more effective and powerful it will become.

In summary, there are many life situations in which we feel frightened. Youngsters are often scared when they leave home for the first time. Serious illness in ourselves, our families, or our friends is frightening. Making such major life decisions as getting married, changing jobs, or moving away from familiar and safe surroundings can be disturbing. There is nothing wrong with having fears about these matters. In fact, such fears can protect us from danger and drive us toward action. Emotions are a problem anytime they are inappropriate to the situation or so strong that they interfere with rational judgment. (This can be true even for love – passion has led to many poor decisions and regretful mornings.) Mankind has not yet evolved to deal with the "dangers" of modern life, and our emotional reactions hinder us from doing so. By taking a number of steps to defuse our emotions and expand our awareness, we can improve our ability to deal with them.

GREED:

or, Bulls and Bears Do Fine,
Only Pigs Get Slaughtered

Greed is all right, by the way. I want you to know that. I think greed is healthy. You can be greedy and still feel good about yourself. — *Ivan F. Boesky* *

For a short period of time in California during 1980, you could not avoid hearing stories about pyramid clubs. At work, on buses, or from persons trying to entice you to join a pyramid club, you heard tales of people who had just made $16,000 by doing so. Eventually, between 50,000 and 100,000 Californians became involved in this scam. Typically cautious individuals would go to their banks and pull out $1,000 in cash, which they would later hand over to strangers whom they met surreptitious in homes, restaurants, and even deserted warehouses. They did this in the hope that they would soon reach the top of a pyramid and have $16,000 handed to them.

The basic scheme of a pyramid is like that of a chain letter. The thousand dollars puts you at the bottom of a pyramid along with 31 other people. You give $500 to the person above you, who recoups the $1,000 he or she put in initially, and the other $500 goes to the person at the top of the pyramid, who gets a total of $16,000. All the persons at the bottom of the pyramid need to find new people to put in $1,000 so that they can move up the pyramid until they reach the top and get their $16,000.

*Commencement speech, School of Business Administration, University of California, Berkeley, l985. Cited in *Newsweek*, December 1, 1986.

Why did people play this "game"? Because they were overcome by greed and the dollar signs they saw before their eyes. They focused exclusively on the $16,000 windfall that they expected to be theirs. They were certainly not looking at the entire scheme and thinking about what was required for it to work. If you take a moment to compute what is necessary to reach the top of a pyramid, you will discover that for each of the new participants to do so, 4,096 new players must be brought in. How many of these people, most of whom lost their $1,000, would have played if they had made this simple calculation?

Both fear and greed cause distortions in our perceptions of situations. *Fear blinds us to opportunity; greed blinds us to danger.* Fear fills our minds with frightening possibilities; greed fills them with fantasies of wealth. Strong feelings – be they greed, fear, or passion – blind us from seeing and reacting to the total picture. We do not think about potential dangers or problems when we are consumed with a burning desire for great amounts of easily attainable money. This leads to trouble because if we develop tunnel vision and see only the positive elements in a situation, we are blind to the negative elements.

Greed is such a well-known stock market mindtrap that a Greed Index has been developed to warn investors of potentially dangerous markets (see Figure 2-1). When the market is high, the desire for even greater gains sucks people in. They are oblivious to the danger of a major decline because they are fixated on making money. As the market continues to climb, the reasonable profits with which they were initially happy are no longer enough for them. It is as if a voice inside yelling "More! More! More!" were pushing them to take greater chances and become involved in riskier investments – which of course have greater potential for losses.

Greedy people have *no patience,* and their desire is fueled by good economic news and ever higher stock prices. Since the stock market

FIGURE 2-1

Greed Index, Often On Target, Sees Upturn Soon Despite Investor Fears

By RICHARD E. RUSTIN

Worried about the chances of worse trouble in the Persian Gulf, major bank failures, soaring interest rates and a return of inflation – and what these might do to an already sour stock market? Not to worry. The Greed Index says that the market already has discounted such horrors, and that the next major price move should be upward, soon.

Despite its flippant name, the Greed Index has proven a remarkably prescient barometer of the market during the past 16 years. It's prepared by Lee H. Idleman, currently executive vice president and research director at Dean Witter Reynolds. (On Friday, Mr. Idleman will join Neuberger & Berman as a partner and research director.)

Consisting of 10 factors, graded 1-to-10, it measures certain statistics and the confidence – or lack thereof – of a cross-section of pros who move the market: financial institutions, money managers and corporate financiers. When their the confidence gets really high, so does the "greed factor," the stock market and the index – "and that's the time to sell," says Mr. Idleman.

Not surprisingly, the index currently is at 31 and nearing its record low of 25 set in August 1970, making it something of a Fear Index as well.

Though the index is depressed, Mr. Idleman asserts that's anything but depressing. Says he: "People are getting more and more terrorized, and that's the best time to buy stocks. I don't think we're going to need much more (downward pressure on the index). The market is pretty attractive. If you want to be a contrary opportunist, you're going to make a lot of money."

Historically, when the index dipped below 30, a major market upturn was just around the corner. That happened right after the 1970 record low, and it occurred again in December 1974, when the index read 28, February 1978 (26) and June 1982 (29).

Source: *The Wall Street Journal*, May 29, 1984.

anticipates the future, it often tops out when the economy is booming. In fact, the failure of the market to rise on good news is considered a dangerous sign by many market watchers. But at such times some market advisers will predict that stock prices will continue to climb. (Have you noticed that, regardless of the market's position, if it has been going up, there is always someone who is ready to predict that it will go 10 percent higher, and if it has been going down, there is always someone who believes that it could still drop another 10 percent?) Investors with money burning a hole in their pockets won't evaluate the situation to see whether this is a good time to buy or a good time to wait. They rush in and buy now because they *feel* that "this is the only chance" they will have, and they buy whatever is recommended. This is why greed causes some people to buy at the top, where less excited and more successful investors are more than happy to sell to them. (More will be said on this in Chapter 4, "Buy High, Sell Low.")

Next we will look at how greed traps us in the stock market through our constant desire for more, our unbridled desire for riches, our envy of the success of others, or our expectations of unlimited success.

MINDTRAP #5:
HOLDING ON TILL YOU GET YOUR PRICE; OR, WAITING FOR GODOT

Greed can ruin people's lives in ways other than financial. For example, Jim has gone out with many wonderful women; unfortunately, none of them was ever quite perfect. Each had some flaw, so Jim would drop her for another woman who in time would also be replaced because she too lacked something. If Judy was beautiful, she wasn't as smart as Jane; if Kim was beautiful and smart, she didn't have Judy's sense of humor. If Maddie was beautiful and smart and also had a sense of humor, she wasn't as young as Melissa. In essence, when it came to women, Jim was greedy. He wanted one person to possess everything he desired in a woman before committing himself to marriage. Not surprisingly, Jim has waited for such a person his entire life and has wound up a lonely old bachelor.

Jim often has the same problem with stocks as he has had with women. He buys a stock at $50 and it goes up to $73. Jim thinks that it will soon be up to $75 and then he will sell. Instead, it drops to $69, at which point he swears that as soon as it hits $73, he will sell. But then it drops to $65, so now $69 looks good and Jim says he will let go of it when it gets back to that. As the stock continues its jagged downward course, Jim always plans to sell it at the previous higher price. He keeps staying a step behind in his expectations about the right price to sell until the stock reaches $50, when he sells so he won't "lose any money on it."

It seems that people who buy or sell something that does not have an unequivocally fixed price often feel dissatisfied with the price they pay or receive. Many of the people I know believe that they overpaid when they bought their house and that they could have gotten more when they sold it. Since the agreed-upon price had been met, they found it easy to believe that there was still room to push that price. The price of a stock is constantly equivocal – a stock is worth whatever someone is willing to pay for it at a given moment. But because stock prices are printed in the paper, it is easy to see them as being more permanent than they are and therefore to wait for a particular stock price to reappear, when in fact it may never do so.

MINDTRAP #6:
WANTING TO GET RICH QUICK; OR,
WHY "YOU CANNOT CHEAT AN HONEST MAN" (W. C. FIELDS)

George has inherited $5,000 from a grandaunt. This pleases him, but he wants considerably more money. When he becomes rich, he will have the fancy houses and cars and the company of attractive women that he desires. He gets interested in stocks as a vehicle for getting rich, and he reads a number of popular books on the stock market. The books are full of stories about people who claim to have increased their money tenfold in the market. He is convinced that he will become one of them. Visions of quickly multiplying his inheritance begin to fill his mind. He feels really good when he pictures himself as rich and successful. In his spare time he calculates how much money he will have as he piles one successful stock market move on top of another. With a large amount of money, he will finally be able to have the things he wants.

To get rich as quickly as he wants to, George will have to leverage his money. Mutual funds and individual stock selections are too slow for him. There is that huge pile of money to be made, and he needs it now. So George decides that the best way to get it is through stock market options, which for a small amount of money would enable him to control a large number of shares for limited periods of time. He calculates ways in which a mere 10 percent increase in a stock price could double his money. If a stock really moves, he could do even better: even a tenfold increase would be possible. Since George's nest egg is $5,000, the first time it doubles he will have $10,000 and the next time, $20,000. If he does that two more times, he will have $80,000 – money that he can really begin multiplying. He sees himself becoming a millionaire in a relatively short period of time.

To get high returns quickly, George invests in very volatile issues. These can go up quickly, which is all George thinks about, but they can go down just as quickly, which he does not consider at all. Since he is convinced that he will be very successful, he purchases large amounts of options. At first, he is right a few times and makes some money. This strengthens his desire to plunge into the market. He then starts losing, and he cannot understand how this could happen to him. He decides it is just "bad luck." Since he is now losing money, it is clear that to get back on his moneymaking schedule, he will have to make even larger purchases. His selections are right some of the time, but usually they do not pan out. George has a ready explanation for each loss and why it won't happen next time. Very quickly he is down to only a few hundred dollars. He decides to invest in the most speculative position he can find, and the last of his $5,000 is quickly wiped out.

George became infatuated with the fantasy of becoming rich. Thinking about it made him feel good. Why should he consider potential problems if this would only keep him from reaching his goal? Negative vibes will only get in your way, according to some of George's self-help get-rich-quick books. But it is not easy to double your money regularly. George was competing with people who traded options as a full-time job, while he was inexperienced and doing it as a sideline. Certainly, the professionals in this area do not double their money in the way George fantasizes he would. But he did not think about the potential problems and dangers when he was filled with greed for all the money that could soon be his.

The books George read had so many examples of people getting rich that George came to see himself as doing the same (which is often the intent of such books). After all, the investors in the books were no better than he is (which is something else that many of such books imply). Books of this kind make little mention of the dangers or problems associated with the strategies they describe because doing so would get in the way of the easy roads to riches that they are promoting. A common theme of many "motivational" programs is to have people focus on the object of their desire: "Imagine the goal – picture it – tell yourself every day that you will achieve it." While this may motivate people, it also leaves them open to losses from bad plans and choices.

Since George felt so confident after reading his get-rich-quick books, he never tried any of their schemes out on paper before risking his money. While playing the market on paper is not the same as risking your money, much can be learned from doing this. For instance, George would have learned in this way that if the recommended techniques were as easy to use as they were said to be, then everyone would be using them. But do not dismiss George and his naiveté too quickly. We disparage get-rich-quick schemes, but we are all vulnerable to their appeal – they touch the greed in all of us. Who would turn down instant, effortless wealth? Lotteries, sweepstakes, penny stocks, and dishonest promotions are successful only because of our own desires and fantasies. W. C. Fields is well known for the statement "You can't cheat an honest man." No honest man will be lured by greed into shady deals. It is also probably true that you cannot cheat a person who is looking for an "honest" profit, since such a person will be keeping his eyes open and will examine the entire financial picture. It is when we are looking for the "dishonest" large return that greed blinds us to the dangers involved. At such times we forget the famous admonition that warns us, "If it is too good to be true, then it probably is."

George's problems with greed were relatively small in scale. A good example of greed on a very large scale is the well known insider trading scandal involving Wall Street investor Ivan Boesky and others. Their actions were certainly a case, not of a need-driven crime, but of a greed-driven crime. Ivan Boesky was already a very rich man when he became involved in illegal insider trading activities. He owned a 200-acre estate outside New York City, Rolls-Royces, impressionist paintings, and all the other trappings of great wealth. But his "passion has been money. Speaking of the sum of $500 million, . . . [he stated,] 'Imagine it in one-dollar bills, or better yet, in a pile of silver dollars. I wonder how tall that would be . . . A Jacob's ladder of silver dollars. Imagine – wouldn't that be an aphrodisiac experience, climbing to the top of such a ladder?'" *(The Wall Street Journal,* November 17, 1986).

Boesky is different from most of us in the extent of his greed, but the basic difference is not quantitative but qualitative. This is a good example of why you cannot cheat an honest man. The honest man, like the dishonest man, feels greed, but he sticks to certain standards. It is the willingness to abandon those standards that makes some people different and criminals, and it is the willingness to abandon standards of prudence and reasonable expectations of profits that can cause the financial downfall of the average investor.

MINDTRAP #7:
BREAKING THE 10TH COMMANDMENT; OR, COVETING THY NEIGHBOR'S HOUSE, WIFE, AND PORTFOLIO OF SUCCESSFUL STOCKS

The stock market has rocketed up during the last year. Friends of yours have doubled or even tripled their investments in over-the-counter stocks. All of your savings are in certificates of deposit or money market funds, earning minimal interest. As you hear about your friends' results, you contemplate how much money you would now have if you had purchased those stocks. You feel that your friends are winning in the race of life, while you are falling further and further behind. Besides, if your money had doubled or tripled during the last year, you could start living the way you really want. Your greed is tickled by the desire to have what acquaintances have. For most of us, this desire results in minor problems. It led to major problems for Martin Siegel, another convicted Wall Street insider, who was partially led into his dealing with Boesky because he "had become awed by the vast wealth he saw Mr. Boesky amassing" (*The Wall Street Journal*, February 17, 1987). Siegel's greed was fueled by a desire so old and dangerous – "coveting thy neighbor's riches" – that one of the Ten Commandments warned against it. Not adhering to that commandment can easily lead us to lose money. This will become apparent as we follow through with our example.

After you have heard about a friend who has done fabulously well in the market, another friend lets you know about one of his new investments and tells you how to get in on it. You can buy stock in Computer Widgets International, a company that is going public. Friends who have been making lots of money in the market tell you that this stock could easily double or triple in price over the next 18 months. There is an exceptionally large potential market for widget chips since all major computer manufacturers could use them to expand the capacity of their systems. Computer Widgets International now has little earnings and considerable debt, but this is not important, because the concept is great and the potential seems unlimited.

As you hurry to invest all of your money in the stock, hoping that you will not be shut out from this great buy, you envisage finally doing as well as your friends. You are already thinking about ways to spend the money you will make. Luckily, you are able to purchase all the shares you want. Over the next few months the price of the stock goes up and you feel wonderful, thinking that it will soon skyrocket as orders for those widget chips come flowing in. Then it starts slipping, but this is not a problem, because within 18 months it will surely at least double. Suddenly it skids to a new low in a week's time. It is going down so fast that you can hardly catch your breath to evaluate the situation. You then read that some Japanese companies are gearing up to produce the very same widget chips. Computer Widgets International claims that this is an infringement of its patents, but the claim is disputed. You do not sell the stock now because if you did, you would lose a considerable amount of money. Its price continues to drop as some large American computer companies announce that they are planning to develop their own widget chips for use with their computers. Computer Widgets International is too small to compete with these companies, and its sales dry up. In time Computer Widgets International files for Chapter 11 bankruptcy and all of your money is gone.

The investment adage "The greater the risk, the greater the reward" needs to be reversed when greed is operating. At such times, when wishful thinking is blocking out negative information and just allowing pleasant ideas to enter our minds, we need to remember that the greater the reward, the greater the risk, and to focus on the risky possibilities. You focused on the fact that Computer Widgets International originated the product, and you paid insufficient attention to the company's drawbacks: its small size, its amount of debt, and its lack of earnings were major disadvantages when it faced stiff competition. Blinded by thoughts about the company's potential, you failed to consider the fact that other companies would be attracted to this wonderful opportunity, resulting in severe competition.

Greed causes us to focus on the potential of our company, while what we need to do is assess the probabilities of achieving that potential. For example, the potential in computers and high technology is great, but a new company will be competing with IBM for that potential. It is difficult to let go of the pleasant feelings associated with greed and to think about unpleasant possibilities, but the price of failing to think about them can be quite high.

MINDTRAP #8:
UNBRIDLED GREED; OR, TREES DO NOT GROW
TO THE SKY ON WALL STREET

You bought Alpha Beta Conglomerate at 13. The stock then dropped to 11 a share as the entire market went through a slump. Since ABC did not go down as far as other companies in the same industry, you believe that when the economy turns around, it will do exceptionally well. This seems like a good time to buy, so you invest a considerable amount in ABC – even purchasing the shares on margin. You are really right this time. ABC becomes a darling of money managers, and in time it is selling for 23 a share. You have almost doubled your money in it, but now you are thinking about how much richer you will be when it hits 25. It has to do this because it is so popular, and all that it has been doing is going up.

About the time you purchased ABC, the whole market started going up. ABC is still going up some, but its rise is getting to be pretty choppy. You have calculated how much money you stand to make when it hits 25, and that projection is still in your mind. The stock starts heading down, but you are not worried, because the Dow Jones averages are continuing to hit new highs, and ABC *will* go to 25. Once again, greed keeps us from looking at negative news or potentially disappointing information, which we need to do to make our best evaluation of a situation. The stock drops to 19 and hangs around there as analysts revise downward their projections for the company. Eventually you sell ABC for 19 1/4, where you feel it has leveled off.

The trap here is a very clear one. Stocks do not go up endlessly at dazzling rates. As the stock market adage goes, "Trees do not climb to the sky." It is difficult to accept this when the trend has been steadily upward. People tend to believe that today's trend will carry over to tomorrow. This usually makes sense just as it usually makes sense to believe that if the sun is shining today, it is more likely than not that tomorrow will be bright and sunny. So if a stock has been going up, we expect it to continue rising. But stocks that have been climbing dramatically eventually become overextended, retrace, and then fall into a reasonable range. It is important to recognize that the extreme prices they have reached are anomalies and not sustainable values. If you keep a stock of this kind, just forget about its highest price. Do not berate yourself with "I should have sold it then," but see the stock as what you purchased it for a long-term investment that you may or may not wish to keep. On the other hand, if you believe that a stock is in an overextended phase, you can try to sell it before it drops, but expect to time that move precisely only through hindsight.

CONTROLLING GREED

To control greed, you must take the same steps that you take to overcome fear: you must become aware of your emotions, maintain perspective, develop a fuller picture of the situation, compile a list of possible negatives, and develop different scenarios for the future. Therefore:

1. Write down your thoughts and feelings.

"This deal is unbelievable. . . I'm going to be able to double my money with no risk. . . I wish I had more money to invest. . . It's another McDonald's in the 1950s. . . I have to get in on it before someone else beats me out."

2. Focus on facts (ferret out wishful thinking).

One way to spark people's greed, and get them to rush in with their money, is to present the situation in a compelling manner. Make investors believe that there is a great opportunity to make money but that unless they act quickly, they will lose out. Also make them believe that there is little risk. These conditions do not allow for calm evaluation of the situation. But in order to make your best decision, you want to take some time and to ask skeptical questions that will subdue your natural feelings of greed. Such questions as the following may be helpful;

- What do I know to be the facts of this situation (items that could be used as evidence in a court of law)?
- What assumptions are being used?
- Why do I have to act quickly?
- How would I evaluate the situation if there were only a chance for moderate profits?
- Why, how, and by whom will the objectives be accomplished?

- What is known about the people running the company? What is their track record?
- Do I have any independent evidence for what I am being told?
- What can go wrong?
- What happens if things do not turn out as projected (which they most probably won't)?

3. Gain perspective.

Put some distance between yourself and the situation. Imagine someone else examining this compelling opportunity, perhaps a scowling banker being asked for a loan or a respected friend whose advice you have requested. If you believe that you give good advice, you might think about how you would advise someone else facing your situation.

4. Compile a list of the positives and negatives.

The more we want to achieve our goals, the easier it is to turn off any information that might get in their way. The positive list will be easy to produce, but it will take real effort to formulate the drawbacks and risks.

Positives	Negatives
Unlimited potential	Highly speculative issue
Stock has been rising	Unproven record
New products to be unveiled	No dividends
Stock well recommended	Unproven management
	High price-earnings ratio
	Low cash reserves
	Unsure what competition will do

5. Anticipate a different future.

This step also involves going beyond the obvious. When everybody is convinced that oil prices, real estate, or the market will continue to go up, it takes real mental effort to come up with possible events that would result in different outcomes. When fighting greed you need to think about the possibility of outcomes different from those that are being presented and about the events that might lead to those outcomes. The following example may sound mildly familiar.

> Oil prices are going up. Predictions of oil reaching $100 a barrel are heard, and you have the opportunity to invest in energy stocks or oil exploration partnerships. You need to ask yourself what might happen to prevent this outcome. You think, "As oil prices go up, people will conserve energy, and this will decrease the demand for oil. High prices will also stimulate the search for new sources of oil and this will increase the supply of oil. As supply increases and demand drops off, the price of oil will decline."

Once you have written down all of your ideas, it is time to think about all the information before you. Evaluating the facts forces you to respond rationally rather than emotionally. This counters the impulse to follow your greed blindly and enables you to arrive at the best decision you are capable of making. Next time you find yourself filled with greed, remember that when you want to catch a mouse, you bait the trap so that his desire does him in. When we are filled with greed, we do not see the entire situation and are likely to take as big a hit as that mouse.

EMOTIONAL CONFLICT:
or, Torn between Greed and Fear

P eople wrestling with a difficult investment decision often take the course described in the following example, as Larry tries to decide whether or not to go into the worm ranching business with his good friend Joe. When Joe first approaches Larry about the scheme and outlines the fantastic possibilities, Larry becomes very excited. This is a chance to make lots of money, work with his good friend Joe, and be his own boss. The potential in worm ranching is unlimited. Once the two of them develop their own spread, they can expand and have worm ranches all over the country.

At the beginning Larry feels very confident about the idea, is committed to the partnership, and is raring to go. But as the time for him to put down his $500 approaches, he starts to feel unsure about the plan. Doubts begin creeping into his mind: "What if there isn't as much demand for worms as Joe thinks? ... What if I lose the $500 that it has taken me so long to save up? ... What do Joe and I really know about the worm ranching business?"

Although initially confident, Larry is now fearful and reluctant to go through with the deal. When it is time to hand over his money, Larry tells Joe he just cannot do it. Joe is furious. He does not understand what happened to the excited partner he had at the beginning. He demands that Larry explain why he backed out at the last minute. Larry is not sure what caused him to change. He is an emotional basket case filled with conflicting feelings. Joe decides that Larry is fickle and unreliable. He throws his hands up in disgust and swears that he will never do anything with Larry again.

When making difficult investment decisions, we sometimes seem to be two different people. Our shifting views are a mystery since outwardly everything seems to be the same. The answer lies in the fact that whenever we are faced with a difficult decision, we experience conflict. Desire pulls us toward acting, and fear pushes us away from making a commitment. Until now, fear and greed have been presented as two separate forces. In reality, they are interrelated emotions that usually pull at us simultaneously. The way these two emotions interact, whipsawing us back and forth, can make our actions seem incomprehensible and irrational. Knowing about their combined effect explains why, for example, investors often pull out at the last minute on potentially lucrative investments – about which they were so positive just a short time before.

Conflict when facing a choice is a problem in all aspects of life. We feel torn between a tantalizing dessert and the fear of gaining weight. A teenage boy wants to ask a pretty girl out but fears humiliation if she says "no". We may desire respect and admiration for our ideas, but we are reluctant to express them lest they be ridiculed. Major life decisions such as getting married, accepting a new position, or buying a house produce conflict because they have positive and negative elements. Let us look at one example to get a detailed feel of what happens.

> Paul and Ann have been going together for some time. They enjoy each other's company, and they have lots of fun when they are together. They have similar interests and outlooks. They are not dating others, and they seem to have no desire to seek out new relationships. Ann is quite committed to Paul and is thinking about marriage. She wants children, and she feels the pressure of the biological clock. Paul does not experience the same sorts of pressures as Ann does. Ann begins talking to Paul about making some commitments. Since neither of them is getting any younger, maybe they should try living together to

see how this affects their relationship. If things work out, then they could think about marriage. Initially Paul agrees; he really likes Ann, and this is the best relationship that he has had in many years. But as they talk more about moving in together and actually start looking for places to rent, things start to change in the relationship. Paul seems more distant. None of the places they look at is "right." Paul's work becomes very important to him, and he finds less and less time to be with Ann. He becomes interested in physical conditioning, begins jogging, and joins a softball team. Ann feels confused and hurt. Whenever she starts talking about living together, the conversation somehow shifts to something else. Little things that Ann does begin to irritate Paul. Ann looks less attractive than she used to, and her friends seem "boring." Paul suddenly notices that one of the women at work is really cute and begins some "innocent" flirtations with her. Ann is becoming more and more irritated with him. They quarrel for the first time. Ann wants to talk about what is happening, but Paul just doesn't have the time. Ann finally gets so frustrated with Paul that she breaks off the relationship.

At first, Paul doesn't seem bothered—in fact, he feels relieved. But soon he begins to miss Ann. He thinks about all of the pleasant times they had together. When he runs across her, she seems prettier than ever. In time he calls to ask her how she is doing and whether she would like to go out to dinner. But Ann says that she is dating someone else and doesn't think it would be a good idea. Paul is heartbroken. All of his love and attraction for Ann begin flowing again. He can't believe that they aren't going to be seeing each other anymore. Now all he wants is to get back with Ann. He calls her and tells her about his feelings. He is ready to live with her, and any place she chooses would be fine. In fact, if she wants to get married, he is ready to do so.

I will let you decide the outcome of this scenario. From a decision-making standpoint, however, it is important to notice the pattern of Paul's feelings and actions. They are not as erratic and irrational as they appear. As the time for making a commitment draws closer, he experiences more fears, is less attracted to Ann, and starts avoiding the situation. As the possibility of living with Ann recedes, his fears die away, Ann becomes more desirable, and he moves toward reestablishing the relationship. This pattern is not unique to Paul but is typical for all of us when we face a situation that includes positive elements that we wish to approach and negative elements that we wish to avoid. We call this the *approach-avoidance conflict,* and its basic patterns have been identified by research psychologists.

The psychologist Neal Miller and his associates illuminated the relationship between fear and desire in a series of very clever experiments. They found that the nearer we come to something desired, the stronger is our attraction to it. In experimental studies they measured the strength of the drive to approach a goal by harnessing animals and measuring how hard they pulled as they came closer to the goal (in this case, food). The nearer the animals came to the goal, the stronger the force of the pull. The truth of the principle established by Miller and his associates was made clear to me a short time after having studied it. A group of friends and I were being given a ride home by a fellow student who hadn't seen his girlfriend for quite a while. He didn't go out with anyone except her, and he really missed her. The closer we got to our destination, the more he talked about her and the faster he drove. It took a few ribald, but true, comments to get him to slow down enough to prevent us from becoming highway fatalities.

FIGURE 3-1

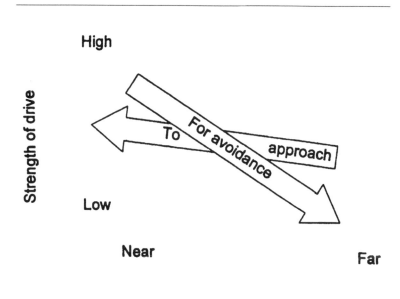

Distance from goal

Miller and his associates also looked at the drive to get away from frightening things. In order to study the strength of the avoidance reaction, a rat was shocked at one end of a maze. The strength of the pull to *get away* was measured by putting the rat back where it had been shocked. The studies showed that the strength of the pull was much greater when the animal was closest to where it had been shocked, and decreased fairly rapidly as it ran away from that point. To see this for yourself, imagine how frightened you would feel if you were face-to-face with a grizzly versus being a quarter mile away and then a half mile away.

When the strengths of the drives to approach and to avoid were compared, a surprising discovery was made. The changes in the strengths of the drives were *not* the same as the changes in the distance from the feared or desired situation (see Figure 3-1). As we come closer to the end point, the pull of desire tends to increase in strength more slowly than the push of fear. (It is important to remember that for most situations in life we are dealing with changes in *time*, not in distance.) This means that, everything else being equal, when we are far away from a decision or action point, attraction will be greater than fear and we will move ahead. But as we get closer to that point, our fear builds very quickly and can overcome our desire, which increases more slowly. It is this quick ascendance of fear that is so confusing to people; it seems to come out of "nowhere" to overwhelm a desire that they have had for a long time. This is why an incredulous bride or groom can be left at the altar after a long, and seemingly loving engagement.

Let us now look at how the approach-avoidance mindtrap can cause problems for investors.

MINDTRAP #9:
UNREALISTIC SELF DECEPTIONS; OR, THINKING LIKE INDIANA JONES BUT ACTING LIKE WOODY ALLEN

When first thinking about investing in the stock market, we are quite a way from having to make the actual decisions of specific stocks to buy in the face of uncertain consequences. This is when we will feel boldest and most confident in ourselves. It may be very easy for a novice investor to see himself as the daring stock market speculator: the swashbuckling Indiana Jones who is not afraid to take risks and spits in the face of fear. But this can be a mindtrap if, as decision time comes closer, we become less like Indiana Jones and more like a Woody Allen character who is afraid of any danger.

This is not to imply that we should try to be something we are not—Indiana Jones if we feel like Woody Allen. To try to be something we are not is foolhardy in the stock market as in all aspects of life. It results in embarrassing moments and foolish acts. The point is that if we act cautiously and conservatively in other aspects of life, then that is probably how we will act in the market. This generalization does not always hold true, but it usually does. So if you are ordinarily like Woody Allen, are you wasting your time thinking you will act like Indiana Jones when investing? If you spend a great deal of time studying how to be a great stock market plunger but will only be terrified when it is time to take the plunge, you are just spinning your wheels. You would be better off investing in a good mutual fund and spending that time with your family or lying out in the sun reading a good book.

MINDTRAP #10:
APPROACHING UNTIL AVOIDANCE TAKES OVER; OR, WHY BRIDES ARE LEFT WAITING AT THE ALTAR

Let us examine how the approach-avoidance conflict might affect you when you buy a specific stock.

Wellington United Bank is one of the largest banks in the country. But like many money center banks, it has made a lot of shaky loans to third world countries. Its management has been less than impressive, though fairly recent changes in investment and management strategies may begin to pay off soon. Within the last week a number of very negative announcements were made about the bank. Federal auditors required that it put large sums aside as reserves against its shaky loans, and this resulted in an unexpected quarterly loss. Rumors are circulating of a cut in its dividend. All of this has resulted in a 30 percent drop in the price of its stock. Many shares have been sold short as some investors anticipate an even greater decrease.

The market has overreacted to the situation, in your opinion, and you are tempted to buy. You think about the bank's long dividend history, its competent if not exciting management, and the fact that all the bad news about it has been reported. Mostly what goes through your mind are reasons why the stock should appreciate. You acknowledge some of the dangers, but they do not seem very significant to you.

Greed drives you to call your broker to buy the stock. But as you start to reach for the phone, your chest begins to tighten and your stomach starts churning. Thoughts of Continental Illinois go through your mind. There were a lot of people who thought a bank that big could not fail. What about all those investors selling the stock short? Maybe they have some inside information that you lack. They are pretty confident that the stock will go down. Why does the price keep going down? Maybe there are more problems than you are aware of? You are feeling more and more anxious about making this investment. As your hand reaches for the phone, the squeamish feeling in the pit of your stomach increases. When you dial the broker's telephone number to get a quote on the stock, your throat tightens and your heart begins to pound. You ask for the current price, but whether the stock has gone up or down, you just can't manage to get the words out of your mouth. Fear escalated very quickly and overcame your greed, so you did not act on your decision.

Overcoming the Approach-Avoidance Mindtrap

There are some steps you can take to help overcome the approach-avoidance mindtrap.

To begin with, recognize where you are on the approach avoidance continuum. If you feel fear suddenly overwhelming you when face-to-face with a decision, then you are on the extreme fear end of the continuum and it is blinding you to the positive elements. Try using the techniques for overcoming fear that were presented earlier. Identify your emotion and the potential mindtrap – *fear*. Then work at remembering the desirable aspects of the situation: "The stock has good upside potential, with minimal downside risk. It aims at a specific niche in the market. Since it will be the first provider of the product, it can build brand identity and brand loyalty."

Let us look at a different type of example – say the chance to buy a new high-tech offering. The initial pitch will be filled with glowing prospects, and you start thinking about how high the stock can go. If you feel euphoric about outcomes down the road-recognize that you are on the approach part of the continuum. Remember that this will change and that the negative possibilities have yet to enter the picture. Now is the time to use the steps outlined for overcoming greed. Identify your emotion and the potential mindtrap – *greed*. Then force yourself to come up with aspects of the situation that counteract your euphoria – "unproven product, unproven management, no earnings, possible new competitors."

It takes hard work to make good investment decisions and to overcome our hindering emotions. We do not want to split our mental energy by trying to do both at the same time. If we are still juggling facts in our mind as the time to make a decision approaches, then we will have diminished energy for the difficult job of combating our irrational feelings so that we can follow through with our choice. By separating these two activities, we can make it much easier on ourselves and increase the likelihood of success.

It makes sense to focus first just on the decision to be made. Once we have made our decision, we can put it aside and focus our energy and attention on the task of resisting the powerful feelings that contradict it. For example, if fear frequently blocks you from acting, then separate the decision-making process from the final action – perhaps by thinking the situation over at night so that in the morning all you have to do is call it in. If greed is your problem (for example, impulsively wanting to commit yourself upon first hearing about a "great deal," and maybe even being pressured to do so), you would want some breathing space to allow some of your fear to emerge. Greed can be a particularly difficult trap if initially you do not have to commit very much money. "Buy now, pay later" can be very seductive and dangerous, as many credit card users have found out. A helpful rule of thumb to use anytime you are in a quandary and are being pressured to make a decision is to buy yourself some time by merely saying, "I would like a day [five minutes, an hour, a week] to think it over." If the person with whom you are dealing will not give you that opportunity, then you know you do not want to get involved with him.

MINDTRAP #11:
CATASTROPHIZING; OR, ONCE AGAIN, THE REPORTS OF MY STOCK'S DEATH HAVE BEEN GREATLY EXAGGERATED

An important point to remember is that as the time to decide nears, fear not only increases in our hearts but also fills our minds with disturbing thoughts. Unfortunately, some of us tend to take any potentially negative or troublesome information and expand on it until it has become a "catastrophe." If a "catastrophizer" is expecting friends for a six o'clock dinner and they are 15 minutes late, he would deal with the situation in the following way. He would begin imagining terrible car accidents. He would have thoughts like these: "They are always on time. . . . Something awful must have happened. . . . Dusk is the most dangerous time to drive . . . . If they were going to be late, they would have called. . . . Maybe I should call them. . . ." He would combine such thoughts with images of fatal car accidents. As our thoughts become more scary, our fear is fed, and this makes our thoughts even scarier. This can build until we are almost overcome with panic. In fact, our catastrophizer is at his wit's end and is ready to call the highway patrol and the hospitals, when his dinner guests arrive for their *seven* o'clock dinner.

Our catastrophizer would react in the same way to potentially disturbing financial news. Let us say that a stock he owns has suddenly started to go down in price. Then reports of unexpected losses appear. Our friend feels very anxious, and his mind begins churning away: "The company will go bankrupt.... The price will drop to nothing.... All my money will be lost.... Why did I invest in this stock? ... I always pick losers. ... Tomorrow the price will drop even more.... Nobody is going to want this stock...." As these thoughts run through his mind his fear escalates. The greater his fear, the more the positive or hopeful expectations are wiped out of his mind. This makes it even harder for him to come to a rational decision about what to do.

One quick way of handling catastrophizing is to ask yourself what you know to be true, that is, what statements you have evidence for. Would those statements be accepted as facts in a court of law, or would they be ruled inadmissible? In the first example, you have evidence that your friends are late for dinner; in the second, that the stock has dropped and there are reports of unexpected losses. Is there any evidence that the dinner guests have been killed in a car accident? No! Is there any evidence that the company will go bankrupt and the price of its stock will drop to zero? No!

A second helpful technique is to ask yourself to come up with reasonable explanations of the situation. The dinner guests (1) were caught in traffic, (2) had an unexpected phone call prior to leaving, or (3) were late in getting home and late in getting started. The stock is going down because (1) rumors will drive down the price and (2) the market is expecting the worst even though the extent of the unexpected losses is unclear.

Another Way to Control Your Emotions

When emotions are interfering with success, some people use their imaginations to help them overcome this problem. Many world-class athletes do this when preparing for events. The first relax themselves (remember the relaxation instructions for coping with fear), and then they picture themselves calmly, confidently, and successfully performing. If this is something you want to try, then take a moment or two and relax yourself. To downplay fear, use your mind to recollect what your feelings and thoughts were like when you were optimistic about the situation. If you need to counteract greed, imagine what you would feel like at the final decision when you have to risk your hard-earned money. If you have made decisions in the past feeling calm and thinking very clearly, re-create that mental and emotional state and then work on your decision. If this has not been the case in the past, imagine yourself feeling no pressures, thinking clearly, and evaluating all aspects of the situation. Once you feel that you are in this calm, clear state, then start figuring out what to do.

Fear and greed wax and wane as the time to act nears. This produces changes in our attitudes and thoughts, as well as our feelings. If we are not aware of this tendency, then we will feel even more confused by the situation and appear irrational and inconsistent to others. It is beneficial to expect these changes and then act to control them so that we perceive a more balanced picture and therefore make the best possible decision.

Buy High, Sell Low:
or, Do I Have It Backward?

"Let me tell you about a great moneymaking opportunity. There is an investment genius who can get you at least a 40 percent return on your money. He speculates in the interbank currency market. You and I haven't even heard of it. But it involves a worldwide network of major banks that buy and sell currency. I don't know exactly how it works, but a lot of wealthy insiders invest with him and are making a killing. The people doing business with this whiz didn't just fall off the banana boat. Some of the real movers and shakers around town have millions of dollars in their accounts with this guy. Even our mayor has made quite a few dollars investing with him. I was lucky and heard about it from a buddy of mine who got involved through a close friend. On top of the great return on your money, the firm's books and records are kept outside the United States and it routes its business through banks in the West Indies and the Channel Islands, so the IRS doesn't have to know anything about this – unless of course you want to tell them. Maybe you have seen his name in the paper; he gives a lot of money to charity. He is very rich, lives in a $750,000 house, owns airplanes and a dozen fancy cars. He doesn't advertise, but he will accept your business if you open an account with him. His firm has a large luxurious office, lots of employees, and computer terminals everywhere."

Would you be skeptical about this kind of opportunity, or would you rush in for those unbelievable returns on your money? Apparently, many good citizens of San Diego, California, could not wait to invest in this type of venture – and it may have cost them $150 million. This was the amount of money that was reportedly lost by people who invested with J. David

Dominelli in San Diego from 1979 to 1983. The people who lost this money were wealthy and very successful individuals. You would think they had heard the cliché "If something seems too good to be true, then it probably is." Certainly, the type of consistently high return promised by Dominelli in a specialized, highly competitive market was too good to have been possible. How could these smart, successful people have fallen for this kind of scam?

What happened was that they fell victim to the same psychological factors that trap so many stock market players and cause them to do exactly the opposite of what it takes to make money in the stock market. The way to get rich in the market is to buy low and sell high. Why do so many people wind up doing the opposite – buying stocks near their highs, suffering through long declines, and finally selling them near the bottom? Maybe you have done this, or if not, then you certainly know people who have. Professionals as well as individual investors are susceptible to this mistake. It is made so often that I have heard people joke about it with friends: "Let me tell you when I sell a stock so you can be sure to buy it, because then it always goes up."

Any pattern of behavior that is this common cannot be happening just by chance. Some powerful psychological influences must be operating to make it happen. To avoid financial losses, it will be very important to learn about the mindtraps operating here and about the underlying psychological principles that contribute to them. As we will continue to see, large numbers of people have been susceptible to these mindtraps and have lost a lot of money because of them. This has not happened just recently but in different centuries and different countries. Why do people continue to fall into these mindtraps?

To help solve this mystery, let us go back to 1920. I would like to introduce you to Mr. Charles Ponzi. He has a great way for you to get rich quick. He also offers you a 40 percent return on your money, and in only

90 days. The way he does this is through International Postal Reply coupons, which are redeemable in stamps. It turns out that you can buy these coupons in countries whose currency isn't worth much, for instance Italy, and then come to the United States and get U.S. stamps for them – worth as much as six times what you paid for them in lira. (This is possible because the exchange rates, which were set previously between governments, do not reflect the current market value of the currencies.) Now that Mr. Ponzi has these American stamps, he will sell them to businesses for slightly less than the Post Office charges for them. A license to print money, according to Ponzi.

Business started slowly for Ponzi, but as word of the incredible return spread, money started pouring into his office. When he announced that the return on investments would go up to 100 percent in 90 days, torrents of money came flooding in. In fact, so much money came in that stacks of bills were just stuck in closets until Ponzi's staff could get to them. Ponzi received so much money that he went out and bought a bank and began talking about huge expansions of his offices.

Ponzi's empire collapsed soon after local newspapers began investigating it. They discovered how it operated and reported the fraud to their readers. It turned out that Ponzi was able to produce those great returns, not by buying postal coupons, but by using money contributed by new investors.

This is the classic Ponzi scheme. Where great returns are promised, early investors get those returns from infusions of fresh funds by new investors. This convinces people that the returns are real, and they leave their money with the operator, confident that they will compound their returns. The operator does not have to pay out very much to initial investors once they are convinced that their money is safe. The few people who want to withdraw their investment are paid off, because there is plenty of money to cover them. But who would want to get out of such a great deal?

The Ponzi and Dominelli schemes duped American investors, but I do not wish to imply that only Americans are susceptible to financial delusions. The good burghers of Holland fell victim to an even greater financial fiasco during the early 17th century. The road to riches for them was investing in tulip bulbs. The tulip had become a craze. Soon people bought bulbs not because they wanted tulips for vases in their homes, but only to be resold at a huge profit. The craze reached such heights that rare tulip bulbs were traded for houses or businesses. This frenzy eventually came to an end, leaving many people considerably poorer.

It seems that some of the psychological influences operating here are the same as those that operate when people buy stocks high and sell them low. This pattern has generally been accounted for through explanations that it is just greed or "crowd psychology." These factors, discussed in other chapters, are part of the answer, but a more complete explanation is necessary to help overcome these mindtraps. Look at what is occurring in such situations.

1. High returns on investments stimulate greed.
2. Seeing others making great amounts of money provokes envy.
3. The investment is felt to be safe – because everybody makes money and nobody sustains losses.
4. The investor is rewarded with high paper profits.
5. Some financial genius or "genius technology" promises the phenomenal return.

Next we will examine a number of psychological influences that feed into these conditions. These psychological influences affect our everyday behavior, but they can also turn situations into mindtraps that get us into financial trouble.

Rewards and Reinforcements

One of the most basic psychological principles is that we are likely to continue doing things for which we are rewarded. Psychologists use the general term *reinforcement* to refer to things that are *personally* rewarding. We use this general term because what is rewarding to you is not necessarily rewarding to me – "one man's meat is another man's poison." I will be using the terms reward *and* reinforcement interchangeably – every reward will be considered reinforcing for the person who receives it.

We continue to work because we are rewarded for it. Some of us work for monetary rewards (we like what we buy with the money we make), while others work for intrinsic rewards, such as the enjoyment of the work itself. Usually we continue to work at our jobs because of some combination of the two. If we work hard and are rewarded for this by promotions, bonuses, or even praise, we are more likely to continue to work hard. If we bust our behinds and get neither extrinsic rewards nor personal satisfaction, in time we will start slacking off.

People gamble because they are sometimes rewarded for doing so. You put quarters into a slot machine because some of the time money comes tumbling out. If a slot machine does not pay off at all, then the gambler will stop playing. This is what psychologists call *extinction* – no longer doing something because there is no longer a reward for doing it.

Buying a stock is an action, and an increase in its price is a reward.

Let us see how this influences three different investors who buy the same stock.

MINDTRAP #12:
REINFORCEMENT; OR, WHY GENERALS ARE ALWAYS PREPARING TO FIGHT THE LAST WAR

Exciting Electronics is a stock with a volatile price history. Changes in the economy are magnified for this company because of the products it manufactures. It also has very aggressive management, and this has further amplified its price swings. During the last few years it went from $5 a share up to $12, then slowly declined to $4, when it really took off. It is now at $18.

Joe buys Exciting Electronics, and it immediately begins its nosedive. He holds on until it comes back in price and performs well – he makes a lot of money on it. What do you think Joe is likely to do if it starts to go down again? He will probably hold onto it, because so far he has been *rewarded* for sticking with it over the long haul. He will probably apply the same strategy to a new stock as well if it starts to go down.

Mary buys Exciting Electronics just before it shoots up from $5, and then she sells it at $11 because she needs the money to buy a new car. The stock soon plummets. Mary makes a very handsome return on her investment, and later she buys the stock back when it is around $6. Next time, will Mary hang on for the long haul, or will she take her profits fairly quickly? Her future strategy will again be influenced by what her rewards were this time.

Pete bought Exciting Electronics before its most recent surge in price. It has gone up ever since he bought it. What will be the chances of his selling it? Pretty slim, unless something pushes him to move. This makes perfect psychological sense, because he has been rewarded for owning it. Why should he do anything different? "Buy and hold" is the strategy he is likely to start using. In fact, this very system was widely used in the 1950s and 1960s by many "sophisticated" investors during a prolonged period of rising stock prices that followed World War II. It was a time of "one-decision stocks" (to buy), when some stocks reached phenomenally high prices that were never again matched. "Buy and hold" was a very successful strategy that rewarded investors for holding on and not selling, and it worked until the late 60s. But when the economic climate changed and prices tumbled and stayed down, those adhering to this strategy lost a great deal of money.*

As you can see from the Exciting Electronics example, each of the three investors made money and developed an investment strategy based on a pattern that had been rewarded – though that strategy was not necessarily the best one to pursue. Emotionally, our gut reaction is to stay with the familiar ways that worked in the past. We feel uncomfortable trying to do something different. Thoughts like "It's always worked in the past. . . . I should do it again. . . . It doesn't feel right to do it this way" may cross your mind. Your emotions and associated thoughts may be in conflict with the rational view that the old strategy just doesn't seem to fit the present economic scene.

Many times, sticking with a successful strategy is reasonable, but sometimes it is not. Reinforcement becomes an investment trap when we do not attempt to evaluate the entire current scene. Instead, we persist in repeating strategies just because they paid off in the past. It will be important for you to identify cases when prior reinforcement may be keeping you on one course, even though your head may be trying to lead you in another direction. To help overcome this mindtrap, you may want to:

1. **Describe the situation.**

   "Thinking about selling stocks because I fear the market may be heading down."

*Many investors are doing the same thing today with mutual funds.

2. **Identify your thoughts and feelings.**

    "Feeling uncomfortable about changing from a successful strategy that has always worked for me."

    "It doesn't feel right.... Why should I change and try something that may not work when this has always worked in the past?... What if the market continues to go up?"

3. **Identify potential mindtraps.**

    "What makes me want to stay on the present course? I have been amply rewarded for holding on to this stock. I feel attached to it and like it."

4. **Gain perspective and develop the most rational strategy for the situation.**

    "If I were starting fresh and did not have this reinforcement history behind me, what would I do? What would I advise a friend to do in this situation?"

MINDTRAP #13:
VICARIOUS REINFORCEMENT; OR, WHY GENERALS ARE ALSO ALWAYS PREPARING TO FIGHT THE LAST WAR OF OTHER COUNTRIES

We do not have to be the direct recipients of rewards to be influenced by them. The likelihood of our following through on a course of action is also influenced by the rewards we see given out around us. This is called *vicarious reinforcement* because we do not receive it directly. We see what happens to others, and then we copy their actions if we see that these are rewarded. This is the psychological principle behind the mindtrap that causes people to buy stocks when they are high and poised to go down.

To get a clearer sense of how vicarious reinforcement operates, let us look at two situations. If you see that a coworker is rewarded with promotions, increases in salary, and bonuses for working hard and if these rewards appeal to you, you will probably work harder. Or if you are playing the slot machines in Las Vegas and the person next to you, who has been consistently getting a payoff from a machine, is called away by his wife, would you not be tempted to switch to his machine?

Vicarious reinforcement is especially powerful in risky situations. Con artists, being excellent psychologists, know this human tendency and therefore use shills. If W. C. Fields wanted you to play the shell game against him, he would draw a crowd and then have an accomplice play the game first. The accomplice would win by finding the pea under the same shell you thought was covering it. Having seen someone else amply rewarded for something you could do, you decide to try. It seems a sure, safe bet. You plunk down a buck, watch the pea, know exactly where it is, pick up the shell, and find no pea. You try again because it was so easy to figure out (maybe you blinked at the wrong moment), and you lose again. After giving Fields some more of your money, you leave, shaking your head and reminding yourself about the evils of gambling.

We base many of our everyday actions on vicarious reinforcement. Most of us like to avoid risks, so we are usually reluctant to be the first to try something. If a new car sounds appealing but is an unproven product, we will let someone else buy it first. After a number of friends have tried the car and been satisfied with it, then we will buy it. A wise and prudent approach.

Let us look at the stock market and apply the principles we have learned so far. Stock market players understand that the market is a risky venture and would like some assurance that they will not lose their hard-earned money by investing in it. The prudent thing to do, obviously, is to watch it for a while. To assure himself of the "safety" of an investment, the "prudent investor" will sit back and watch others make money on it. Such vicarious reinforcement, however, is useful only when we are dealing with a static entity such as a car. We can assume that the car we will buy six months from now will be much the same as the one coming into the dealer's showroom today. But the stock market is a constantly fluctuating dynamic entity. It is likely to be completely different six months later. So our prudent investor will watch an individual stock, or the market, go up and up to be sure he is safe. When he has seen others make money and is convinced that he can invest with little risk, he is ready to plunge in. Markets do not climb to the sky, however, so just as he is convinced that it is safe to go in, the market may be ready for a downward correction. *It is precisely when one is convinced that there is no risk in a risky investment that such an investment is usually the most dangerous course to pursue.*

There is good reason to believe that our prudent friend may be hit by a double whammy when he finally decides to invest. Having seen his friends make lots of money and having heard about how high the market has gone, he is probably looking for good returns, so he may invest in speculative stocks. After all, why invest in stocks if they only yield the same return that you would get from a savings account? When the market corrects, the high-flying stocks are the ones that are most likely to drop most. So our prudent friend watches his investment plummet. He is upset and completely befuddled by the situation. He took all the precautions and still failed miserably. He swears off investing in the market.

We can now see why people buy stocks when these stocks are high. They do this for the same reasons that people fall victim to Ponzi schemes or other types of scams. Vicarious reinforcement makes such purchases seem safe and thus reassures them and inhibits their fears. The people who lose their money in Ponzi schemes are cautious individuals who do not usually take risks, but whose hesitancy is worn down by seeing others well rewarded. By the time the cautious investors get involved in these schemes, all of the easy money has been made. By waiting, in fact, they end up making the riskiest investment of all.

MINDTRAP #14:
PUNISHMENT; OR, WHY THE MARQUIS DE SADE
WOULD HAVE LOVED WALL STREET

Now that we understand some of the psychological reasons for buying high, we will examine why people sell low. The psychological principle operating here is called *punishment*. This principle, the exact opposite of reinforcement, holds that we are less likely to do things we are punished for. Again, it's a simple and obvious principle. If your hand is slapped when it is caught in the cookie jar (punishment) a few times, you will stop taking cookies.

Losing money is punishment for most people. Owning a stock that is going down in price can be brutally punishing. On top of the financial loss, it is bruising to our egos. But few of us would sell a stock just because it went down within days of our purchasing it. We would tend to hold on to it. If the losses mount, our punishment continues. We begin to feel terrible about this stock. We hate looking at the financial pages to see how the stock is doing. We may cringe if we hear or see ads for our company. It is easy to despise the stock after it has been down for a long time. The stock represents not only a financial loss but a constant reminder of our "stupidity." Finally, for one reason or another, the stock may take a large drop one day. We decide that we just cannot take the punishment anymore, and we sell.

Just as trees and stocks do not grow to the sky, most stocks do not sink below the earth. Markets eventually turn, often after producing the deep losses that are so punishing to investors. In fact, it is often after such a "blowout" that the market turns, and takes off in a major rally. But our poor, pummeled investors have sought refuge from further punishment and sold their stocks. They have completed the cycle. Reinforcement got them to buy high, and punishment got them to sell low.

MINDTRAP #15:
VICARIOUS PUNISHMENT; OR, WHY WE DO NOT BUY LOW

We now know some psychological reasons for buying high and selling low. But why do we *not* buy when the price is low? The psychological principle operating here is called *vicarious punishment*. If you just saw someone get a ticket for jaywalking, would you cross the street against the light while the police officer was still around? Of course not! When stocks have been going down and you have been seeing people lose large sums of money in the market, will you jump in with both feet? The psychology of vicarious punishment inhibits you from investing in a market that has been going down. Observing others being punished for investing increases our tendency to avoid investing, and at such times there are usually no factors operating to stimulate our greed. Again, the principles that are generally helpful in dealing with a static situation cause us to miss out in the ever-fluctuating world of stocks.

The same steps that have been previously recommended can also be used to deal with the problems of vicarious rewards and punishments.

1. **Describe the situation.**

   "Market has been going down. . . . People have been losing money in stocks. . . . Because of this, advisers are bearish and expect the decline to continue."

   "Market has been going up. . . . People have been making money in stocks. . . . Because of this, advisers are pretty bullish and expect the risk to continue."

2. **Identify your thoughts and feelings.**

   "Afraid to invest because everybody has been losing money."

   "Very confident because everybody has been making a killing."

"This is not a good time to buy because the experts say the market will go down further. They are even talking about the possibility of a depression. It would be stupid of me to risk money in this scary climate."

"This is a great time to buy. The economy is booming. Everyone expects the market to continue climbing. My friends have doubled and tripled their money in these new high-tech firms. The markets have to be higher a year from now."

3. Identify potential mindtraps.

"Vicarious punishment leading to aversion about buying stocks."

"Vicarious reinforcement leading to conviction of success."

4. Maintain perspective and develop the most rational strategy for the situation.

"If I were starting fresh and did not know what has been happening with others, what would I do? What would I do if I had not been reinforced [punished] for my previous stock selections? What would I advise a friend to do in this situation?"

MINDTRAP #16:
SELLING STOCKS TOO LATE; OR, ONCE AGAIN, WHY BULLS AND BEARS MAKE MONEY IN THE MARKET AND ONLY PIGS GET SLAUGHTERED

Bernard Baruch was once asked how he became so rich in the stock market and his answer was, "I always sold stocks too soon." Why don't we sell when our stock is high and we have made a profit? One psychological answer is that the stock's increasing value has reinforced our keeping it. This strengthens our "commitment" to holding on to it. We feel attracted to the stock, and selling it runs counter to the rewards we have received. Further, since the stock has been going up in price, we tend to expect this to continue because, as discussed earlier, once a trend has been established, people expect it to continue.

Unfortunately, our grip on the stock will often not be loosened until it has dropped in price. But this may have been a large drop, for we have weathered small drops in the past. A large drop may be required to really punish us for holding on. So how do we make money in the market? By selling too soon and overriding the expectations and feelings that tell us to hold on for an ever-continuing price rise.

MINDTRAP #17:
INFLUENCE BY PRESTIGE; OR, HOW THE SCARECROW GOT SMART IN THE LAND OF OZ

In the Ponzi scheme, the mastermind of the venture may be described as brilliant or a genius. This is done because *we are more likely to be moved by a message if it comes from some knowledgeable or prestigious source* than if it comes from the average guy on the street. If I tell you that a fact about the stock market was discovered by a professor of computer science at MIT, you will be more likely to believe it than if I tell you that it was discovered by my barber. People will use advanced degrees as a way of buttressing their positions, even though a Ph.D. or an M.B.A. is no proof of knowledge or wisdom. Only for the scarecrow in *The Wizard of Oz* has a degree been a substitute for brains. We should focus on the message and discount the authority of the source presenting it. Ask yourself whether you would accept what you have been told if you heard it from your barber rather than from a "genius" with a "proven" history of success.

MINDTRAP #18:
DEFINITIVE ADVICE; OR, IF YOU DO NOT KNOW HOW
TO PRONOUNCE A WORD – SAY IT LOUD

You are in a quandary about what to do in the market. It seems even more confusing than usual. You are fully invested, have made some nice profits, and are feeling very apprehensive. You are thinking about selling but are not sure that this is the right time. Market watchers have mixed opinions about the market's future course. Some are predicting a further rally, while others believe a correction is due. You then hear a market strategist authoritatively state that the market has been overbought. He says that his indicators are giving a strong signal that a correction of at least 300 points is due, and he is warning people to sell immediately. What are you going to do about your stocks?

Hearing that strongly worded statement can easily push you into selling because we are more likely to believe a message if it seems to clarify an uncertain and ambiguous situation. If we know what is going on, we will trust our own judgment and not need the "experts" to help us. But if we are not sure what to do in the face of an ambiguous situation, we are likely to believe someone who gives a firm answer. (Propagandists know that when people are confused, they are more willing to accept simple lies that appear to answer complex and confusing situations.) To help you overcome this mindtrap, remember that it makes sense to be skeptical about people who say that they know the unknowable – no matter how sure they sound.

In summary, we see that through chance we can be reinforced to follow strategies that were successful previously but may not succeed in the future. Vicarious reinforcement can lead us to invest too late (that is, to buy high) because it overcomes cautiousness by mistakenly reassuring us of the safety of the safety of our investment. Punishment for owning stocks that have gone down can drive us to sell at low points in market cycles. Vicarious punishment can keep us from buying when prices are low. We are susceptible to believing a message if it seems to clarify an ambiguous situation, is uttered firmly, and is delivered by a supposedly knowledgeable or prestigious source.

OTHER EMOTIONAL MINDTRAPS:
or, Beyond Fear and Greed

A newspaper reporter asked J. P. Morgan, the famous banker, what the market would do tomorrow. He replied, "It will fluctuate." This is certainly a basic truth about the stock market. As those prices swing two steps forward, one step back, three steps forward, five steps back, investors may go on a roller coaster ride of thrills, excitement, hope, anxiety, despair, relief, and joy. This can be a dangerous ride for investors because it is while under the immediate influence of those emotions that people often take foolhardy, impulsive, or costly actions that they later come to regret.

To be successful in the stock market, we need to be reasonable and rational, rather then swayed by our emotions. In the 19th century Baron Rothschild stated that the time to buy stocks is when there is blood in the streets – that is, when others are totally caught up in feelings of panic. Even positive emotions can trap you; in fact, John Templeton, founder of the very successful Templeton Funds, warns pleased investors to be most on their guard when stocks are up. Complacency can as easily lead to erosion of your profits as fear can lead to missed opportunity.

As you have already seen with regard to fear and greed, in order to avoid being overwhelmed by emotions, you need to learn to anticipate when they can carry you away and then work at controlling them. This requires assessing situations realistically, focusing on the facts, not on hopes, dreams, or fears, and then keeping the facts in proper perspective. In this chapter a number of troublesome emotions are examined.

MINDTRAP #19:
HOPE SPRINGS ETERNAL, BUT YOUR LOSSES ARE MOUNTING UP

Hope is the expectation that our actions will lead to a desired outcome. Given the uncertain world we live in, hope is an essential commodity. The hope of someday being the football hero is what keeps the third stringer plugging away through difficult drills. Visions of being a prima ballerina keep young dancers working at their craft. The person who puts down a dollar in the state lottery is happy thinking about what to do with the $10 million he hopes to win.

We also have high hopes every time we buy a stock. Unless success were expected, no new investment would ever be made. For example, an investor has heard good things about the future prospects of Volatile Vectors. This company is well established in its field, has a new president who is intent on expanding into new growth areas, and has a history of steady growth. It is about to come out with some really innovative products that are projected to triple its profits within the next two years. On the basis of these facts, our investor is filled with hope about the company and buys the stock at 19. Within two months it climbs to 22. Our investor is happy, and now he hopes it will soon go to 25. He is not aware of any new reasons why it should; it would just make him very happy if it did.

Unfortunately, the price starts dropping. At first, our investor is not concerned, because the stock market as a whole is declining and the stock is selling for more than he paid – as if this makes the decline any less significant. When the stock begins dropping more sharply than the overall market, our investor feels a little uncomfortable, but he remains hopeful. He reminds himself of the dynamic president, of the great new products that will be coming on line soon, and of how these products will fuel a rise in price. As the price declines more rapidly and drops below the price paid, our investor feels trapped. Rather than questioning the reasons behind the price drop and considering what actions to take, he begins to experience a different type of hope – wishful thinking. Now he hopes that the economy will turn up soon or that the company will become a takeover target, causing its price to zoom. Finally, hope dies away and self-recrimination creeps in. Why didn't he sell when he had a nice profit? Maybe he should sell now at a large loss. The stock then drops – bang! bang! bang! – by four points within three days. Reports of the company's serious losses are covered in the paper the following day. The company is being run in a pretty sloppy fashion by the new president, who is big on ideas but poor on follow-through and management.

Hope was a mindtrap because it stopped our investor from realistically assessing the stock's declines. There are always reasons for the movement in a stock's price. We do not have to accept those reasons, but it is important to be aware of them and to evaluate them. Hope means focusing on our desires. If the stock is up, we *want* it to go up more, and if it is down, we *want* it to go back up – this is what will make us feel better. When filled with hope, we do feel better, but hope is not what drives a stock's price up. Hope causes us to focus on our feelings and not on the facts. A little bit of hope, like the proverbial little bit of salt, can be helpful. But just hoping for things to get better in the face of a deteriorating situation lessens our ability to deal with it. It is a naive and immature reaction to an emotionally troublesome situation. We may feel better, but our financial state will suffer.

To get a handle on hope and the other emotions to be covered, you should use the same general steps that were recommended for dealing with fear and greed.

1.   Write down what you are feeling and thinking.

"I wish my stock will go up to the price I purchased it for, so I can unload it."

"I am hopeful that the market will soon take off and my stock will go up with it."

2. **Write down the facts.**

-Stock going down.

-Decrease greater than typical for market.

-Volume of trading increasing.

-New dynamic management.

-History of steady growth.

3. **Compile a list of the positives and negatives.**

Positives	Negatives
New products on line	Price declining
New, though unproven, management	Large volume of selling Excessive rate of decline
History of steady growth Great potential	Rumors of problems

4. **Gain perspective.**

Ask yourself how some unbiased observer would evaluate the situation or how you would evaluate the situation if you did not own this stock and someone asked your opinion about it. Then you might ask yourself whether there are any measures you can take to help you evaluate the situation. For example, could you ask your broker what he or she thinks is happening. What would a respected, knowledgeable friend or adviser do to better evaluate the situation?

After going through the above steps, it is time to make your best guess about the chances for the stock, based on all the facts you know. You might conclude that this stock seems to have relatively little chance of going up since it has considerable downward momentum, many more people are interested in selling it than in buying it, its actions are confusing, and you would never consider buying it if you didn't already own it – it seems a much riskier and more dangerous proposition than you thought initially. You hope that things will improve, but you see no reason for expecting this to happen. Even though you do not want to deal with this mess, you realize that you would be better off if you did something than if you did nothing at all.

As will be discussed later, the difficulty people often have in selling losing stocks can lead to even greater losses. It is important to view this difficulty within a proper perspective. You have to admit:

> "I made a mistake in buying this stock. This is neither the first nor the last mistake I will ever make. I may lose 20 percent of the money I invested. There have been many stocks on which I have made that much. This loss represents less than 1 percent of my total worth. I make more money in a week than this loss represents."

You then decide whether to sell, hold, or buy more.

MINDTRAP #20:
DENIAL; OR "ME OBSESSED WITH SEX? YOU'RE THE ONE WITH ALL THE DIRTY PICTURES"

A psychologist is testing a man by showing him a series of Rorschach inkblots and asking him what he sees in the different designs. The man sees sexual images and scenes in every inkblot. When they are finished, the psychologist comments to the man that he seems rather obsessed with sex. The man is incensed and angrily snaps back, "Me obsessed with sex? You're the one with all the dirty pictures!" We laugh because the man is denying something obvious about himself, but *denial* is a psychological phenomenon that can occur in all of us. It is a psychological mechanism that closes off emotionally disturbing information, thoughts, or feelings (though only rarely to the extent displayed in the joke).

An actual stock market example of denial involved a friend of mine, a very intelligent psychologist who invested all of his money in a stock recommended by a stock analyst friend (the most tempting type of tip – "special information"). When the psychologist first bought the stock, for 36, it was projected to reach 60 within a few years. As its price kept going down, he bought more and more of it because it had been so highly recommended. He made his last purchase of the stock when it was 17 1/2. The stock then kept going down. When it was 12, I talked to him about his plans for the stock. "I'm holding on until it reaches 60," he said.

This response went beyond hope, and fell into denial because it functioned to close off emotionally disturbing information and feelings about the stock. The size of his loss was emotionally to much for my friend, so he was denying that there were significant reasons for the price drop, that the company had suffered major losses and was now in serious financial trouble. Nobody likes to experience the pain of major financial blows, but when we close ourselves off from reality, we are likely to promote worse losses. *Clinical experience shows that the psychological and emotional damage resulting from a problem is experienced whether or not we deny the problem.* Burying one's head in the sand does not change the reality of the situation. The problem only festers. In time it just hurts us more. Focusing on the facts of a situation may be painful in the short run, but in the long run it will yield greater psychological and financial payoffs. If we face a bad situation, we can still salvage something from it, but if we deny its existence, it can continue to deteriorate until there is nothing left to save. For example,

Volatile Vectors can go from 20 a share to 10 a share before the bad news becomes public knowledge. If we sell and it then goes down to 2, we have avoided a loss of $8 per share – as much as we would gain by buying a stock for 10 and having it go to 18. Denying the reality of the situation and keeping the stock is the same as buying a new stock and having it go from 10 to 2.

In addition to the steps recommended for dealing with hope, two additional steps may be helpful in opening up denial's blinders.

1. **Look for some danger signs.**

    If none come to mind, this is itself a danger sign. Every situation has some problems or issues of concern.

    If you feel no anxiety or concern about an investment, you may be denying problems or just closing yourself off from potentially useful information. There are risks to all investments, and the necessity of climbing a "wall of worry" about those risks was covered earlier.

2. **Develop a list of possible negatives.**

    Use your imagination and work hard to come up with potential problems. If you cannot do this, then ask someone else to do it for you.

MINDTRAP #21:
BEING OVERWROUGHT WITH ANXIETY; OR, WHY THE MARKET REACTS LIKE A LITTLE OLD LADY WITH SHAKY KNEES

Uncertainty is almost always unsettling. Imagine that you are rushing to the airport to catch a plane for a very important meeting. You feel anxious – your stomach is churning, tingling sensations shoot through your arms, your shoulders and chest tighten, and drops of perspiration form as you worry about getting there in time. But if you knew that you had already missed your plane, you would probably feel resigned to the situation and be much less upset. With rare exceptions, ironically, we find it less disturbing to actually experience what we are afraid of then to be anxious that it might happen.

This fact about human nature can make some people vulnerable to an unexpected mindtrap. Many investors will not consider selling a stock in which they have a paper loss. As long as the stock is selling for less then they paid for it, they are experiencing the feared outcome, so they have no decisions to make and nothing to worry about. It is only when a stock appreciates in value that they begin feeling anxious, because then they have decisions to make. So after sitting with a losing stock for years, people may sell out at the first sign of improvement and miss out on a large run-up because it is more comfortable to sit with a losing stock than to be anxious about a winner.

Since the stock market anticipates the future, it is always a bet on an uncertain outcome and therefore an anxiety-producing situation. Because many investors are high-strung, constantly on edge, and easily spooked by sudden price movements, the market has been described as "a little old lady with shaky knees." The anxiety of these investors is understandable since they may be dealing with large amounts of their own money or with hundreds of millions of dollars of other people's money. Any sudden event, such as an outbreak of war in the Middle East, a serious health problem of the president, or even a sell recommendation by a market guru can lead investors to jump in and out of the market precipitately. Panic selling may occur, driving the market way down; or large-scale purchases may be made because of a fear of missing out on a major advance. The maxim that the *market hates uncertainty* is a good one to keep in mind.

People's aversion to anxiety often leads to overreactions by the market. Rational investors can profit from this *if they keep* in mind *that the market usually overreacts* because investors anticipate a "terrible event," one much worse than what is likely to occur. Stocks often, though not always, go up after the actual "bad news" is reported, as recently occurred with the stocks of some major banks when they announced billion-dollar write-offs of their third world loans and their prices rose. Another example is the precipitate drop of Union Carbide's stock when news of the Bhopal disaster hit and the absence of any effects when the company was actually dealing with its liabilities for the catastrophe.

People react so excessively to anxiety because anxiety is a particularly odious emotion. A telling statement about its aversiveness occurred during World War II. Being a fighter pilot was exceptionally anxiety producing. Every mission involved the danger of being shot down. The anxiety of some pilots became so intense that they chose the certainty of death by flying into a mountain side over the continuing anxiety about being killed or maimed. Similarly, after the 1929 stock market crash, some investors who had lost most of their money jumped out of skyscrapers because they were anxious about becoming "poor." (It was uncertainty about their status rather than actual poverty that led them to jump, since they still had far more money than the truly poor, who just kept trudging along.)

Since the market fluctuates, its next move is almost always uncertain. But this inherent uncertainty is what provides the potential for making money; if there were no risks due to uncertainty, there would be little potential reward. Investing in the market inexorably leads to some anxiety; however, it is important for the investor that the anxiety not become excessive and hinder his or her judgment.

Excessive anxiety generally hinders our judgment and decision making. Recall times when you were very anxious about making a decision. At such times it may be hard for you to sit still. You go over the same issues again and again. The more uptight you become, the more difficult it is for you to concentrate on and evaluate information. If you are anxious about the market, your mind may race from one alarming economic scenario to another. In time your anxiety may become so high that it is difficult for you to make simple decisions. You may then act impulsively and make a poor decision. On the other hand, you may freeze and be unable to make any decision, while the market continues moving against you and compounds your losses. During war extreme anxiety may result in shell shock, a condition in which individuals become paralyzed and can do nothing.

To be a successful investor, you must control your anxiety rather than allowing it to control you. But the control of anxiety is an acquired skill, not an innate ability. This skill involves learning to analyze the problem and then taking steps to deal with it. The process is somewhat complicated because, as you will see next, we may feel anxious for more than one reason. But the basic approach for overcoming anxiety is the one that has been suggested for dealing with other troublesome emotions and involves the following steps.

1. Write down your thoughts and feelings.

"I am worried that XYZ will keep going down in price. . . . I am feeling anxious because I am uncertain whether this investment will work out. . . . I am scared that the market may turn down."

To diminish your anxieties, focus your mind on them and bring them into conscious awareness. Articulating anxieties dispels them from our minds, much as turning on the lights makes actual scary shadows disappear. For example, you may feel afraid that you will lose all of your money and wind up in the poorhouse, but once you say this, it obviously sounds ridiculous. The thought "I am going to be proven a failure just like my . . . always said" may be quite disturbing when it is in the back of your mind, while actually stating that thought makes it appear rather unimportant. Since articulating anxieties makes them appear less frightening, you want to write them down on paper.

2. Write down the facts of the situation.

"The market is down 150 points."

"My stock lost four points during the last 10 days."

"There are reports that the Federal Reserve Board may change its monetary policy."

A concrete statement of the facts of the situation is much less frightening than the irrational fears we carry in our minds. These facts are what you want to focus on, and they, not the irrational fears, should be the basis of your decision. Too often, unfortunately, we are fearful of events that have not happened and are very unlikely to happen. Thinking about such events colors our view of the present and increases our anxiety about the future. To our detriment, we often imagine the worst outcome, not the most likely one, and needlessly scare ourselves out of an advantageous position. Therefore, we always want to:

3. Maintain perspective.

Think about the *most likely* consequences of the event or situation you are anxious about.

For example, if you are "worried that there will be a drop in the dividend and this will cause the price of the stock to drop," try to state as specifically as possible how great you think the drop will be. Do you expect the stock to go down 90 percent? 50 percent? 25 percent? 10 percent? "I am worried that the stock will go down in price" is not precise enough. Once you recognize that you are reacting as if the stock will go down 90 percent but that you really believe it will go down 25 percent, you will see that your emotional reaction is out of proportion to the expected event and your anxiety will diminish.

In order to change your perspective on stock losses, always think of those losses as a percentage of your total wealth. It is much less disturbing to lose one half of 1 percent of your net worth than to lose a specific number of dollars.

MINDTRAP #22:
OVERCOMING SUPERSTITIOUS BEHAVIOR; OR, LETTING BLACK CATS CROSS YOUR PATH ON WALL STREET

Sometimes we may feel anxious about a move because of a similar previous move that turned out badly through no fault of our own. It may have been a well-thought-out move, but "bad-luck" stemming from political events or other circumstances caused us to lose money by making it. Past misfortunes in certain situations can lead to the avoidance of similar situations; for example, if you have lost big on bonds, you may be rather anxious about buying them again – even though the situation may now be completely different. Avoiding innocent situations because such situations have been associated with unfortunate events in the past is superstitious behavior. It is like avoiding the paths of black cats because long ago something bad may have happened to someone who crossed the path of a black cat. Such superstitious thinking is what makes people say things like "I lost money in gold mine stocks [or over-the-counter stocks, high-tech stocks, airline stocks, or any other possible group of stocks], and I am never going to go near them again." It is, of course, a mindtrap, because your prior experience has nothing to do with whether your present investment choice is a good one.

To help you overcome this mindtrap, imagine how you would feel if your ill-fated earlier move had been *successful*. For instance, "If I had made money on bonds before, I would be very enthusiastic about bonds now. Things look twice as favorable for them now compared to last time."

MINDTRAP #23:
GROUP INFLUENCE; OR, WHY IT'S HARD TO SING
"I'M DOING IT MY WAY"

A spaceship hovering over earth beams you up. The friendly spacemen acknowledge your presence as they go about their duties on board. You are terrified at first, but gradually you calm down. After a while the lights dim and the spacemen walk toward a large doorway. Before going through the doorway, each of them twirls two times and then touches a spot near the door. The last few spacemen gesture for you to follow them through the doorway. When you get to the doorway, will you twirl two times and touch the spot before going through? Most probably.

Although we may often believe that the stock market is inhabited by strange creatures whose ways are quite peculiar, that is not what you were intended to learn from your adventure aboard the spaceship. The purpose of that experience was to teach you that whenever we are faced with an uncertain situation, such as predicting the market, we tend to observe how others react to the situation and then follow their lead.

This attraction to the opinion of others helps explain such speculative frenzies as the tulip craze in the 17th century, or the growth stock craze in the late 1960s, or later real estate speculations. If everyone is saying that you cannot lose money in real estate, or that "gold will go to $1,000 an ounce," or that growth stocks are the only investment, this influences our perception and makes it hard to act contrary to the prevalent view. After all, if everyone perceives gold as a good investment because "it is going to $1,000 an ounce," this becomes our perception of reality – which is our reality – and we base our investment decisions on that perception.

Moreover, it is comforting to have agreement on a point of view. *The confidence produced by consensus tends to decrease our fear and allow our greed to take over.* Unfortunately, too many people have followed the group's judgment, felt quite comfortable and confident in that position, but then lost considerable amounts of money. For this reason, the "contrarian" school of investment thinking recommends going against the general consensus and what the experts advise. While this may be a good approach, it is much easier stated than followed. Let us look at an everyday example. You are thinking about buying a new car, something everybody has an opinion about. You like the ride and feel of a Toyovo, but most of the people you consult say that the Toyovo is unreliable and that you ought to buy a Honsun, which has a higher rating in *Consumer Reports*. You will feel a great deal of anxiety about your decision if you buy that Toyovo, because your decision runs counter to the majority opinion.

The influence of the "crowd" is so great that even in unambiguous matters people are influenced by others to an almost incredible degree. Verification of this fact comes from a psychological study (Asch 1955) in which people were shown lines of three different lengths and asked which of those lines was the same in length as a fourth line. This was a simple task because all four lines were in front of them, and under ordinary conditions mistakes were made less than 1 percent of the time. But in a group with six people who purposely gave an incorrect answer, 37 percent of the time people would go along with the crowd and give the wrong answer – even though the lines were right in front of their eyes. Imagine the impact of other people's opinions in something as unclear and confusing as the stock market. In fact, when anxious and uncertain about any decisions, investment or otherwise, we are likely to search out the company and opinions of other people because this reduces our anxiety. Anxiety, like misery, loves company, and this makes us vulnerable to the opinions of others and works against our being contrarians.

MINDTRAP #24:
A FOOLISH CONSISTENCY IS THE HOBGOBLIN OF
LITTLE MINDS (RALPH WALDO EMERSON)

Over the last 50 years psychologists (e.g., Heider 1946; Festinger 1957) have developed theories about the fact that *people seek consistency in their lives and are motivated to reduce the psychological disharmony produced by inconsistent beliefs, at attitudes, and relationships.* We want consistency among our beliefs ("I love my parents. . . . I love my fiancé. . . . My parents should like my fiancé"). Inconsistency among our beliefs produces consternation, so if it exists, we will work mentally to get things back in balance (e.g., "When my parents get to know my fiancé better, their feelings will change"). Numerous experiments, many of them exceptionally clever, have proven this fact and shown how it affects us in a variety of situations.

People respect the opinions of experts, who, after all, are supposed to know best. So if an expert espouses a point of view or suggests a stock, our desire for consistency would cause us to value that opinion or recommendation highly. Yet there is a great deal of evidence (Dreman 1982) that the opinions of stock market "experts" often produce poor results. So once again, when we feel comfortable and safe because we are following "expert" advice, our desire for consistency may be frustrated because we do poorly and have difficulty understanding why.

A common dilemma occurs if you like your broker (adviser) and the broker recommends a stock you are unsure about. You may then alter your opinion about the stock ("Maybe it is a good opportunity") or about your broker ("Maybe he doesn't know that much"). It may not be necessary to change your opinion if you can come up with an inclusive consistent attitude such as this: "No one is ever completely right in the stock market. Sometimes my broker will be wrong, and sometimes I will be wrong, and yet we both may still be competent." In this way you can avoid having to attitudinally throw out the baby with the bath water.

The desire for consistency is one of the reasons it is difficult to be a contrarian. When investing, think of the "experts" as being your "parents" and of the stock you want to buy as being your "fiancé." You feel comfortable when the "experts-parents" like your "fiancé-stock" but anxious when they do not. If you felt anxious about deciding on a car, think about how uncomfortable you would feel if your investment opinion were contrary to that of the experts and the way the market was moving (you are bearish, but most advisers are bullish and the market continues to go up). Wouldn't you feel pretty shaky about your view if day after day the action of the market went against your judgment?

Psychologists have found that *people want not only consistency between attitudes but also consistency between attitudes and actions.* They have discovered that this desire for consistency can lead to unusual changes in people's attitudes. In a classic study by Festinger and Carlsmith (1959), for example, two groups of people were given a very boring task to do. Later the people in one group were each paid $1 and the people in the other group were each paid $20 to tell others that the task was interesting. After they did this, their "true" feelings about the boring task were ascertained. The people who were paid $1 found the task more interesting than did the people who were paid $20. Why did this happen? If you "lie" for $20, you have a good justification for doing so, but there is no good reason to lie for $1. So to make their beliefs consistent with their actions, the people who were paid $1 had to change their attitudes.

The fact that people change their attitudes to make them consistent with their actions has important implications for the investor. For example, if you are 100 percent invested in the market, in order to be consistent with your actions, your beliefs about the market will need to be bullish. You will be more likely to accept bullish rather than bearish news. You will also be more likely to focus on and remember optimistic indicators and opinions. Remember that your perceptions and judgments regarding the market cannot be objective, even though you may feel that you are unbiased. When you are presented with new information that confirms your position, you take it at face value, whereas you critically scrutinize contradictory evidence (Lord, Lepper, and Ross 1979). But what you need to do is the opposite: you need to critically examine the supporting evidence and to be more accepting of contrary facts.

In order to avoid being trapped by your previous actions, remember to compensate for the inherent bias toward consistency as follows:

1. **Write down your positions and actions as well as the views of the "majority."**

   "I am fully invested in the market and have bought a lot of stocks recently."

   "The consensus of the experts is bullish."

   "High corporate profits will drive the market up."

2. **Analyze how these positions, actions, and views are influencing you.**

   "I feel very optimistic."

   "I want to buy more before the market goes up again."

   "I feel like buying tomorrow."

   "I feel like buying a lot of XYZ Company."

3. **Remind yourself of the consequences of your actions.**

   "I want to hear positive news and expectations about the market. It would be difficult for me to change positions now that I am committed to being bullish. I should not regard my judgments as being completely objective – I will lean toward bullish sentiment."

4. Gain perspective.

Use your imagination and picture yourself in different financial positions – for example, 100 percent out of the market or 50 percent in the market. Under each of these conditions, what would your predictions about the course of the market (or of an individual stock) be? Compare your various conclusions, and use that comparison to make your final judgment.

MINDTRAP #25:
OVERCOMING DEPRESSION; OR, WHAT TO DO
WHEN YOU FEEL BLUE

Whenever we suffer a significant loss, we become depressed. We know that this holds true not only for such losses as the death of a loved one but also for blows to our self-esteem, such as being passed up for a promotion, and for financial losses, such as taking a bath in the market.

There are a number of symptoms of depression that may be news to you. Let us examine a hypothetical case. Joe loses a large amount of money investing in a speculative high-tech company. Afterward, thinking about the money he lost makes him feel sick. Over the next weeks he continues to dwell on the loss. He becomes more withdrawn, spending hours at home sitting in front of the TV screen. He is no longer interested in reading the papers and keeping current on financial news.

He begins doubting his ability, "Maybe I'm not cut out to be a successful investor. . . . Maybe I'm not smart enough." He starts feeling generally pessimistic, not just about his own situation but about world events as well. At work he is more irritable with coworkers and shorter than usual with friends. Fears that he never had before begin to bother him. He feels unhappy and dispirited. In a word, Joe has become depressed.

When we are depressed, not only do we feel blue, but a number of other symptoms can occur as well, including increased irritability, apathy, lethargy, anxiety, pessimism, and, in serious cases, sleep, appetite, and weight problems occur. Depression can compound an investor's difficulties by adding to his or her financial loss an impaired capacity to make judgments and act decisively. People do not make their best decisions when they are filled with doubt, lack confidence, and take a generally pessimistic view of the world. This problem could be particularly tragic if suffering through a bear market or major corrections has made an investor depressed and that depression keeps him or her from participating in the eventual upturn.

The period that followed the great stock market crash of 1929 illustrates the effects of depression on investors. There were certainly many very depressed investors at that time and for good reasons. If you were invested in the market on Black Thursday, October 24, 1929, you were in for some trouble. Let us say you owned AT&T, General Electric, and U.S. Steel. AT&T dropped from 272 to 232, GE from 314 to 221, and U.S. Steel went from 204 to 167 one month later. Clearly, those hefty losses could bring you down. But if you kept your head, looked forward and not backward, and became a bear, as did Joseph Kennedy, President John F. Kennedy's father, you could have sold those stocks short and then in 1932 bought AT&T for 104, GE for 15, and U.S. Steel for 27. You would then have been a very rich person rather than a depressed poor one.

One thing you can be sure of in the stock market is that some of your selections will not work out and you will suffer losses. **The steps previously described can help you minimize the impact of losses and the depressed feelings that follow them.**

1. **Write down your feelings and thoughts.**

    "I feel unhappy and depressed."

"I feel I can't do anything right."

"I am doubting my ability. . . . I feel that everyone is smarter and more capable than I am."

2. **Focus on the facts.**

    "I am feeling depressed because the stock I paid $17 for has been going down ever since I bought it and is now $13.50. This represents a loss of _____ dollars."

3. **Develop perspective (in terms of time and in terms of the amount of the loss as a percentage of your total net worth).**

    "This paper loss represents less than one tenth of 1 percent of my net worth."

    Ask yourself whether you will be upset about this in the future. "I will not be upset about this in a week, and I will probably have forgotten about it within six months." Then is it worth getting upset about something that you won't even remember six months from now?

    Do not engage in self-recrimination and put yourself down for buying the stock. "I will not insult myself under the circumstances I made the best decision I was capable of. If put back in the same situation and knowing only what I knew then, I would make the same decision again. It is only through hindsight that I recognize it was a mistake."

4. **Make plans for the future.**

    Study the situation to find out why you were wrong and what you can learn from your mistake so that you will not make the same mistake next time. "I acted too impulsively. I cannot act just on the basis of a hot recommendation."

    Look toward the actions you can take to improve things in the future.

"I think the stock will just sit there for the next year. If I can find something that will give me a better return than this stock, I will sell the stock and invest in that."

If you are depressed, it is a good idea to take a vacation, put some fun back into your life, begin exercising, and generally try to act as if you were not so down. If the problem continues, you should consider getting professional help.

MINDTRAP #26:
OVERCOMING REGRET; OR, YOU CANNOT DRIVE DOWN WALL STREET WHILE LOOKING BACKWARD

Regret is an emotion of sorrow or remorse over one's actions or inactions. It can be considered a "cousin" of depression. Whether or not we experience regret depends to a great extent on how we perceive a situation. For example, you and a friend share a taxi to the airport to catch 5 P.M. flights to different destinations. You are caught in traffic and don't arrive until 5:30. You discover that your friend's flight left as scheduled but that yours took off just five minutes ago. Why are you likely to be more upset than you friend? You were both late, you both missed your flights, and both of you had expected to miss them. Your mental reference point, however, is now different from that of your friend. It appears that you were closer to catching your flight, so you feel more upset (Kahneman and Tversky 1982).

In the stock market, *regret and fear of regret can be costly mindtraps for people*. For example, you have been following Nifty Products for some time, you consider it a good investment, and you decide to buy it after seeing it bounce between 19 1/4 and 20 1/4 for weeks. You call up your broker, only to learn that the stock jumped to 21 in the last 15 minutes. You regret not having purchased it 15 minutes earlier and call off the whole transaction.

Nifty Products closes the day at 22, and it is up to 24 1/2 by the end of the week. You were upset about not purchasing it 15 minutes earlier, but if it had been at 21 for the last two weeks, you would have purchased it. As with missing the airplane flight, it doesn't matter whether you are 15 minutes late or two weeks late – a miss is as good as a mile. The question is whether Nifty Products is still a good stock to buy at its new price. You have forgotten that the 19 1/4 - 20 1/4 range was an arbitrary reference point – you just happened to choose it. From a different perspective, the fact that the stock broke through its trading range could be seen as a very positive sign supporting its purchase. Regret means that you are looking backward, but stock market decisions should always be based on looking forward – what the future price of a stock will be, not what the price was yesterday.

People tend to experience less regret when they act in a conventional way rather than in an unconventional way. For example, if you buy the stocks of large, well-known companies and they go down, you will feel less regret than if you incur equal losses in penny stocks that nobody ever heard of. After all, who could have imagined that blue-chip stock going down? Fears of regret place pressure on investors to follow the crowd and accept conventional thinking. If you do that and you are wrong, at least you will not be alone. If you follow your own unconventional beliefs and your stocks go down while "everyone else" is doing great, you lose both money and face. If you follow the crowd, however, and your stocks go down, you only lose money (Kahneman and Tversky 1982).

In summary, *the mindtraps produced by regret and the anticipation of regret slant stock market decisions toward inaction, conventionality, and the general consensus.* Regret inhibits us. It is an unnecessary emotion that only produces trouble. It is important to keep in mind that we always make the best decision that we are capable of. Sometimes a decision does not work out, but that does not negate the fact that under the circumstances, given what we knew at the time (without benefit of hindsight), we made what seemed to be the most reasonable choice. If we were to go back in time, be faced with the same problem, and know only what we knew then, we would always make exactly the same decision. This basic fact frequently needs to be repeated in order to overcome the nagging hindrance of regret.

PERSONALITY INFLUENCES:
Who You Are, and Not What you Know, Can Lead You Astray

"Know thyself." – *Inscription over entrance to the Temple of Apollo at Delphi*
"The unexamined life is not worth living." – Socrates
"If you do not know who you are, the stock market is an expensive place to find out." – Adam Smith, *The Money Game*

We all face the same array of potential investments, yet no two of us make the same choices. What determines how people invest? Clearly, the desire to make money is a driving force, but it is only one part of the answer. Other desires, needs, attitudes, and characteristic ways of doings things – our personalities – all affect our choices. Events from the formative years of childhood and adolescence can cause people to act in nonrational ways that interfere with success in life and in the stock market.

A tragic example of this is Martin Siegel, one of the Wall Street insiders convicted in the Ivan Boesky scandal. At the time he was apprehended for illegally passing information to Boesky, Siegel was a star on Wall Street. The Harvard Business School graduate was smart, charming, creative, respected, and admired. In terms of outward appearances, he had it all: a beautiful wife, a fabulous house, an incredibly remunerative job – he was earning over $2 million a year. He didn't drive to work – he helicoptered in. Why did he jeopardize all of this by getting involved with Ivan Boesky? To answer this question, we need to take a closer look at the man and his personality. Although Siegel presented the image of confidence and success needed for his work and career advancement, he was also described by someone close to him as "the most insecure guy I have ever known" (*Washington Post*, February 17, 1987). The roots of his insecurity lay in his upbringing. He grew up in modest, middle-class circumstances, but his family struggled with financial problems that culminated in his father's filing for bankruptcy when he was in his early 40s. "It led Marty constantly to be insecure. No matter how much money he had, he didn't have enough" (*Washington Post*, February 17, 1987). "Friends say that Mr. Siegel was haunted by the fear that someday, like his father, he would fall just as he reached the prime of life" (*The Wall Street Journal*, February 17, 1987). Siegel desired financial security in order to avoid the failure his father experienced. This led him to become entangled in the insider trading schemes. So after working exceptionally hard his entire life to avoid financial failure, he suffered an even worse fall. At 38, after pleading guilty and facing a jail sentence, he forfeited $11 million when he resigned his position at Drexel Burnham, had to sell his beautiful house, and paid $9 million to the government.

Next we will explore how personality mindtraps can influence investment decisions. When reading about these mindtraps, see whether you can identify any characteristics that apply to you. This is a cost-free opportunity to develop ideas about how your personality may be impeding your investment success. Remember, the stock market is an expensive place to find out about yourself.

MINDTRAP #27:
THE "GAMBLING INSTINCT"; OR, IT'S LAS VEGAS NIGHT ON WALL STREET

Sid is a successful businessman who runs his own small company. He has been much happier since he stopped working for a large corporation. Working for someone else was very hard on him. He is very impatient, and it was frustrating for him to wait and get approval before he could take action. Sid is energetic, talkative, and outgoing. He is always checking on things or talking to someone. His employees say they would get more done if he would just leave them alone. His wife is worried that he drinks and smokes too much, but he says it helps him unwind.

Sid has done well since he has been out on his own, and he has been able to put aside a fair amount of money. Now he wants to invest his money. Stocks and bonds have no appeal for him, but he has become fascinated by, and obsessed with, call and put options on stocks. These can show large percentage changes in value on a daily basis. It is this "action" that Sid loves. He calls his broker three and four times a day. He wants to call more often, but he tries to control himself. He listens to the news hourly to catch the latest Dow Jones averages. This is not all pleasure for Sid. He worries about his investment choices, but the action perks him up. The action – the quick changes in value, getting fast feedback on whether he has won or lost, and constantly mulling over what to do next – occupies his attention. It is important for him. He is happy when he wins, upset when he loses, but he continues to invest even though he loses more than he makes.

If asked to explain his investment strategy, Sid would claim that he is merely trying to get a good return on his capital. From the way he invests, however, it is clear that what he is doing is closer to gambling than to investing. Investing this way must be meeting some psychological needs, since it is certainly not meeting any financial ones. Why is Sid falling into this gambling mindtrap? His childhood provides some clues.

Growing up was a very lonely and bleak time for Sid, who did not have many childhood friends. His parents were not very loving, and the family was poor. This has left a deep emptiness inside him. The action of the market is a means for masking his feelings of insecurity, anxiety, and unhappiness. The emotional ups and downs resulting from quick market moves and the many calls to the broker divert him from his disturbing feelings, but the diversion is costly.

While Sid is an extreme example, the gambling aspect of investing is part of the stock market's attraction for many people. However, responding to the seduction of picking the long-shot winner, the excitement of uncertainty, or the lure of quick riches will undermine our success. This was stated very elegantly by the economist John Maynard Keynes, a very successful stock market speculator who spent only a half hour every morning (in bed) evaluating the markets. Keynes said, "The game of professional investment is intolerably boring and overexacting to anyone who is entirely exempt from the gambling instinct; whilst he who has it must pay to this propensity the appropriate toll."*

Sid has the "gambling instinct," and he is paying the "appropriate toll" for it, though he does not realize this. It is hard enough to be a successful investor when our only goal is to make money. Trying to combine that goal with the fun of Las Vegas makes it particularly difficult to come out ahead. As will be discussed later, successful investing requires work – developing goals, developing a plan for achieving those goals, and engaging in systematic, structured activities to carry out that plan. This is different from tossing the dice and waiting excitedly to find out whether you have won or lost. Gambling can be appealing, so when investing, we need to be sure that we are not falling prey to the gambling instinct.

MINDTRAP #28: PERFECTIONISM; OR, I WOULD RATHER BE RIGHT THAN MAKE MONEY

Maybe you know someone like Dan. His motto is: "If anything is worth doing, it is worth doing well." He applies that motto to everything he does – his work, home repairs, even mowing the lawn. He has found supervisory positions hard to handle. He has high expectations of the people who work for him, and he gets too involved in the details of their

---

*Cited in Adam Smith, *The Money Game*, New York: Random House, 1968.

work. He has difficulty in delegating responsibility, and he has been criticized for oversupervising.

Dan is not disliked by his coworkers. They respect him because he is honest and consistent and does not play favorites. He sticks by the rules and tries to be fair, and he is always harder on himself than on others. The people around Dan all say that he is a perfectionist, and though he does not like to admit it, he knows that this is true.

Dan's perfectionism, his need to make the "right" choice, has hindered him from making successful financial decisions. For instance, when first starting to invest, Dan spent a great deal of time researching mutual funds. He finally narrowed down his choices to two funds. These funds were almost identical, and Dan could not choose between them. As he agonized over their prospectuses, the stock market went up 100 points. Instead of just buying one fund or the other or just splitting his money between the two, Dan spun his wheels for weeks and lost the chance for significant appreciation in either fund.

Dan's perfectionism immobilizes him because he is afraid of making a mistake—choosing the "wrong" fund. This fear of making a little mistake causes him to make the big mistake of not investing. Dan's focus on not making mistakes—rather than on succeeding—is costly for him. In sports, or any other activity, *the person who is afraid of losing is usually defeated by an opponent who concentrates on winning.*

What are the roots of the perfectionism that is creating so many problems for Dan? It is clear that he has very high standards and that he applies them to both himself and others. His parents also had very high standards. They would openly criticize one and all for not meeting their expectations. When Dan was a child, his parents always pointed out his mistakes, but they rarely praised him for what he did correctly. He became very cautious and inhibited because he did not want to be criticized.

As we have seen, Dan approaches the stock market in the same way that he approaches everything else in life, applying the same unrealistic expectations to himself here that are causing problems in other areas of his life. His perfectionism impels him to expect to buy the "right" stock at the "right" time. What immobilizes him is his fear of doing the "wrong" thing – making a mistake. Dan is in a contradictory bind; his high expectations lead him to want high returns, but his reluctance to take risks limits his potential success.

Perfectionism leads to a loss of perspective both in life and in the market. Perfectionists can become so focused on a small point, say buying at the "right" price, that they miss the larger picture, a runaway bull market that is shooting up all prices.

MINDTRAP #29:
NOT ACCEPTING RESPONSIBILITY FOR ONE'S ACTIONS; OR, "THE DEVIL MADE ME DO IT"

Phil is an engineer who knows his job. He is not the world's best engineer, but he is not the worst either. He is conscientious, he tries hard (sometimes too hard), but no one likes to work with him. He's a nice guy, he's fun to go out with for a drink, but at work he is an irritant because nothing is ever his fault. Every mistake he makes is caused by other people. Either they told it to him wrong, or they should have explained it better, or he had to rush, and if they were more organized, he wouldn't have fallen behind like he did.

When investing, Phil also never makes a mistake. Yes, he does lose money on investments, but it is just never his fault. His broker talked him into buying, or if his wife wasn't so jittery about the market, he would never have sold.

The roots of Phil's inability to accept responsibility for his actions lie in his childhood. His parents were very critical and blaming. Phil would be severely reprimanded and punished for the slightest mistake. He was even made to feel guilty about things that weren't his fault but were problems for his parents. Anything they did not like, they blamed Phil for.

It is understandable why Phil now denies responsibility for any of his mistakes, but this robs him of the opportunity to learn from them. You learn from your mistakes only if you study them to find out what went wrong. You can then work to avoid repeating a mistake the next time a similar situation pops up. But if you deny having made mistakes, you will not learn from them and you will be doomed to repeat them.

MINDTRAP #30:
MY MIND IS MADE UP, DON'T CONFUSE ME WITH FACTS

Ann is a computer programmer. She enjoys her job very much because she is intelligent and likes to work alone. She has always had difficulties with people in positions of authority, such as teachers or supervisors. She bristles at being told what to do, and she is very sensitive to any hints of being patronized. Her supervisors have recognized this about Ann, so they give her a wide berth.

As an investor, Ann has very definite opinions about the stock market. She believes that the market is run primarily by insiders and that the small investor needs to be constantly alert to their machinations. She tends to disbelieve most of the recommendations offered by brokerage firms. She is convinced that those recommendations reach the major clients first and that by the time they get to the average investor, it is too late to buy.

Ann has some very strong views about economics and about how the stock market should act. Those views usually lead her to positions contrary to the ones taken by most market followers. In order to maintain her views, she focuses on a few bits of supportive information that buttress them. This means that she usually ignores contradictory information and discounts the views of most economists and stock market experts. She can ignore, for example, obvious signs that a bull market will continue and focus instead on a few minor indicators pointing to the contrary conclusion. Occasionally she is right and profits from her views, but most of the time she is wrong and loses money.

Ann's approach to life was established through her interactions with her mother – a young divorced woman who raised Ann entirely by herself. Ann's mother was suspicious, distrustful, and controlling. Ann was constantly subjected to lies and to exaggerated threats of the harm that would result if she did not go along with her mother's wishes.

These experiences had a profound effect on her, and she now reacts in the same way to others as she once did to her mother. She is suspicious and guarded, and she is very distrustful of what people say. She expects them to be devious rather than forthright. She assumes that the opposite of what someone says is likely to be the truth.

Although she does not realize it, Ann is very arrogant about her stock market opinions. In dismissing the views of those who hold opinions different from hers, she ignores the fact that intelligent, thoughtful people have studied the same array of information that she has and have come up with different and well-reasoned conclusions. These people may not be right, but it is a mistake to ignore their ability and the amount of effort they have expended. Whenever we cavalierly dismiss opposing views, we are falling into that same mindtrap of arrogance. Opposing views are food for thought that need to be considered and digested. You are unlikely to learn very much new from people who already agree with you. Listening to opposing views keeps you sharp and on top of things. A friend of mine says, "You have to keep an open mind, but not so open that your brains fall out altogether," and that is not a bad maxim to keep in mind for the stock market.

MINDTRAP #31:
DEPRESSIVE PERSONALITIES; OR, IT LOOKS LIKE
RAIN ON WALL STREET IF YOU ALWAYS HAVE A
BLACK CLOUD HANGING OVER YOUR HEAD

Depression was discussed earlier as a reaction to situations involving loss. It is a feeling that everyone experiences at times; for some people, however, depression is more than a transient mood. Instead, it is a style of life. This can be due to an inherited genetic predisposition to depression, family interaction patterns, tragic life circumstances, or a combination of these. The depressed person does not experience life as being particularly happy, although he or she may not be unhappy. People who are chronically depressed feel that they are "just going through the motions...... neither happy nor unhappy," "having a bad case of the blahs" – no oomph, no *joie de vivre*. They experience very little fun or excitement in their lives because they find that most things are just not very pleasurable.

Unfortunately, such people often come to have a very negative view toward life. Their expectations for the future take on a decidedly pessimistic slant. Will things improve? "Probably not." What's the state of the world? "It's going to hell in a hand basket." When viewing situations, they focus more on the problems than on the potential. Will the economy improve? "There sure are a lot of problems out there – foreign competition, incompetent politicians, and the confusion in Washington." (These problems can be safely mentioned because they are always present.)

The pessimism of these people contaminates their perceptions of their situations and their abilities. Should you buy now? "No. It's too late. I've missed the right time to buy like I miss out on most things in life." You think XYZ has great potential, and it looks cheap. "If XYZ was any good, other people would have discovered and bought it. It wouldn't be this cheap if there weren't some problems."

This type of thinking hinders these people in three ways. First, it keeps them from being more than marginally successful. They expect any success to be short-lived, so if a stock they own is up, they move quickly to sell it before it goes down. This keeps them out of the major moves and the super-successful stocks whose prices double, triple, or do even better over the years. Second, it undermines their confidence in their own judgment. As we have seen, the stock market is an anxiety-filled place so investors have to be self-confident to do well. If they are not self-confident, they will constantly be scared out and sell low. Third, it makes a bearish viewpoint appealing to them. While being a bear can produce some success in the market, historically the market has gone up, not down. Bear markets can be sharp and treacherous downturns, but they are relatively short-lived, lasting on average only 1 1/2 years, whereas bull markets last much longer. So being constantly bearish means betting against the general trend of the market and therefore being a loser over time.

Chronic depression is different from the other personality styles that are presented here in that it may have a genetic and biochemical basis. It should be assessed by a professional, and medication may be required to overcome it.

MINDTRAP #32:
LOW SELF-ESTEEM; OR, "I WOULD NEVER BELONG TO ANY CLUB THAT WOULD HAVE ME FOR A MEMBER" (GROUCHO MARX)

Paul is 33 years old, lives off a family trust, is single, and dates quite a bit. He is attracted to detached and distant women and works very hard to win them over. He wines and dines them, and takes them to the best restaurants and expensive resorts. In these relationships he always feels insecure and inferior and his anxiety leads him to constantly try to impress his dates. However, if one of these women should become interested in Paul, a strange metamorphosis takes place. His feelings change abruptly. While previously all he sought was signs of acceptance and love, now he no longer cares. Since he no longer feels attracted to the woman, he soon ends the relationship.

Groucho Marx once said, "I would never belong to any club that would have me for a member." Paul has the same attitude about himself. He is not interested in any woman who is attracted to him. Why does he have this attitude? The answer is that he suffers from low self-esteem. Since he thinks poorly of himself, he subconsciously concludes that there must be something wrong with any woman who is attracted to him.

Paul's low self-esteem also interferes with his approach to investing. Paul has been speculating in the market for years. If asked why he invests, he would answer, "To make money, get a good return on my investment." Overall he has lost a considerable amount of money in the market, yet he continues to follow the same game plan. Why does he continue to follow this losing plan? The answer is that he is thinking less about the chances of a stock going up than about how brilliant he will appear to others for having made unlikely choices.

Paul wants people to think he is smart and competent. He feels happy fantasizing about the admiration and respect he will receive when telling friends about his successes. More than making money, he wants the recognition from others of his ability. He has been known to pass up good investment opportunities because they would not appear to be brilliant moves. Why should he buy stocks during a bull market – anyone could do that? Why should he buy obvious stocks, such as IBM, when choosing them does not require real intelligence? Instead, Paul buys two types of stocks. The first type consists of risky new issues that he thinks could skyrocket in value – "I want to get in on the ground floor of the next IBM." The other type consists of stocks that are out of favor with investors and have been sinking in price – "turnaround candidates that could really surprise you." Both these types of stocks have the possibility of achieving spectacular returns, but they also run a high risk of losing money.

Investing well is hard to do, even if your entire focus is on making money. Whenever other agendas enter into the process, such as proving your worth or ability, your chances of doing well will decrease. It may be worthwhile to review whether anything other than financial influences affects your stock selections. Even if you merely like to talk about your good or bad luck with stocks, your stock market decisions could be influenced by the attention you anticipate from telling others about the choices you make. This could prevent you from making optimum choices.

MINDTRAP #33:
FEAR OF SUCCESS; OR, HOW TO SNATCH DEFEAT FROM THE JAWS OF VICTORY

Martha is a computer analyst for a large corporation. She is very conscientious, thorough, and diligent in her work, and she applies these same qualities to picking stocks. She makes well thought-out selections, but they just don't seem to work out right. For example, a few years ago she bought stock in a waste management company because she concluded, after considerable thought, that the disposal of industrial waste was a major societal problem and would need to be addressed. The stock's price fluctuated around her purchase price for a while and then began drifting down as the entire market went down. Unlike most investors, Martha was not perturbed by these paper losses and resigned herself to losing money. After staying down for months, the stock's price finally started climbing and eventually it exceeded the purchase price. As the stock continued to go up, Martha began worrying that it might soon fall in value and she would be stuck with a loss again. So she sold the stock, feeling relieved about not incurring a loss and happy about making a small profit. The stock's price remained stable until reports of higher profits were announced. Then it really began climbing, and it continued to climb for months and years.

Martha next bought stock in a women's clothing company. She did so because she liked the company's clothes, because she had noticed that many women were choosing these clothes, and because some research had indicated that the company was sound. The stock began going up in price within a few weeks of Martha's purchase. Within three months she had made a profit of almost 30 percent on the stock. She then decided to sell the stock before something happened and she lost her profit. It turned out, however, that Martha had picked up on a major shift in shopping preferences. The company achieved spectacular profits, and these fueled a more than 200 percent increase in the stock price in a few years' time.

When investing, Martha reacts to success by anticipating failure, and this keeps her from being successful. She feels anxious when her stocks show profits, so she soon sells them. It never occurs to her to buy more of stocks on which she has been proven right, or even to continue to hold on to such stocks while their prices are still rising. Snatching defeat from the jaws of victory is something Martha has done often in her life.

Martha developed the pattern of undercutting herself as a protective mechanism against her mother, a very insecure woman who was sensitive to any hint of criticism or inadequacy. When playing such games as Monopoly or Scrabble with her children, she would always try to win. If she lost, she would become defensive and irritable, and soon Martha would be punished for some newly discovered offense such as not having cleaned her room well enough or being careless.

From childhood on, Martha learned that winning was not worthwhile. She was taught that her successes hurt others and made them angry at her. As an adult, she is not made happy by her achievements because her life experiences have led her to feel uncomfortable about success. If she does succeed, she anticipates that something will soon spoil her success – criticism, anger, or new problems. Therefore, she always does something to avoid achieving noticeable success.

When Martha is investing, the same psychological patterns recur. She is not particularly troubled when she does not succeed. Success makes her feel anxious, however, because she expects unpleasant consequences to result from it. That is why she accepts having her stocks go down but soon sells them when they go up. A rule of investing is to cut your losses and let your profits run, but Martha's fear of success causes her to take exactly the opposite approach. Her expectations cause her to exclude certain ideas from consideration, such as buying more of a stock that is appreciating in value. This again limits her ability to do well in the market.

Martha is an extreme example, but it may be worthwhile for you to examine your own feelings toward success and failure. If being successful makes you feel somewhat anxious, embarrassed, or guilty, those feelings could hamper your success. You may be excluding certain stock choices or selling successful picks too early because of them.

MINDTRAP #34:
BLIND OPTIMISM; OR, "WHAT, ME WORRY?"

Tim is one of those people whom the gods have smiled upon. He is exceptionally smart and very talented, and he has been successful in almost everything he has tried. He was raised by loving, doting parents who thought that everything he did was wonderful.

Not surprisingly, Tim has an exceptionally optimistic outlook on life.

Whatever the problem, he assumes that it will all work out just fine. This has always been the case for him. No matter how difficult an assignment he has been given, he has always been able to accomplish it. Projects have required time and effort, and have engendered some anxiety along the way, but everything has always worked out for him.

Tim is not perfect. There are areas in which he does poorly. For one, he gives terrible advice. He makes snap judgments, which pose no problem for him because he is so competent that regardless of what he does, he will be successful. But when others try to follow his advice, they often run into trouble because they are less capable than he is.

Since Tim has never had to learn to make thoughtful analytic judgments, his success in the stock market has been limited. His general optimism and lack of thoughtful analysis combine to leave him open to buying impulsively when he hears good news or is given tips. He therefore often buys stocks at the top. If the stocks start to go down, he does not worry, because things "always work out" and the stocks will go up again. What Tim forgets is that he is not running the companies whose stocks he bought, so he cannot make them "work out."

As Tim's example shows, it is possible to be too optimistic about the market. Stocks fluctuate, and they do so for numerous reasons. One needs to deal with down-trends as well as up-trends. A person who is overly optimistic will tune out important negative information that needs to be heard. Also, the stock market game is much too difficult to be dealt with impulsively and cavalierly. Some time and effort are required to learn and play the game.

OVERCOMING PERSONALITY MINDTRAPS

As we have seen, our individual personalities and life experiences influence our approach to investing and can become obstacles to our success. In psychology these patterns have been called "games" or "scripts," but they just describe ways of acting that have been established during our formative years. In order to develop some hypothesis for why we behave as we do, it is useful to first think about how our parents approached situations and how that may have influenced us. For example, if you had a parent who was critical and perfectionistic, you may be approaching life, and investing, in the same way. To help identify such patterns, think about and jot down what types of people your parents are, how they raised you, their attitudes toward money, and how any of this could be creating mindtraps in your investing.

Personality of father (e.g., perfectionistic):

_____

_____

_____

_____

Personality of mother (e.g., pessimistic):

_____

_____

_____

_____

Parental expectations of you (e.g., high expectations):

_____

_____

_____

_____

Reactions to success (e.g., ignored, praised, success expected):

_____

_____

_____

_____

Reactions to mistakes (e.g., severely criticized):

_____

_____

_____

_____

Attitudes toward money (e.g., money very important, loss of money seen as a major catastrophe):

_____

_____

_____

_____

Other relevant attitudes (e.g., expectations of total self-reliance – no help with decision making):

_____

_____

_____

_____

This can start you thinking about how you react to risk, loss, success, errors, and any other issues that could be hindering your success. In the next chapter we will look at other attitudes that hinder people when investing and describe some ways to overcome them. As you go through this book, jot down any mindtraps to which you may be susceptible. People are often reluctant to do this, but I believe that you have to do it if you really want to overcome those investment mindtraps. What you are reluctant to do, with respect to developing self-awareness, may be what you need to do most.

ATTITUDES:
The Rose Color in Our Glasses

I magine that you are going to the top of a skyscraper on a crowded elevator. You are at the front of the elevator facing the door. As you stand there, minding your own business, someone jabs his umbrella into your leg. You are taken aback by this and move over. A few seconds later he jabs you again. Now you are starting to feel angry. If he does it one more time, you are going to give it to him. He then jabs you one more time. This is it. You are really steaming now, your hand tightens into a fist, you turn around ready to confront this SOB – and you see that he is a blind man who was accidentally poking you not with an umbrella, but with his cane. What has happened to your anger? It has disappeared. But why? Your calf still hurts. The reason you are no longer angry is that your *attitudes* about the situation changed when you saw that the man was blind. This shows how powerful our attitudes can be and how much they influence our emotions, decisions, and actions.

People sometimes find it hard to understand how our attitudes influence the way we act and feel about things. It is easy to assume that the events of life cause us to react the way we do. People say such things as these: "Judy really makes me mad"; "My job is killing me"; "My kids drive me crazy"; "The market is ruining my stomach." Remarks of this kind imply that the events themselves cause our reactions. But how can this be? Not everyone responds in the same way to the same events. Things that cause great turmoil for one man are shrugged off by his neighbor. A stock market situation one person responds to with panic is greeted as a great opportunity by another person. So it cannot be just events that cause our reactions to situations; our attitudes are also involved.

This influencing of our attitudes happens because when we think about things, we use language. We are wired in such a way that language has the power to produce emotional reactions in us. For example, if I were to tell you that a good friend of yours had been seriously injured in an automobile accident and was now undergoing emergency surgery, you would experience a powerful emotional response. Your heart would start pounding, blood might drain from your face, your blood pressure would shoot up, and you might feel faint, apprehensive, and anxious. What would have produced these powerful emotional reactions? Have you seen your friend in the hospital? No. Have you seen the smashed-up car? No. Just my words produced these reactions. When we think about things, we use words and images, and it is those words and images going through our minds that produce the reactions. Certain attitudes are so entrenched and well developed that we run through them almost instantaneously. We are unaware that we have assumed attitudes; we feel that we are just perceiving reality. But it is still our attitudes that account for the emotions we feel.

Sometimes people have mistaken attitudes, attitudes that do not reflect present reality, but they continue to operate on the basis of those mistaken attitudes. In my clinical practice, for example, I see people who will do anything to avoid a confrontation. They tell me they "can't stand fighting," so they never assert themselves. They give good reasons for this position (fighting doesn't solve anything, it only makes matters worse); after some exploration, however, we discover that the underlying attitude is that "no one should ever be angry with me." This attitude often develops during childhood, when it can be very threatening to a child's security to have a parent be angry. Obviously, this is not a realistic attitude for an adult; however, since these people are not consciously aware of the attitude, they never examine its validity – they just feel terrified about displeasing others. Only after they have identified and questioned the attitude can they begin to change. A friend of mine makes this point by saying, *"It is not what we don't know that hurts us; it's what we 'know' that ain't so that does us in."*

Next we will examine some common attitudes toward investing and observe how they can mislead investors.

MINDTRAP #35:
"I HAVE TO..."; OR, HOW TO PRESSURE
YOURSELF INTO A LOSS

Joe and Bill are good friends and have known each other for a long time. They have similar interests, and they are both fairly competitive. This has contributed to their success in school and in their careers. Over the last few years Joe has put together some savings, and now he wants to invest in the stock market. He is interested in the market because his friend Bill, who inherited some money a few years ago, has been investing in the market for a while and has been telling Joe about how well he has been doing. Joe is determined to do at least as well as Bill, but he would really like to beat Bill at this new game. Since Bill is already ahead, Joe believes that there is no time to lose. He feels that he is as smart as, if not smarter than, Bill, and so should be at least as successful as Bill.

Joe contacts Bill's broker. Feeling that he has to start off by hitting some home runs, he tells the broker that he wants to invest in stocks that have a chance of really taking off. "No widow and orphan stocks for me," he says. The broker suggests a few aggressive stocks. Joe not only buys the stocks the broker recommends but also chooses some high-flyers himself, based on information from newspapers and magazines. Yet it seems that just as soon as he buys a stock, its price goes down. On the average his stocks are down 25 percent after a couple of months. Now he no longer wants to beat Bill; he would just like to get his money back. Then the entire market stages a rally and all of Joe's stocks go up. But they are not quite up to the price he paid for them. He is sick of these stocks and sorry he ever started to play the market. He is just waiting for the stocks to reach the price he paid so he can unload them and recoup his losses. Unfortunately, the market takes a major dip and the stocks quickly fall in value. Joe feels sick about this; he feels trapped and helpless. Finally, he cannot take it anymore and sells all of his stocks at roughly 50 percent of what he paid for them. He swears off ever investing in the market again. He cannot face his friend Bill for months because he feels so embarrassed and down on himself.

How did Joe's attitudes contribute to his losses? Joe had three different attitudes about the situation that greatly influenced his actions:

Attitude 1: "I have to do better than Bill."

Attitude 2: "I have to be successful in a hurry."

Attitude 3: "I have to sell my stocks for at least what I paid for them (I cannot take a loss)."

You will notice that all of Joe's attitudes include the words *have to*. Similar words could have been used, such as *must, got to,* or *need to.* These words all have the same implications as *have to.* In order to understand how the words *have to* affect our actions, let us look at their meaning–remember, words by themselves can produce powerful emotional reactions. We have to have food, air, and water. Unless we have these things, we die. Thus, when we tell ourselves that we "have to" have or do something, the implication is that the situation is urgent–a life-and-death matter. This is rarely the case, but we always tend to feel extra pressure when we think we "have to" do something. A good way to understand this is to imagine how you would feel if your boss came over and said, "You have to get this done by 3:30" versus how you would feel if he said, "I want you to get this done by 3:30." Most of us would feel less pressure in the second case than in the first, even though the two situations are identical. No one will die if the work is not done by 3:30. The boss just wants it completed by that time. Too many people have gotten ulcers rushing to meet a deadline, only to see the finished work sit on someone's desk for a few days. When the boss says, "You have to get this done by 3:30," what he really means is that he wants it done by 3:30, but because of the words *have to,* we perceive the situation as being more urgent than it really is.

I can remember doing this to myself. I would wake up feeling relaxed and refreshed. Then as I drove to my office, I would think over all the things I "had to" do: write a letter, make a phone call, see someone in the hospital, pick up milk on the way home, and so on. By the time I would get to work I could feel the tension across my shoulders. Were these things that "had to" be done? If I were sick and didn't do them today, couldn't I do them tomorrow or the next day? Yet by telling myself that they were "have tos," I was turning them into unreasonable, urgent demands on myself, and my body was responding to that perception.

Joe's perception of reality was that he had to do better than Bill, that this had to be done quickly, and that he had to sell a stock for no less than it cost him. Doing anything else was inconceivable to him. His actions are completely understandable, given his attitudes about the situation.

Our attitudes function like lenses or filters in front of our eyes. Unbeknownst to us, they alter our perceptions. For people who are color-blind, the world appears as black, white, and shades of gray – that is their perception of reality. People who are born nearsighted perceive most of the world as being fuzzy; only when they begin wearing glasses do they become aware that their perception has been inaccurate. Our attitudes are the lenses and filters that cause us to perceive reality in the way we do. It was no more a part of Joe's perception of reality that he had other options than is the color purple for people who are color-blind.

How can we overcome attitudes that may get us into trouble with investments or in life? One effective technique for overcoming any unnecessarily disturbing attitudes is to analyze the situation on paper. To do this, you will want to take the following written steps.

1. **Identify the event.**

   "Bill is making money investing in stocks."

2. **Identify your attitudes.**

   "I have to do better than Bill."

   "I cannot sell a stock for less than I paid for it."

3. **Identify your perceptions/emotions.**

   "I am feeling pressure, a sense of urgency."

   "I feel trapped, helpless-that I have no options."

4. **Identify the actions that result from your perceptions/emotions.**

   "I have to buy a lot of stocks quickly."

   "I have to hold stocks until they are selling for at least at

   what I paid for them."

5. **Identify the realities of the situation. (Put down just**

   facts – no opinions – e.g., the type of statements that would be acceptable to a court of law.)

   "I have money I want to invest."

"My stock is now worth $ _____."

6. Assess the rationality and logic of your attitudes.

A simple way to do this is by prefacing each of your assumptions with a "Why." "Why do I have to do better than Bill?" "Why is this an emergency situation?" "What's the hurry?" "Why can't I sell a stock for less than I paid for it?" Then think about how a rational individual would assess the situation.

7. Reassess your attitudes and draw practical conclusions from your reassessment.

"I do not believe it would be reasonable for me to rush in and buy a lot of stock all at once. I do not have to equal or surpass Bill. What is likely to happen to someone who is starting out in a new venture? Usually such a person makes mistakes as he learns. Rarely is anyone successful at something the very first time he tries it. I should expect to make wrong decisions at times, and it would be reasonable for me to take a loss."

Since your illogical attitudes are long-standing and well entrenched, it is important to go over the new reasonable attitudes repeatedly so that you reprogram yourself with them.

8. Develop your new game plan.

"What is a reasonable course of action? It would be to go slowly, not put all my eggs in one basket, and learn about investing before I jump in with both feet."

MINDTRAP #36:
NEEDING TO SELL STOCKS FOR AT LEAST THE
PURCHASE PRICE; OR, RIDING LOSERS TOO
LONG

Among Joe's troublesome attitudes is one of the most costly and
pervasive mindtraps of all investors, and it is worth examining just by itself.
The investor perceives that he or she has no alternative but to hold on. This
attitude can be phrased in various ways: "I cannot sell a losing stock"; "I
have to hold on to a stock until its price is at least what I paid for it." The
words *have to* and cannot imply that there is no other option. However,
although you "have to" rush an injured child to the hospital, you do not
"have to" continue owning a stock. The unfortunate investor stuck with
this belief can hold on to a bad stock for years and years until it finally inches
back to the price he paid for it.

As already stated, a common Wall Street tenet is that you should **cut
your losses and let your profits run**, but "have to" and "cannot" prevent
you from doing this. The need to question this attitude has already been
discussed, but a new attitude needs to be articulated and frequently
reiterated. We all *want,* and initially expect, our stocks to go up, but this is
a far cry from "having to" keep them. The attitude you should inculcate
upon your mind is: "I want my stock to go up, but I *will* sell it if it goes below
_____." In this way you are programming yourself to avoid the "have
to" mindtrap rather than falling into it. Through repetition you need to
program yourself with a well thought-out personal plan (covered in the
next chapter), specified individual strategies, and rules for action so that
they displace your irrational attitudes. Another way of programming
yourself to avoid major losses is to develop this attitude: "I *will* not hold on
to a stock once I believe the probability of its going down is greater than
the probability of its going up." Once again, you are using a strong attitude
– I will not – to avoid a common mindtrap.

"Have to" attitudes can cause trouble in all aspects of life, not just in the market. In my clinical practice I see lots of people who suffer from stress-related problems. These are normal people–people like yourself and your neighbors – who do not have serious psychological or emotional problems. Yet these normal, sane people will put incredible pressure on themselves and then do totally irrational things. For example, they will speed and drive recklessly, not because an emergency has arisen, but because they "have to" be on time. This is something that most of us have done. We have endangered ourselves and others by speeding because we were late for an appointment, a meeting, or a date. Why have we done this? Because we believed that we "had to" be on time – we defined and perceived the situation as an emergency. Rushing a seriously injured child to the hospital is a life-and-death situation in which it makes sense to drive this way. But it makes no sense to speed if we are late for a doctor's appointment, a date, or a business meeting. But if the "emergency" lens is in front of our eyes, we will respond in the same way to such a situation as we would to an injured child needing to be rushed to the hospital.

It is a well-known fact that *we tend to make better decisions when we are calmer than when we are under extreme pressure.* Since the uncertainties of the stock market are often an unavoidable source of anxiety, it will benefit everyone to remove unnecessary, self-induced pressure. The "have tos" are one way in which such pressure is created, the following mindtrap is another.

MINDTRAP #37:
GUILT; OR, THE TYRANNY OF THE SHOULDS

Marvin has been investing in the market for some time. He studies the markets intensely. He reads *The Wall Street Journal* daily, studies stock market magazines such as *Barron's,* and watches business shows on television. Although he makes some money in the market, Marvin is almost always disgruntled and unhappy. When stocks are going down, he is reluctant to buy them because they may drop even further. When they rally, he does not buy them because he believes that stocks should be bought when they are low and that once they have started to go up, it is too late. He is then angry at himself for not having bought earlier.

A typical pattern for Marvin is to watch a stock go down in price for a while. He then starts thinking about buying it, but he cautiously waits for it to bottom out. It does so one day, and then it starts going up. By this time Marvin believes that it is too late to buy it – that he should have bought it at its low price (buy low, sell high). He then watches the stock shoot up by 35-50 percent or more and kicks himself the whole time for not having bought it on the day it bottomed out.

Occasionally Marvin buys a stock out of sheer frustration or impulse, rather than when the price is at its low. The stock then rises, and Marvin is faced with another dilemma: When should he sell it? He has owned stocks that have doubled in price, but he has always been reluctant to sell them because they might go even higher. Let us say that he buys a stock for $20 and it goes up to $40, a nice return on his investment. But then the stock goes down to $35. Marvin is again angry with himself, this time for not selling at $40. He swears that if the stock reaches $40 again, he will sell it. Unfortunately, when it rallies, it only goes up to $38, before dropping to $33. It hovers around $33 for a while, and Marvin is now kicking himself for not selling at $35-$38. This time he swears that when it reaches $35, he will sell. This pattern is repeated as the stock slides lower and lower, finally dipping below $20. Marvin feels that he could never sell it for less than he paid for it, so he ends up being stuck with a losing stock for years.

The two major attitudes that undermine Marvin are:

1.   I should buy only at the bottom.

2.   I should sell only at the top.

The operative word here is *should,* and like *have to,* it gets people into a lot of trouble. I think the best way to get a sense of how "should" affects us is to think about the Ten Commandments: Thou shalt not kill, thou shalt not steal, and so on. Today we would put it this way: "You should not kill, you should not steal." You can see that the word *should* implies that we are doing something wrong, that we are being bad. When we do something wrong, we feel guilty. As a "should" goes through our minds, we start to feel guilty. Think about how you would feel if I told you, "You really should talk things over more with your spouse. You should exercise more." Most of us feel a twinge of guilt when we are reminded of such things.

Since Marvin's stock market decisions are so greatly influenced by "shoulds," let us go through the steps that would help him overcome this attitude.

Event

Stock goes up.

Attitude/Lens

I should have bought.

Perception/Feeling

Can no longer buy. Depressed. Guilty.

Action

None. It is too late to buy this stock because it has already started to go up.

Fact

Stocks can be bought and sold anytime the stock market is open.

Rational/Logical Assessment

How can anyone know whether a stock has reached its high or low level? It is only after the fact that we know this. So I am setting up impossible criteria for myself. I will feel guilty all the time if I attempt to act in accordance with this attitude.

Conclusion

I will always buy stocks for more than their ultimate lows and sell them for less than their highs. The rise of a stock above its low will be a sign for buying it. The price of a stock in relationship to its high will not be my primary reason for selling it.

New Game Plan

My decisions about buying and selling stocks will depend on other factors besides the top and bottom price. I will use a *system* for identifying times to buy and sell.

The "have to" and "should" mindtraps result from the effects of words on people's emotions and actions. The next set of mindtraps are caused by the assumptions inherent in different attitudes.

MINDTRAP #38:
ONE-TRACK THINKING;
OR, GETTING DERAILED BY THE EXPRESS

Jill has been investing in the stock market for 15 years and is happy with her success. She had to learn some painful lessons when she started, and she lost a considerable amount of money trying to get rich quick. She has one rule of investment now, and that is to always buy at low price-earnings ratios. (The price-earnings ratio, or P-E, is the ratio between the price of a stock and its earnings.) Following this rule, Jill has consistently done better than bonds or money market instruments.

You might ask how this qualifies as a mindtrap since Jill has been successful. It is a mindtrap because of her "always" (or inverse "never") filter. The "always" filter functions to exclude a number of potentially successful stocks from her perception. As far as she is concerned, those stocks do not exist, and since she will never be aware of them, she can never purchase them.

Event

Growth stock recommended.

Attitude/Filter

Always buy low P-E stocks.

Perception/Feeling

Does not register. Smug self-assurance ("I know how to do this").

Action

Buy only low P-E stocks.

Fact

There are many ways to assess the potential appreciation of stocks.

Rational/Logical Assessment

Do I gain anything by limiting myself to only one set of rules for picking stocks? Can this be the best way at all times?

Conclusion

I will try to use what seems to be the most promising approach for me at any point in time.

New Game Plan

I will try the strategy that in my opinion best fits the situation.

People joke about never saying never and caution us against taking rigid, absolute positions. Yet once patterns of action become successful, it is easy for us to fall into mental ruts and maintain those tried and true ways. Constant vigilance may be not only the price of liberty but also the price of stock market success. The star stocks of yesterday can be the fallen stars of tomorrow. Openness to new information and the mental agility needed to process are essential in a constantly changing world.

MINDTRAP #39: HOLDING ON TO OLD BELIEFS; OR, JOINING THE WALL STREET CHAPTER OF THE FLAT EARTH SOCIETY

John was a yuppie before the term was invented. He was a baby-boomer, but while many of his generation were involved in alternative lifestyles or political movements, John was taking the opposite path. In life, and as an investor, John tended to be cautious and prudent. He began investing in bonds, and in time he became quite knowledgeable about them. Eventually he began buying and selling bond futures. John's conservatism allowed him to do well. He became fairly successful in anticipating changes in interest rates and profited from this. When interest rates started climbing during the 1970s, John followed the trend, sold, and made money. When they reached a plateau at historically high levels, John decided that bonds could not go any lower. (The value of bonds is inversely related to the level of interest rates.) He believed that if interest rates rose further, the economy would be crippled because no one would be able to afford new mortgages and because the interest on major purchases would also become excessive. Assuming that this could not happen, he bought more bonds. His choice was rewarded when interest rates took a minor dip, but then they started to rise again. Convinced that this was a temporary aberration, John bought more bonds. Interest rates continued to climb, and the value of his bonds plummeted. Unable to give up his belief that interest rates could not go higher, he bought still more bonds. Ultimately John learned – it was a costly lesson – that interest rates, like everything else, will do what *they* are going to do, not what we decide they will do.

The mindtrap John fell into was the belief that we can know what can and cannot happen. John had never witnessed the kind of event that took place, so he could not draw on his experience to envisage this possibility. The fact that other countries had experienced much higher interest rates, so it was possible for our country, was beyond him. We may all agree that certain things are unlikely to happen, but once we step over the line from probability to *certainty*, we are in deep trouble.

Event

Interest rates rising.

Attitude/Lens

Interest rates cannot go higher.

Perception/Feeling

It is not possible for interest rates to go higher. Great confidence in this belief.

Reality

The direction and amount of interest rates are dependent on market forces.

Rational/Logical Assessment

How do I know when interest rates will peak? One can never be sure that anything will never happen.

Conclusion

I will think about the probability of various things happening. This way I still have opinions, but I realize that anything can happen.

New Game Plan

I will set down what I think the probability is of something happening. I will also recognize that there are no sure things, and I will always be open to new possibilities. A closed mind is dangerous.

For a considerable period of time, a lot of people believed that the earth was flat, and this belief greatly influenced their behavior – they would not sail too far from shore, and so on. It is very difficult not to be limited by our experience and perceptions, but the effort to keep an open mind to new thoughts and possibilities will pay off handsomely.

MINDTRAP #40:
UNDERESTIMATING THE UNPREDICTABILITY OF STOCKS; OR, FORGETTING MURPHY'S LAW

Judy was another novice who decided she would get rich quick by investing in stocks. She began playing the options market, basing her purchases on the high and low price of a stock during the preceding year.

For example, if General Motors had had a high of $75, a low of $60, and was now selling for $67 1/2, Judy would decide that within the next six months GM must sell for at least $75 again. She would buy an option to purchase shares for $70 a share five months from now, for which she would pay $1. For her to make money, GM would have to be higher than $71 a share by that time, which Judy was convinced must happen.

The belief that something "must" happen is similar to the previously discussed belief that things can, or cannot, occur. John and Judy – were both unrealistically certain about the future. Neither of them was prepared for an unexpected occurrence, one that might overturn their "certain" conclusions. Remember Murphy's famous law (Whatever can go wrong – will go wrong), and think about what unexpected "wrong" things could upset your investment strategy.

Event

GM selling for $67 1/2 after trading in a range between $60 and $75.

Attitude/Lens

GM must go higher than $75.

Perception/Feeling

The stock is certain to exceed its previous high. This is a money-making transaction.

Reality

The direction and range of stock prices are dependent on market forces. Stock prices can go anywhere.

Rational/Logical Assessment

How do I know GM will go higher? One can never be sure that anything will ever happen.

Conclusion

I will think about the probability of GM going higher. I will keep in mind that someone is selling the option to me whose opinion is the opposite of mine. I have to be open to the possibility that GM will not reach, let alone go beyond, $75.

New Game Plan

I will develop a list of reasons why GM might go over $75. I will also come up with a list of reasons why this might not happen. I will then decide what the chances are that the stock will exceed $75. if I still decide to make this purchase, I will be alert to any of the things that could stop my prediction from coming true.

Since certainty in one's opinion regarding the stock market is an obvious mindtrap, a simple way of combating this attitude is to remember that the person at the other end of this trade is equally convinced of the opposite opinion. Why?

MINDTRAP #41:
CONFUSING INTELLIGENCE AND PERSONAL WORTH WITH STOCK MARKET SUCCESS; OR, YOUR IQ DOESN'T GO UP AND DOWN WITH THE DOW JONES AVERAGES

Don is a successful businessman who recently started investing in the stock market. When he was in high school, he held two part-time jobs.

After graduating, with average grades, he took a full-time job and held on to one of his part-time jobs. After a few years he started his own small business, and then through very hard work he built it into a successful small company. He was proud of what he had accomplished, but he also felt insecure about his abilities because he lacked a college education.

Don began his investing by buying a lot of shares in one company. Unfortunately, it was a poor choice and he lost money. He took this personally, and his ego was bruised by the loss. Since he was not the type of person to passively accept this loss, he decided that he was going to get his money back quickly. In his next stock purchase he doubled the amount of his investment, so that even a modest rise in the price of the stock would be sufficient for him to recoup his loss. This choice did as badly as his first, so now instead of a small loss he had a sizable one. Don was smart enough to realize that continuing to double his investment every time he suffered a loss would make no more sense in the stock market than at a blackjack table. He changed strategies and developed a diversified portfolio. This allowed him to make a reasonable return on his investments.

Two attitudes led Don to double the size of his investment after his initial loss. The first attitude centered on his feeling of being a failure and involved such thoughts as these: "Losing money like this shows that I am not very smart. . . . If I were more capable and better educated, this would not have happened. . . . Getting the business going was just luck." Don took his loss personally because he saw it as a reflection of his intelligence and ability. When he lost he felt like a failure, but if he recouped the loss, he would not feel as bad about himself. While this attitude is common, it is completely illogical. Don's abilities are the same whether the stock he buys goes up or down. His IQ does not go up when he makes a profit, and it does not go down when he takes a loss. However, if he believes that a loss proves his "incompetence," he will feel bad about himself and act in irrational ways that produce further losses.

The second attitude that led Don to double his investment was the desire to recoup his loss. That desire dictated his move. Remember, he took such a large position in the second stock, not because it was reasonable to do so on the merits of the stock itself, but only because he wanted to recoup his loss.

Let us quickly analyze these attitudes.

Event

Money lost from a stock purchase.

Attitude/Lens

This shows how stupid I am. I am a failure.

I must make up for this loss with my next transaction.

Perception/Feeling

Incompetent. Worthless. Inept.

Must find opportunity to redeem self. Must act quickly.

Reality

One decision was unsuccessful.

Rational/Logical Assessment

Why does one mistake mean I am a failure? Everybody makes mistakes when it comes to the stock market. My intelligence and ability are the same whether or not my decision works out. My IQ does not go up when I am right, and it does not go down when I am wrong.

Conclusion

One stock market decision, whether right or wrong, is not enough for me to judge my ability in the market. I will have to see how successful I am after a number of decisions. Even if I do not turn out to be a successful trader, this does not mean that I am stupid or a failure. It just means that my particular abilities are not useful for trading stocks. My business success shows that my abilities are valuable in other areas. No one is good at everything. I should not let my desire to redeem myself and do well influence my opinion of the merits of opportunities.

New Game Plan

My decisions on what and how much I buy and sell will depend on each stock. I will not let previous success or failure enter into my decisions.

I have listed below a variety of attitudes toward investment that I have read about or heard of. The list is not meant to be inclusive. See whether any of the attitudes listed seem to fit you. If there are any other attitudes you can think of that apply to you, write them down. Then go through the exercise for overcoming an attitude and see what you come up with.

- I cannot sell a stock for less than I bought it for; I cannot take a loss on a stock.

- I have to make _____ percent return on my money.

- I have to do better than... (my friend, money market rates, mutual funds, etc.).

- I have to buy at the bottom.

- I have to sell at the top.

- I should have bought it when it was lower.

- I should have sold it when it was higher.

- I should own only low P-E stocks.

- I should own only growth stocks.

- I should own only stocks that pay a high dividend.
- The insiders/experts control the market, so the little guy doesn't stand a chance.
- The experts don't know anything and are always wrong (extreme contrarian view).
- Never buy a stock recommended by a broker.
- Brokerage houses spend fortunes on research; they know more than I ever can.
- I am smarter than "they" are.
- I have to make up for my loss with this new stock.
- . . . . cannot happen.
- . . . . must happen.
- I cannot make a mistake; I have to make the "right" decisions.
- What will people think of me if I lose money?
- It is awful/terrible/horrible to lose money.
- I cannot stand being criticized for making a mistake.
- I am going to make a quick killing in the market.
- I love the excitement of the market.
- People will respect me more if I make smart moves in stock market.
- The more money I have, the more worthwhile I am as a person.
- How a stock performs reflects on me as a person.
- If I am too successful, people will not like me/will be angry with me.
- My stocks should not go up too fast; something bad will happen if they do.

If you hold any of the above attitudes or if you have identified other attitudes that you hold, go through the exercise outlined below. It will give you greater insight into how you process information and provide you with a way of overcoming your biases.

Event:

_____

_____

_____

Attitude/lens:

_____

_____

_____

Perception/feeling:

_____

_____

_____

Action:

_____

_____

_____

Reality:

_____

_____

_____

Rational/logical assessment:

_____

_____

_____

Conclusion:

_____

_____

_____

New game plan:

_____

_____

_____

MINDTRAP #42:
OVERATTACHMENT TO BELIEFS; OR, GOING
DOWN WITH YOUR SHIP ON WALL STREET

Once we have committed ourselves to beliefs, we develop an attachment toward them that can get us into as much trouble as the beliefs themselves. Once we have espoused to a set of beliefs or committed ourselves to a course of action, we seem to find it very difficult to change gears. We have trouble admitting we were wrong, that we have changed our minds, that we see things differently now than we did before.

In these respects, Mahatma Gandhi was an extraordinary exception as the following story illustrates. When Gandhi was fighting for Indian independence from British rule, one of the tools he used was long protest marches by thousands and thousands of people. On the day such a march was to have begun, but Gandhi called it off. When asked by a subordinate how he could do this, in view of the fact that people had given up jobs and come from great distances in order to march, Gandhi answered, "My commitment is to truth, not consistency." If we were in Gandhi's place, how many of us would have had the courage to tell those people that we had changed our minds? Very few political leaders whom I know of have ever made such admissions. Too many leaders go down with ill-conceived policies rather than admit that they have made a mistake.

While few of us have to make decisions that affect the lives of thousands of people, our decisions can affect the family coffers to the tune of thousands of dollars. Unfortunately, in making such decisions, too many of us are committed to consistency rather than truth. But in the stock market one must have the ability to turn on a dime and the wisdom not to do this continually.

One way to help untie ourselves from our commitment to consistency is to use our minds and the power of our imagination. It is important to know that once we have taken a certain position, we will be reluctant to alter that position even if our views have changed. One way to free ourselves from that reluctance is to imagine what we would be likely to believe and do if we held an opposing position. For example, an investor sold stock short because he believed that the market would go down. As conditions changed, he began to doubt that this would happen, but he did not change his position because he was "committed" to the bearish point of view. To help overcome this mindtrap, he could imagine a scenario in which he is long (owns stocks) and ask himself how he would feel under this condition. His answer is that he feels very confident about being long – in fact, he wants to buy even more stocks. Now that he knows how he feels doubtful when short and confident when long, he merely asks himself whether he would rather be confident or doubtful. Since he would rather be long and confident, this approach allows him to overcome the mindtrap and change his short position.

It is important to remember that we always have a choice in the stock market. The difficulty comes in being willing to use our freedom to choose and not be trapped by commitments. Once you are committed to any position, you will find it harder to change your views. Let your imagination help you by assuming that you have adopted other positions and see which of the various positions you have considered feels most comfortable to you. That position is most likely to reflect your best judgment. Remember that you want to be committed to truth and profits, not to consistency and losses.

Personality and attitudinal factors can hinder effective investment decisions. Our attitudes influence the way we process information and therefore how we perceive the world. Our emotions and actions then follow from our perceptions of situations. We often react emotionally first and then marshal reasons, sometimes even fallacious ones, for the particular position we have reached. For example, we have all at times responded emotionally to controversial issues and then come up with arguments in favor of our positions. If you do this in the stock market, you risk losing your money rather than an argument. That is why *it is a good idea to imagine yourself with an opposite point of view and see what arguments you can develop for it. Remember that when you buy a stock, someone is selling it who has good reasons for doing so. Then compare the two positions, decide which is more reasonable, and act accordingly.* The game plan you use should reflect your best evaluation of the situation based on an evenhanded view of the facts.

GOALS AND PLANS:
Overcoming Emotional
and Psychological Mindtraps

The game of professional investment is intolerably boring and overexacting to anyone who is entirely exempt from the gambling instinct; whilst he who has it must pay to this propensity the appropriate toll." Keynes based this statement on his personal experiences as an investor and not on some theoretical point of view. He studied the markets one-half hour every day (in bed according to legend), and this enabled him to achieve exceptional success in the stock market and also to help his college manage its endowment very handsomely. Although this quotation from Keynes was used earlier in connection with the "gambling instinct" mindtrap, the view of investing that it expresses will also serve as a most appropriate focal point of this chapter on a general approach to overcoming mindtraps. This chapter will focus on the words, "The game of professional investment is intolerably boring and overexacting," which will serve as the foundation of our approach for overcoming many of the emotional and attitudinal mindtraps we have discussed.

These words suggest that to do well in the market, you need to view it as a job – not as an adventure. It is a job that you know well and have done for a while, and it therefore seems boring and overexacting. Like most jobs, it is not only often tedious and unexciting, but it also involves too much paperwork and excessive review. You have to put a specified number of hours into both your job and your investing. Finally, you do your job because you are being paid to do it, and you have to see the stock market in the same way—as something you do for money.

In many ways, needing to "work on investing" is similar to needing to "work at a marriage." We have all heard the cliché, but what does working at a marriage mean? People enter into a marriage with subconscious expectations and opinions about how the two partners should act, based on their observations of their parents' marriage. Since the two partners grew up observing different styles and patterns of husband-wife interactions, each of them will have different expectations and opinions about the way spouses should act (the wellspring of marital quarrels). A successful marriage requires both of them to change those expectations and opinions. This requires them to do things that do not come naturally, which is not easy. If it were easy, there would be far fewer divorces. Investing also requires changes in deep-seated expectations and opinions. You have seen how "normal" ways of making decisions can produce disaster in the stock market. Successful investing frequently requires major departures from those normal ways, and this too requires effort.

That is why treating investing like a job is helpful. You do your job assignments regardless of whether they are difficult and require effort. Therefore, think about structuring your efforts at investing as you would structure a job assignment. Set aside specified times for the task based on your goals, your investment plans, and your ability. (Keynes required one-half hour every day.) But putting in time is not enough. As with your job, you need to measure and evaluate your performance against a set of specified expectations. This requires you to regularly review your stocks and their performance.

GOALS

To start, identify your investment goals. "I want to become rich" is acceptable as an overall goal, but you want to break this goal down into precise sub-goals that can be measured. These subgoals can be such statements as "I want to double my money in a year" or "I want a 15 percent return on my investment." Be precise. People are often reluctant to be precise when they set a goal because they then believe that, unless they achieve it, they have failed. A goal is merely a target, a destination you would like to reach. Remember, the goal is something you made up. It is not inscribed on stone tablets. Your goal yesterday does not have to be your goal today. You have the right to change your mind if you perceive things differently. Since the financial markets are constantly in flux, it is reasonable to change your goals as conditions change.

Specifying measurable goals is a useful technique for managing your time and improving your decisions. For example, once you have identified your goals, you can exclude many investment areas and focus your attention only on the areas relevant to your goals. Thus, if you want to double your money within a year, you can exclude conservative types of investments and focus entirely on more speculative types. Similarly, if all you desire is a very conservative return on your investment, you do not need to know anything about commodities, futures, or over-the-counter pink sheets.

Write down your investment goals.

Goals:

_____

_____

_____

_____

_____

_____

_____

_____

ACTION STEPS

Now that you have identified your goals, your next step is to figure out how you are going to achieve them. This typically involves acquiring information and planning your actions. If your goal is to get to San Francisco, you can do this in a variety of ways. You can fly, drive, take a train, or even hitchhike. Each of these ways will get you to your goal. The same approach would apply for investment goals. For example, if your goal were to make 15 percent a year on your investments, your action steps might be:

- Investigate the historical rates of return on various investments.
    Mutual funds
    Annuities
    Bonds
    Stock market (as measured by a broad index such as the S&P 500)
- Identify the risk factor.
- Compare different options.
- Develop a plan.
- Make purchases.

Your next step is to specify the actions necessary to achieve your goals. Remember that just as there are different ways to get to San Francisco, there are different ways to achieve your financial goals. But it will be easier to accomplish them if you have developed a specified set of action steps. For example, the action steps in your plan can range from talking to a stockbroker, to reading financial journals, to talking to officials of a company you are thinking about investing in, to developing an intricate computer-based trading system. There is no one right way, but you need to identify what your personal action steps will be.

Now write down the action steps that your goal requires.

Time
Frame

Action steps:

_____

_____

_____

_____

_____

_____

_____

_____

_____

_____

_____

_____

YOUR INVESTMENT STRATEGY

Your most important step is to clearly specify your investment *strategy* for buying and selling stocks (bonds, mutual funds, etc.). Most investors have some vague sort of "plan." I recommend that you write your plan down so that you can evaluate it and follow it better. Everyone's plan will be different and there is no "right" one, but you want to develop the most rational plan you can and then follow it *consistently*. You should do this now, when you are not being buffeted by greed, fear, or other emotions. Since you are devising the most rational strategy for achieving a specified financial goal, you will avoid being trapped by many personality factors or personal agendas.

Your plan may be as simple as following your broker's or adviser's recommendations. If that is what you have decided, you are free from having to think or read about the market or even from having to follow the actions of your stocks (just make sure you know when your maven is taking a vacation). You are now free to give more time to your family, your hobbies, or your job. On the other hand, you may devise a complex plan for buying and selling that will require many hours of work. But once again, you will have devised a working system that tells you when to buy and sell. Remember, you can change your goals and action steps as often as you wish. In fact, I would hope that your goals and stock market strategies have changed as a result of what you have already learned from this book about yourself and the mindtraps to success. Hopefully, they will be changed further after you read the remaining chapters on perception and decision making.

If you plan to make your own decisions, then your plan should have the following rules, at minimum:

- Under what conditions will you enter the market?
- What will your rules be for aborting you position?
- When will you take your profits – under what conditions?
- What will your money management or asset allocation rules be?

These are the rules that determine the size of your position in the market. If you need more information on how to do this, see Dr. Tharp's material in the recommended reading.

For the time being, write down your stock market plan.

Plan:

_____

_____

_____

_____

_____

_____

_____

_____

_____

_____

While you are developing your goals and plans, keep in mind reasonable time frames for achieving them. (As a rule of thumb, I ask people to triple their estimates of how long it will take to complete the various action steps the first time through, because typically people under estimate the difficulty and complexity of these steps.) You can then specify target dates for completing each step. It is useful to record these dates on a calendar, because otherwise it is easy to slide past them without being aware that you are falling behind.

Once you have an estimate of how long it will take you to complete the action steps required by your plan, remember that time is money. If your nest egg is sitting idle while you complete the initial action steps, this will cost you money. (It is often worthwhile to have the first action steps deal with how to maximize the return on your investment while you follow through with the other action steps.) As you monitor the rate of your progress toward achieving your goals, remember that if you are not making the progress you anticipated, you may want to reassess your initial action steps.

ESTABLISHING YOUR INVESTMENT PLAN

Having developed your list of action steps, you now have to follow through. As discussed earlier, this requires a regular commitment of time. The amount of time you commit can be brief or lengthy, depending on your goals and plans. But when will it be? Write it down.

Most readers will not follow through with this structured commitment of time for one month, and perhaps not even for one week. What makes such follow-through difficult is that people are creatures of habit. If there is anything more difficult than breaking an old habit, it is starting a new one. But I can guarantee – one of the few investment guarantees you will ever get – that you will be more successful if you develop good investment habits and systematically apply them. Here are a few suggestions on how to develop your new investment habits.

Try to find something that you already do regularly, and then have your investment time precede that. For example, if you read the paper regularly, do not allow yourself to read it until you have studied the market. After years of working with people on changing habits, I can almost hear you protesting that you don't want anything to interfere with your pleasure in reading the paper – can't your investment time be tied to something else? The answer, of course, is yes, but the paper is a good choice precisely because it is such a desired and powerful habit.

Another way to establish a new habit is to start small. If your goal is to spend an hour a day working on investment, begin by doing this for 15 minutes, or even 5 minutes, to establish the habit. When the time you spend on investment begins to feel like your regular routine, then gradually lengthen it – to 30 minutes, to 45 minutes – until you put in the full hour.

Once you have developed an investment plan and established regular procedures and times to complete them, you will need to monitor your performance. View your performance in the same way as you would view the performance of an employee whom you are supervising. Check regularly to see whether you are following the instructions of your investment plan. If you find that you are slipping, you may decide to change the plan – perhaps it is too complicated or time consuming. If you discover that things are not going well, see whether you can find any flaws in your plan. Monitor and keep regular records of your performance in the market – this can be done weekly, monthly, quarterly, or yearly-and then compare it with your goals and perhaps with some standard, such as the S&P 500 or the NYSE, AMEX, or NASDAQ averages. If you want to increase your money 15 percent in a year and after a year you find that you are not even close to this goal, this is very important feedback. It suggests that you reevaluate your goals and action steps. You will have learned some things during that year, so a new game plan may be not only warranted but also more likely to succeed.

You will need to be very disciplined to follow your plan. Your individual mindtraps – fear, greed, perfectionism, and so forth–will work to pull you away from it. When this happens, identify the mindtraps and counteract them in the ways that have been described. Up to now, a variety of "individualistic" mindtraps have been presented. In the next chapter, covering cognitive processes, "universal" mindtraps that affect how all people process information and make decisions will be covered.

INFORMATION PROCESSING:
or, Caveman in the Computer Age

The year is 10,000 B.C. One of our ancestors is out hunting for food. Dressed in animals skins, he stalks his prey, ready to hurl a poised weapon at it. He has been hunting for many hours, but he still moves cautiously through the forest in quest of signs of his prey. He sees a broken branch and then a footprint in the mud, and he hears a rustling sound as he closes in. Eventually hunger and persistence produce the desired result.

Thinking about these events can help us understand some potential mindtraps that investors encounter when they hunt for stock market profits. Notice that the hunter is presented with bits of new information sequentially – the broken branch, the footprint, and so on. As we go about our days, we are also presented with bits of new information sequentially. For example, while driving to work in order to earn money for tonight's dinner, you see a green light, so you proceed; then the brake lights on the car in front of you go on, so you slow down; later traffic is stopped in your lane, so you move over. In the same way new information will be presented to you for the rest of the day, you will evaluate it, and then you will make adaptations based on it.

Since historically this is the way human beings have most often been presented with new information, people are very good at processing information and thinking things through in a step-by-step logical sequence. We can usually solve difficult problems methodically by figuring out the first part, then the second part, and then the part after that. Great achievements have been made in such fields as mathematics, science, business, and engineering by dealing with very difficult problems or tasks in a logical, step-by-step fashion. Even if you did not know anything about construction, you could build the most elaborate house if I told you step-by-step how to do it. It might take a very long time, but the house would be built in just the same step-by-step way that the pyramids and the Taj Mahal were built.

But what if you are now facing a different type of problem? For instance, what if, instead of trying to build a house, you are trying to choose a new one to live in? This problem is different because you cannot deal with it step-by-step. When choosing a residence, you need to consider many factors simultaneously–neighborhood, distance from work, price, interest rates, quality of schools, style of house, number of bedrooms, and so on. Each house differs from other houses along these dimensions. Try weighing just some of these factors against one another for five houses – neighborhood versus distance from work versus price versus quality of schools versus style of house. (In some ways this decision is easier to grasp since by reading what has to be done, you are receiving data in a sequential manner rather than looking at five different houses and trying to weigh all of the information in your mind when you get home.) If you are like most of us, it is easy to feel overwhelmed by the problem, start to get a headache, throw up your hands, and decide that your old house is just fine. Investing in the stock market is this type of problem. Many factors must be weighed and balanced against one another when a stock is chosen.

How do we go about solving this type of problem? Few of us can identify all of the factors on which we base decisions, let alone articulate how we go about making those decisions. But understanding how we process information and where potential problems lie in our processing of information can improve our decision making.

MINDTRAP #43:
OVERESTIMATING THE MIND'S CAPABILITIES

Charley is very proud of his intellectual abilities. He has frequently been complimented on his "good mind." Charley believes if he just reads everything about the stock market that he can get his hands on, his mind will digest all of it, objectively evaluate it, and then spit out "THE ANSWER" (e.g., buy IBM Monday at $173.25) that will lead to stock market success. Is this feasible? We can get some help in answering this question from two studies (Slovic 1969; Slovic, Fleissner, and Bauman 1972) that have looked at how stock market professionals analyze and make predictions about a stock's success. In the first study one broker identified 11 factors that he thought needed to be considered in predicting a stock's future value.* Unlike Charley, this broker did not follow "everything" in a helter-skelter manner but instead specified what he thought were important contributing influences. Researchers then presented him and another broker with information on the level and trend of the 11 factors and asked them to rate the prospects for future growth of 128 companies.

A number of interesting findings emerged from the study. First, even though the broker said that all 11 factors were important to him in judging stock, in fact only 6 and 7 factors, respectively, were important to him and his colleague when rating a stock. While in theory the broker believed that all of the factors should be considered in practice he found it too difficult to use them all simultaneously. This finding suggests that we ought to identify a handful of factors that we believe most useful for predicting a stock's gains, and just try to work with these. We then need to see what

---

*The 11 factors were yield, near-term trend, earnings trend, past year's performance, profit margin trend, earnings per share yearly trend, price-earnings ratio, shares outstanding, resistance trend, support trend (the last two are technical factors), and sales volume trend.

factors were used when previously choosing stocks. By keeping track of the factors used in our stock choices, in time we will find out which ones we are actually using and which ones we merely believe useful.

Bombarding ourselves with voluminous, unrelated information does not mean that this information will be processed and used. A study by Oskamp (1965) disclosed why this approach may be appealing. The study found that giving psychologists more information did not improve their judgments, but it did increase their *confidence*. We may feel more confident if we have "read everything," but this is a mistaken confidence that could cost us considerable money if we do not examine the factors we are using to make our judgments.

People like Charley fool themselves into thinking they are capable of making more involved and complex judgments than they are capable of making. Even when the professionals in the Slovic study were reviewing specific, identified factors, they did not use all of them in making their judgments. When processing information, we are very good at juggling one ball at a time, and typically this is all we need to juggle. Sometimes, however, a situation like investing in the stock market requires us to juggle a number of balls at a time. We are not very good at this, so we usually juggle some of them and drop the rest. Unfortunately, we often believe that it is important to juggle all of those balls and that we are doing so, when in fact we are not. Instead, we are wasting time.

MINDTRAP #44:
BEING OVERWHELMED BY INFORMATION; OR, NECESSITY IS THE MOTHER OF SELECTIVITY

More investment information is available than can be listed, let alone read, digested, and evaluated. The daily newspaper informs us of the latest Dow Jones averages, along with the price of gold, bond prices, changes in the value of the dollar vis-à-vis foreign currencies, inflation rates, changes in the leading economic indicators, the number of housing starts, and on and on and on. If we seek out information about the economy, the stock market, and companies, the available material is endless. Just keeping up with *The Wall Street Journal, Barron's, Forbes, Business Week, Fortune,* industry journals, and newsletters is at least a full-time job. From the vast array of available information, investors must decide what is meaningful. List the factors that *you* believe are important for making investment decisions. (Be ready to add to your list as you identify other important factors.) In this way you have clearly identified what factors you believe are important and you can incorporate those factors into your system. This will enable you to choose more consciously what information you want to filter out. This should allow you to use your available time to focus on the information you have decided is important. For example, if you decide that information about takeover prospects is not meaningful for you, then decide to exclude reading anything about them.

Meaningful factors

_____

_____

_____

_____

_____

_____

_____

MINDTRAP #45:
THEORETICAL BLINDERS; OR, WHAT YOU THEORIZE IS WHAT YOU GET

Your "theories" about the stock market are how you relate the factors you consider important with market changes. Now that you have identified part of your "theories," there are a number of mindtraps that you can fall into.

News Release

MBI today announced the introduction of a new computer. The company believes that this long-awaited product will not only allow MBI to maintain its present market share but will also enable it to enter new market areas. Enthusiastic analysts said that the new computer meets most of the expectations about this long-awaited product.

Upon reading this hypothetical article, two hypothetical equally experienced and knowledgeable investors immediately called their brokers. One bought 100 shares of MBI, while the other sold 100 shares. Why did these two investors respond in an opposite manner to the same piece of information? Because they had two different *theories* about the stock market. The first investor subscribes to the theory that you should "buy on the rumor, sell on the news." He believes that anticipation drives the price up beyond what is reasonable, so that when the expected event finally occurs, there is a letdown and the price drops. The second investor saw the news item as a sign that MBI continues to be an excellent growth company, with even higher earning likely because of the new product, and therefore, according to his theory, a stock to buy.

All theories describe the relationship between prior and later events. We then use that relationship to predict what will happen in the future.

Our theories do not have to be well formulated sets of laws like Newton's laws of physics, they can be informal and limited in their scope. Once we accept a theory, however, it affects our perception of the present and how we process information in the present and predict outcomes in the future. When scanning information, we home in on facts that our theory designates as important and pay no attention to information that is important according to someone else's theory.

Jill's story, discussed in Chapter 7, is an example of how a stock market theory influences perception. She is an investor whose investment theory is to buy only stocks with low P-Es. She has been successful with this approach and therefore has never deviated from it. As she scans the stock market, she notices only what is occurring with low-P-E stocks, and she sees verification of her theory in case after case. It is amazing to her that others do not see the validity of her approach but continue to make their choices in other ways.

Jill faces a number of potential problems resulting from her narrow perception of the market. Since only successful instances of her theory are registering with her, *she is unaware of how successful other theories may be.* While her theory has been successful, other theories may have been even more successful, and she may therefore be missing some wonderful opportunities. *She may also have become overconfident in her approach*, and this may make her even less likely to find out about other ways of thinking and evaluating the markets.

Another example of adhering to a theory too strongly is the investor who focuses entirely on monetary factors in predicting future inflation and thereby fails to recognize the effects of rapidly falling energy prices. This single-minded monetarist might continue to predict higher inflation when the opposite is occurring. This does not mean that monetary factors are useless predictors; what it means is that a single theory is limited and can only describe part of what is actually happening. Yet another example is that of the technical analyst who is wrong because he focuses on technical indicators that are no longer working in the same manner as they have in the past (see Figure 9-1).

In summary, theories bias our perceptions of situations and thereby produce a biased view of the world. Those biased perceptions can in turn reinforce our belief in our theory. The theory-perception-theory cycle can make us become more and more rigid in our attitudes and therefore less open to potentially useful information. It is important to understand that theories are not absolute truth, but rather tools for understanding the world. Like all tools, they have limitations: they can be very useful for some tasks and useless for others.

MINDTRAP #46:
NOT ACCEPTING THE LIMITATIONS OF THEORIES; OR, THE PETER PRINCIPLE STRIKES AGAIN

Like all other tools, theories are *man-made* inventions that *attempt* to describe, in a concise way, relationships that we believe exist in the world. These theories then allow us to make better predictions and have better control over future events. Even widely accepted theories, such as those of Newton and Einstein in physics, are not gospel; they are shorthand, often mathematical, descriptions of certain relationships that occur in nature. They describe some part of the relationships that exist in the world, but they can never be all-inclusive because the world is too complicated to predict with 100 percent accuracy. That is why there are almost always exceptions to or restrictions on theories and why there are often so many conflicting theories. This holds true for economic, political, and psychological theories and for almost any other kind of theory we may espouse. These limitations of theories lead to two mindtraps.

FIGURE 9-1

Market Signs: Call Them Unreliable

Predicting Direction of Stocks Is Tougher Than Ever, as Indicators Become Distorted

ABREAST OF
THE MARKET

By BEATRICE E. GARCIA

Staff reporter for The Wall Street Journal

The thermometer says high fever but the patient feels cool. Looks like the thermometer is busted.

Many analysts and investors are discovering this these days as they try to take the stock market's temperature with indicators that are no longer reliable.

For instance, one measure has been telling analysts for more than 17 months that institutional money managers don't have enough cash on hand to keep buying more stock. Yet the Dow Jones Industrial Average has soared 53% in that period as plenty of money flowed into the stock market, most of it from institutions.

This and other once-worthy indicators have been distorted by the development of new trading strategies and the introduction and widespread use of new investment vehicles such as futures and options on stock indexes, as well as the characteristics of this bull market - which is unlike any Wall Street has seen in 20 years.

"There are different ways of playing the game and (investor) psychology could be skewed a bit," says Ralph Acompora, a technical analyst with Kidder, Peabody & Co. in New York.

The least reliable measures currently are many that attempt to ascertain investors' "sentiment" and appetite for stock. Among them: short-selling activity, institutional cash holdings and the ratios of bulls and bears in the market.

Short selling involves borrowing shares and selling them, making a bearish bet that their price will fall; the shares then could be bought back at a lower price. If the price rises, the investor loses when closing out the position. Short selling can be a way of speculating on the overall market, or of simply hedging a position in a particular stock.

The expansion of the options market and the creation of futures on stock indexes, such as Standard & Poor's 500-stock index, have given investors new ways to speculate and hedge. As a result, short-selling indicators have gone awry.

The short-interest ratio, which relates short sales outstanding to average daily trading volume, "used to be the closet thing to a bell going off on Wall Street," says Ralph Bloch, a technical analyst with Moseley Hallgarten Estabrook & Weeden in Chicago.

A ratio of 2 means that it would take

investors two trading days to cover their short positions by buying stock. A ratio of 2 or more was considered a bullish sign since such purchases would tend to drive stock prices higher. But since September 1983, the ratio has been well above 2, not signaling any of the market weakness that occurred periodically through September 1985, when the last rally began.

This indicator is distorted by the increase use of options and futures. Simultaneously taking offsetting positions in options or futures can make many arbitrage techniques relatively riskless. Those contracts provide ways of covering short positions that don't necessarily involve buying stocks.

Odd-lot short sellers, very speculative investors who short stock in other than round 100-share lots, long ago earned the reputation as horrendous market timers. They would usually sell many shares short just as a market advance was about to start. Analysts and conservative used to track what odd-lot short sellers were up to, and then do the opposite.

But the growth of the options market gave these speculators a somewhat less expensive arena to play in. Since 1976, odd-lot short sales have declined so sharply that tracking them offers few insights today.

Many indicators that have gone haywire were developed in the late 1960s and refined through the 1970s when the stock market was stuck in a trading range between 600 and 1000 on the Dow Jones Industrial Average.

Some analysts see the current bull market as an extended cycle in which the price peaks and valleys are trending higher and higher. Comparisons are being made to the market of the 1920s and to the prolonged advance from the late 1940s to the late 1960s, when prices climbed with few setbacks.

The survey of investment advisers taken by Investor's Intelligence of Larchmont, NY, has shown a high percentage of bulls in the stock market since mid-1984. Analysts used to consider such high readings an indication that just about all the bulls were in the market, leaving few buyers left to push stocks higher.

But the current market "can tolerate bullish unanimity," says Robert Ritter, a technician with L.F. Rothschild Unterberg Towbin. It's the kind of prolonged bull market that comes around once in a generation, he adds enthusiastically.

The current environment of low inflation and declining interest rates has "created a flight of money into the stock

market" from bonds and tangible assets such as commodities and real estate, explains Newton Zinder at E.F. Hutton in New York. That's why the market has been rallying steadily, even though institutional equity managers have had less than 8% of their assets in cash or money market instruments, which in the past had proved to be a bearish indication.

Increased trading in low-priced second-ary stocks has been traditionally regarded as a sign of speculation and a clue that the end of a market advance might be close. The "speculative index," which measures combined American Stock Exchange and over-the-counter volume as a percentage of Big Board activity, picked up a buying frenzy in 1983 when it shot above 75%; shortly afterward, the market fell back.

Yet the index isn't reflecting the current surge in the OTC market. Joseph Barthel, a technical analyst with Butcher & Singer in Philadelphia, contends that the speculation in this market is in blue chip stocks. He compares the current move to the early 1970s, when high-quality growth stocks were selling for 60 to 90 times their companies per-share earnings.

"The job is just getting harder," Mr. Barthel says.

What indicators *are* working?

In the past few months, oil prices have been one of the best short-term indicators. Many stock traders and portfolio managers closely monitor the price changes of the most actively traded crude oil futures contract on the New York Mercantile Exchange for a quick fix on where stock prices are headed. As oil prices plummeted, stock prices soared - except for oil issues, of course.

Still reliable are indicators that point out which industry groups and individual stocks are outperforming the market, as well as which ones may be shooting up too much too quickly. Edward Nicoski, a technician with Piper Jaffray & Hopwood in Minneapolis, says these "relative strength" indicators "tend to keep us in the strong sectors of the market and momentum tells when we're starting to reach extremes."

He says these indicators correctly warned him of an imminent peak in secondary stocks in mid-1983. These indicators now are showing some extremes among blue chip issues.

"You'll want to have some core holdings in the blue chip sector, but investors need to start moving down into second-and-third-tier stocks in some industries," he says. "For instance, rather than owning Eli Lilly and Merck, which have surged in the last six months, start looking at generic-drug companies, some biotech firms and health management organizations, which have just started to move."

The first mindtrap is wanting theories that are simple, completely accurate, and universal (and when the theories relate to the stock market—surefire ways for us to get rich quick). The people who fall victim to this mindtrap will not accept the inherent limitations of theories and instead try to stretch them to cover more and more ground. Soon good, limited theories are in shreds because of their use in inapplicable areas in the hope of making them more powerful than they are. When theories are stretched to explain everything, even useful theories lose their predictive power. In a kind of Peter Principle, overextended theories rise to their level of uselessness.

The second mindtrap is discarding a theory that is not 100 percent accurate as not being "true." Instead of trying to understand how such a theory might be helpful (where, when, and how it might be used) the people who do this proceed to the next theory, which they then discard because it is not 100 percent accurate either. They continue to believe that one *right* theory will solve all stock market riddles. More might be gained by asking the harder questions about a theory – such as whether it works better in a bull market or in a bear market or for what type of stocks and under which conditions it works best – rather than simply whether it is 100 percent right.

In summary, accepting a stock market theory will affect your perceptions. You will home in on the factors that the theory suggests are important and you will "see" the times that the theory worked out. At the same time you will be oblivious to other influences that affect the overall market or the price of an individual stock. Since there are many conflicting stock market theories, it should be borne in mind that adherents of the different theories will be perceiving the stock market differently and drawing different conclusions. This is why there are always bears in the most powerful bull markets, and vice versa. It should also be borne in mind that all of the stock market theories are limited in their usefulness, though most of their proponents do not mention this, and that their limitations as well as what they are predicting should be considered. For example, the current "hot" theory may work well for stocks in a bull market but not for stocks in a bear market, for gold, or for bonds.

Overcoming Theoretical Mindtraps

In order to clarify your theories about investing, answer the following questions. What, according to your theories, are the particular events that are predictive of changes in a stock's price? What changes do your theories predict? When will your theories work best?

Theories

_____

_____

_____

Key predictive events

_____

_____

_____

Predicted changes

_____

_____

_____

Limitations

_____

_____

_____

What has been covered so far is how we select the information we use. Next we will look at how we process that information and the mindtraps that this produces.

MINDTRAP #47: OVERESTIMATING OUR ABILITY TO ANALYZE A COMPLEX SCENE

Our friend Charley has learned the error of his ways and now recognizes that he cannot just read everything and come up with "the answer" that will make him rich. He sees that he has fallen into the mindtrap that computer types call the GIGO phenomenon – garbage in, garbage out. Continuing to study the stock market, he identifies a half dozen factors that he believes influence a stock's rise and begins monitoring them. Those factors might include number of shares traded, projected earnings, dividend rates, the direction of interest rates, the health of the economy, foreign competition, the strength of the dollar, expectations for the industry group, and the position of the company in its industry group. But Charley realizes that it is not enough to consider those factors individually, because a change in one can have important implications for the meaning of another. He agrees, for example, with those who hold that the decline of a stock on high volume is more serious than a decline on low volume. He now sees that it is necessary to look at the "whole picture," or configuration, not just at individual factors. This is the "art" of picking stocks, and he is going to become a great artist.

While the ability to look at the whole picture may be very important, how good are people at doing this? If we look again at the two studies of brokers mentioned earlier, we find that they made only six or seven types of *interactional* judgments of factors and that these interactional judgments contributed relatively little to their final judgments. Research has shown that the professional decisions of physicians, psychologists, and financial professionals are subject to the same limitations. These professionals also tend to do less configurational thinking than they think they do and make simpler examinations regarding the presence of important factors than they think they make.

In summary, the results indicate that the brokers greatly simplified the task of putting information together. Their conclusions were based primarily on an inspection to see whether what they considered important was happening – e.g., dividend yield high, price-earnings ratio low, near-term prospects good – and then adding up the six or seven factors they examined. Of course, some factors might be considered more important than others – for example, near-term prospects might be considered twice as important as the past year's performance and therefore given twice the weight. Interactions between factors – e.g., the effect of a price decline on low volume as compared with the effect of a price decline on high volume– were examined, but such interactions had a smaller impact on the brokers' final judgments.

I believe that these studies should warn investors against overestimating their capabilities. We need to limit the number of factors we weigh to a reasonable number since none of us can keep a large number in mind. When we make a decision it will probably be based primarily on a handful of factors, with minimal consideration of how those factors interact with one another. If we try to consider how all of those factors could interact, we get that really bad headache and decide to just follow cousin Fred's tip on a stock he heard about from his accountant.

It seems important that investors keep all relevant information on paper in front of them. Using pencil and paper (or a computer if you are so inclined), simplify the task of evaluation by breaking it down into a search for the occurrence of certain factors and of any important interactions between them.

IDENTIFYING PREDICTIVE CUES

To help flesh out your "system" for the market, list the predictive factors used in "theories," which should include the "meaningful" factors you derived earlier. Next, estimate the weight you would give each of these factors in predicting the success of a stock, the direction of the market, and so on. If you think that the weight assigned should depend on the interrelationships between factors, write those interrelationships down and assign your weights accordingly. Remember that there aren't going to be as many factors as you think. You may also wish to review some of your previous decisions and see what factors played a part in them. Now you have a list of cues that you pay attention to, a method for processing that information, and some sense of the weight you give it when you make your decisions. How those cues are used to make predictions about investments is covered in the next chapter.

10
PREDICTIONS:
The Heart of Investing

It is a typical morning. You get up, shower, dress, have a quick bite to eat, and are off to work. As you head out, heavy gray clouds on the horizon catch your attention. You think about hunting for your umbrella, but you decide not to since it rarely rains this time of year. Once you are in your car, the radio gives the latest traffic conditions. The freeway is very congested, so you take city streets, expecting them to get you to work faster. When you arrive – late – at work, there is a pile of things for you to do, including a number of phone calls to return. You make a quick judgment about which are most important and start with those. Later you notice that the boss is in a bad mood. You have been thinking about asking him for a raise, but this does not seem to be a good time. As you are pondering the matter, a buddy comes over and asks who you like in Sunday's game. After this matter has been concluded, you get down to work.

You have just started a typical day. Notice how many predictions you have already made and how little attention you have given to the process of making them. Most of us go about our days completely unaware of how we make most of our predictions, let alone of any flaws in the way we make them. Unfortunately, the same things typically hold true for our investments.

At the heart of every investment decision is a prediction. Purchasing a stock says that this choice will achieve a greater financial return than comparable options. How much attention do you pay to how you go about making your financial predictions? Too often, such predictions are made in a vague, passive almost unconscious manner: "I think the stock market is going up. I should buy some stocks now. I read some good things about ABCD Company in the paper today. Maybe I'll buy some of it." Thus it should not be too surprising that people tend to be rather poor predictors, and consequently poor investors. *To improve your predictions, you must learn about the process of making a prediction and then about mindtraps that hinder good predictions.*

What happens when me make a prediction? Basically, we assume a relationship between cues – meaningful bits of information, such as higher projected profits – and some future event, such as an increase in the price of a stock. We rely on two sources of information for making predictions:

1. Current information from our environment – for example, clouds, a report on the car radio, or the throbbing vein on the boss's neck.

2. Relevant information from memory – for example, you recall what weather patterns are typical for this time of the year, what the freeway is like when traffic is heavy, and what happened the last time someone asked the boss for a raise when he was in a bad mood.

When making investment predictions, we are influenced by:

1. Current information – for example, a broker's recommendations, news of changes in interest rates, reports of a company's profits and projected earnings, and changes in technical indicators.

2. Relevant information from memory – for example, how the stock market responded to similar changes in interest rates in the past, how well this broker's recommendations succeeded in the past, what you remember about a company, how accurate the previous earning estimates of a company's officials have been, how a company previously fared at the beginning of the business cycle.

For most of us, relating present events to past memories is a "passive process." We engage in that process unthinkingly – whatever comes to mind is what we use to make our predictions. For example, if a broker calls and recommends a stock, we think, "His last recommendation worked out OK; I'll take a chance and buy 100 shares." But what we need instead of a passive and haphazard way of making decisions is an active, purposeful, and systematic decision-making approach that enables us to thoroughly assess the meanings and implications of various facts.

One such approach is to have a prepared list of the questions that you want answered about new information. Your list might include such questions as:

- What has happened (changed)?

- What is really different as a result of this event – that is, why buy the stock today rather than yesterday, or next week, or next month?

- What are the consequences of this event?

- How will other things – the company, the economy, the stock market, investor psychology, etc. – change as a result of this event? (Try to come up with as many potential changes as possible.)

- When have similar events occurred in the past?

- What happened as a result of those events?

- Where can I find more information about all of this? (You can use sources besides your memory.)

- What stocks will be affected by all of this, and what changes in my portfolio would be advisable?

Such active, purposeful, and systematic evaluation and prediction should be included in your plan or system for investing in stocks. But now that you have a sense of how the process of predictions works and of some ways to make that process more efficient, there are also a variety of mindtraps to watch out for.

MINDTRAP #48:
IRRELEVANT PREDICTIONS; OR,
LOSING SIGHT OF WALL STREET'S BOTTOM LINE

When making predictions, the most important thing you should keep in mind is precisely what you are trying to predict. When you invest in the stock market, you are not necessarily choosing the best company, the smartest management, or the most profitable concern. You are predicting which stock will go up the most (relative to other concerns that you may have, such as some dividend return or relative risk). The cues you use to predict this outcome may or may not involve traditional methods of evaluating a company, but they need to include cues that look at how other investors will evaluate a stock. Many advisers forget this and then complain that the market does not "appreciate" a recommended stock or understand the "true value" in a company. This is why there are "undervalued" companies, but such companies may be undervalued for a long, long time. A stock, like everything else in life, is worth only as much as somebody will pay for it.

MINDTRAP #49:
FORGETTING THAT JUST BECAUSE LIFE USUALLY
TROTS ALONG DOESN'T MEAN THAT IT WON'T
OCCASIONALLY BREAK INTO A GALLOP

Most of us live our lives in the slow lane-that is, we expect and react to a slow-moving and therefore fairly stable world. This expectation is reasonable because the world generally is relatively stable. If you want to predict tomorrow's weather, your best predictor is today's weather.

Seasons change slowly; we do not go directly from winter's cold to summer's heat. What will your health, wealth, and relationships with people be tomorrow? Most likely, pretty much what they are today. Unfortunately, or perhaps fortunately, the same unsolved problems will still be there for you to deal with.

A mindtrap that is easy for us to fall into is to react to an unstable, fast-changing environment as if we were still dealing with our usual slow-paced world. The U.S. automobile industry in the 1970s is an excellent example. Slow change in car design had been a successful pattern for 50 years. When radical changes in gasoline prices produced a very rapid shift in consumer demand, U.S. automakers continued to build gas guzzlers that consumers no longer wanted. When investing in the stock market, you are dealing with an environment in which you can usually take some time before acting but in which abrupt shifts may require an immediate response.

This seems to have been the case for quite a while. In *Reminiscences of a Stock Operator,* published in 1923, Edwin Lefevre said that the successful stock market speculator "cannot bet on the unreasonable or on the unexpected. . . . He must bet always on probabilities – that is, try to anticipate them. Years of practice at the game, of constant study, of always remembering, enable the trader to act on the instant when the unexpected happens as well as when the expected comes to pass." If our approach is to expect slow change and therefore the opportunity to slowly evaluate the facts before we decide to act, then we will be left at the post some of the time. The difficult distinction to make is whether we are dealing with an abrupt shift, such as the gas crisis or a dramatic change in Federal Reserve policy, or with the more typical slow change that is most representative of our lives.

MINDTRAP #50:
OVERREACTING TO NEWS; OR, WHY MOMS AND
DADS HAVE GRAY HAIR

Your teenage daughter is out on a date. She is supposed to be home by midnight, but she is late. You are not too worried at first, but as the hour gets later and later, you become more and more anxious. As even more time passes, you become convinced that something terrible has happened. You are getting ready to call the police when your daughter waltzes in. She accuses you of overreacting again just because she is a "little" late, and she has a ready explanation for why she was not home earlier.

It is very frightening to have something happen to one's child. The strong emotional reactions that this possibility produces have a profound impact on our judgment that does not exist when our feelings are not involved. For instance, if I were to ask you how likely it is that a teenage girl will come home late from a date, you would probably answer that it is very likely. But when the girl is your daughter, your judgment regarding the odds of this happening goes out the window – you are convinced that something terrible has happened. Ignoring the general likelihood that something will happen, the base rate, is a human flaw in prediction that we will come across repeatedly as we examine investing mindtraps.

The stock market, like a parent waiting for a long overdue teenager, has a reputation for overreacting to events, whether they be news events, such as disasters or illnesses of political leaders, or market rumors involving potential takeovers, new products, or new technologies. This reputation is in fact deserved according to a well-researched study (DeBondt and Thaler 1985). Accordingly, the authors hypothesize:

(1) Extreme movements in stock prices will be followed by subsequent price movements in the opposite direction.

(2) The more extreme the initial price movement, the greater will be the subsequent adjustment.

These researchers believe that the tendency of the market to overreact is also an explanation of the low-P-E phenomenon – namely, that stocks with a low ratio of price to earnings produce larger risk-adjusted returns than do high-P-E stocks (Basu 1977). They argue that "companies with very low P-E's are thought to be temporarily 'undervalued' because investors become excessively pessimistic after a series of bad earning reports or other bad news. Once future earnings turn out to be better than the unreasonably gloomy forecasts, the price adjusts. Similarly, the equity of companies with very high P-E's is thought to be 'overvalued,' before (predictably) falling in price."

When we overreact, we minimize information about the overall odds (base rates) of something happening and give excessive weight to the latest event. This is true both for people acting individually, such as parents predicting the worst when a teenage daughter is late in coming home, and for people acting in the aggregate in the market and dumping a stock because profits for a quarter were less than expected.

MINDTRAP #51:
FALLIBLE RECOLLECTIONS BUT COMPLETE
CONVICTION; OR, DANGER: MEMORY AT WORK

After information is deemed meaningful, relevant incidents, prior cases, and other bits of information are recalled before predictions are made. The mindtrap operating here is one's memory. We all know that we can forget things, but we assume that what we recall is accurate. This is not so. A widely accepted, though erroneous, belief is that we store exact replicas of our experience and knowledge in our memory and that when it is time to recall something, we bring up this stored "copy." Therefore, if we remember something, it must be true. But this is not how our memory works. Instead, *what happens is that we store bits of "meaningful" information and when we recall something, pick out such a meaningful bit and reconstruct the rest around it.* You can prove this for yourself by recalling some important scene from your childhood or even some recent event that you were involved in. In your recollection you see yourself, but this would not be possible if it were an exact copy, since we do not watch ourselves as we experience life. Your memory has to be a reconstruction of the scene or event. Since we reconstruct what we remember, our memories are not exact replicas of the facts and are subject to significant error. *Misremembered facts are much more common than we are aware and can be costly* if a stock market choice is based on them. Your being convinced that something is accurate is no proof that it is. Bets have been made and lost because both parties are convinced that they remember something accurately – but at least one of them is always wrong. Write down what you remember, and then check it out. A little humility and verification of facts could save you a considerable amount of money.

MINDTRAP #52:
MAKING ROUGH GUESSES RATHER THAN PRECISE PREDICTIONS; OR, USING A DULL BLADE RATHER THAN A SHARP ONE CAN NICK YOUR PROFITS

We are aware that a prediction is a guess about the likelihood of something happening. During a typical day we may make such predictions as these: "John has a good chance of getting a raise"; "Our team is more likely to win than lose Sunday's game"; "It is a sure thing that Smith will be elected." Such imprecise predictions do not communicate information very well. If I say that the Los Angeles Raiders are a "sure thing" to win the Superbowl, what does this mean? Do they have a 100 percent chance, a 90 percent chance, or a 75 percent chance? The best way for me to clarify my meaning is by expressing it through numbers. Numbers provide very precise information: an 81 percent chance is clearly better than an 80 percent chance. When I use the 80 percent figure, you know that I am saying that if a situation is repeated 100 times, on the average this outcome will happen 80 times and not happen 20 times. An 80 percent chance is not a sure thing: on the average the outcome will not happen one time out of five.*

Most of us make pretty rough estimates about a stock when we decide to buy or sell it. We think that the "market may go down" or that the stock "has a good chance of going up," but we tend to be sloppy in making our predictions. While it takes a little more mental effort to put our guesses into numbers, it is very advantageous because it allows us to clearly compare our predictions about different situations. If you think that one stock has a 75 percent chance of going up and that another has an 85 percent chance, your decision about which stock to buy has been greatly simplified. This is easier than trying to decide between two stocks that have a "good chance" of increasing in value.

How do you go about putting a prediction into numbers for example, that, as measured by the DJIA, the stock market is likely to go up 10 percent within the next two months? Since we live in a technological age, we need a machine to do this. We will therefore construct a probability-making machine. Imagine a fancy piece of equipment that looks like a big gum ball machine filled with black and white gum balls. We design the machine so that it will randomly spit out one ball. We set varying odds in the machine by having different numbers of black and white balls totaling 100 in it. If we want a 50 percent chance that the machine will spit out a

---

*This means that the first time you take the chance it may not happen even though it has an 80 percent chance of happening and that it may happen the fifth time after having happened four times. This is true because it is only on the average that it happens four out of five times. Sometimes it may happen 10 times in a row, and sometimes it may not happen 5 times in a row.

black ball we place 50 black and 50 white balls inside the machine. If we want a 60 percent chance, we will use 60 black balls and 40 white. If we want a 99 percent chance, we will use 99 black balls and only 1 white ball.

Now that you know how to set the machine, here comes the hard part. You need to imagine that some dire outcome is in the balance, such as losing your home or a large sum of money. Whether you lose it is to be decided by either whether the stock market goes up or whether a black ball pops out of the machine. You are to choose which of these outcomes will decide your fate. Before making your choice, you would want to know what odds the machine is set for. If there were a 99 percent chance of a black ball popping out, you would of course choose the machine, and if there were only a 1 percent chance, you would choose the stock market. (Remember, you believe that it is likely to go up.)

Your task is to derive the probability that you would set the machine so that it makes no difference whether you choose the odds in either the machine or the stock market. Since you believe that the stock market will go up, you would of course choose it over any probability setting of less than a 50 percent chance. But would you choose it over the machine if the machine were set for a 60 percent chance? If you would, then you are saying that you believe the stock market has a better than 60 percent chance of going up. Would you choose the stock market if the machine were set for a 90 percent chance? If not, this means that you believe the stock market has a chance of going up that ranges between 60 percent and 90 percent. You then continue to narrow your odds until you are undecided between the machine and the stock market. Let us say that at 75 percent there is no advantage for either the machine or the stock market. This is your subjective probability estimate that the stock market will go up 10 percent within two months. You may not be able to pin your probability estimate down to a precise percentage, but if you get it within a range of five percentage points, say 70-75 percent, you still have a much better sense of your estimate than "I think it will go up."*

Take a few minutes to practice using your probability machine.
Figure out your estimates of the following:

The stock market will be up 10 percent
  in three months.
  in six months.
  in one year.
The stock market will be up 25 percent
  in three months.
  in six months.
  in one year.
The stock market will be down 15 percent
  in three months.
  in six months.
  in one year.

MINDTRAP #53:

MISUNDERSTANDING UNCERTAINTY;
OR, WE ARE ONLY AS GOOD AS OUR INFORMATION

We are uncertain about what the stock market will do, not because the
stock market is unpredictable, but because we never have enough
information to predict exactly what it will do. There are always reasons
why things happen, but we are uncertain about what will happen because
we are not aware of all the reasons. *If we had all of the necessary information,*

---

* See Behn and Vaupel (1982) for a more detailed explanation of this and of how to use decision
trees.

prediction with complete accuracy would be easy. We are uncertain because we lack sufficient information. A simple example will show this. If I asked you to predict your grade on a test you were taking tomorrow, your answer would involve a considerable degree of uncertainty. You know the extent of your comprehension of the material on which you will be tested, and you would use this information to make your prediction, but you are uncertain because you do not know what will be asked. If you also knew what the questions would be, then you could predict your grade with close to 100 percent accuracy. If I asked you whether the Dow Jones Industrial Average would go up tomorrow, you might answer that there was a 50-50 chance, a sensible answer if you had no information leading you one way or the other. But if you knew that a drop in interest rates would be announced tomorrow, your answer might be that there was a 90 percent chance for it to go up.

Uncertainty is often incorrectly interpreted to mean that things happen by chance, that is, without any cause. This implies that chance or bad luck is operating when our predictions do not work out; in fact, however, this happens because the predictions are based on insufficient information. It is important to understand that *our predictions are only as good as the information we have available.* People with more information are more likely to make better predictions than people with less information. A common stock market application of this principle is the use of insider trading, the buying and selling of a company's stock by its corporate officers, as a gauge of how well the stock will do. It is assumed that insiders know more about a company that others do, so that their purchases or sales of its stock are good predictive cues about the future value of the stock. (Of course, such information is not an infallible guide.) When you hear any prediction about the stock market, you want to know what information supports the prediction.

MINDTRAP #54:
UNRELIABLE INFORMATION; OR, WOULD YOU BUY A USED STOCK FROM THIS MAN?

You get a tip about a company from a friend who works there. He tells you that it will have much greater than expected earnings next year. Since higher earnings are indicative of higher stock prices, you buy as many shares as you can. Is this a sensible thing to do? When assessing information, you need to look at two aspects. First, *is the information predictive* – are higher earnings followed by higher prices? Second, *is it reliable?* Reliability is the degree to which a statement accurately describes what is or has happened.

The reliability and predictability of information are interrelated. The less reliable information is, the less predictable the outcome becomes. If information is completely unreliable, then it has no predictability. This seems quite obvious, yet in our daily lives we typically do not separate reliability from predictability when evaluating data. Tips are very attractive because we believe them to be predictive. How many of us would try to assess the reliability of the tip mentioned above? Would we ask our friend how he knows about the earnings, from whom he heard it, or why he alone knows it? Most of us would be so thankful to get this "inside" information that we would never think of questioning its reliability.

When making any investment decision, you face the problem of reliability. A stock market analyst states that the market will change course because of a shift in investor sentiment. This turnaround in sentiment can be predictive, but how reliable is the indicator being used?

A common mindtrap is the assumption that any information presented to us possesses some reliability. We tend to believe something if we read it – hence the warning "believe nothing you read and only half of what you see." The Big Lie technique was used by Hitler's propagandists because if you hear something often enough, you begin to believe it. Skepticism regarding information is almost always helpful. You can obtain a different perspective on a situation by merely asking yourself such questions as these: "Why is this true?" "How does... know this?" "Why could this be false?" "Does... gain any advantage from spreading this information if it is false?" Clarifying the reliability of information can make you a better predictor and therefore a more successful investor.

MINDTRAP #55:
EXTREME STATEMENTS CAUSE SHIFTS IN REFERENCE POINTS; OR, WHY NEGOTIATORS FIRST ASK FOR THE MOON

Often people base their estimates (what the DJIA will be a year from now, the value of a used car, or a company's future earnings) on some initial value (today's DJIA, the price of a new car, or the company's earnings this year). They make adjustments from the initial value to derive their estimates. The initial value you start with will bias your estimate toward that value—higher initial values result in higher estimates than lower initial values (Slovic and Lichtenstein 1971; Tversky and Kahneman 1974). A higher asking price for a house will tend to result in a higher offer.

A stock market newsletter says that, contrary to the opinion of other analysts, ABCD Company will earn $3 a share next year, up from $1.50 a share this year, because of a large turnaround in profits from one of its subsidiaries. If this report is true, the stock, currently selling at $15 a share, could easily double in price within a year. You are tempted to go out and buy it, thinking that even if it only earns $2 a share, this could result in a nice 33 percent appreciation in its price within a year. You might easily forget that if the report is unreliable, it is worthless.

MINDTRAP #56:
WISHFUL THINKING BIASING PREDICTIONS; OR,
"MY HORSE CAN'T LOSE"

At the age of 60 Bernard Baruch, a Wall Street legend, wrote a memo to himself about analyzing the stock market. The memo included this admonition:

> "Judgment: Consider all the facts – meditate on them. Don't let what you want to happen influence your judgment" (Grant 1984).

Probability and decision theory have certain rules for improving the accuracy of predictions, and Baruch was independently formulating one of the basic rules. That rule, which can be thought of as the "no wishful thinking" rule, calls for independence between our preferences and our probability judgments. This means that you do not let your desire to have something happen (say your desire to have the price of your stock go up) interfere with your judgment of the probability of its happening. While this appears obvious, research (McGuire 1960) has shown that it is a difficult rule for people to follow. *When people make probability judgments, they deem desirable outcomes more probable than undesirable ones.* Since our "wishes" can easily influence our predictions, some preventive steps previously presented to counter consistency bias will help you obey the no wishful thinking rule. When predicting whether a stock you already own is still a good investment, imagine not owning the stock and see whether you come up with the same prediction. When predicting whether a stock you want to buy would be a good investment, imagine what your prediction would be if you were stuck with it. This technique will help you keep preference and prediction separate.

MINDTRAP #57:
AGREEMENT AMONG EXPERTS; OR, HOW CAN 12
PH.D.S BE WRONG?

A consensus among experts that something will happen – for example, that the Dallas Cowboys will win the Superbowl – is regarded by us as a rather powerful indicator. If a number of knowledgeable individuals independently look at the various aspects of a situation and come up with similar predictions, this instills confidence in us. We tend to assume that all of these experts observed the teams and based their conclusions on their independent observations. If, on the other hand, the opinions of these experts are not independent, but instead all reflect the same information or bias, then their consensus is a less powerful predictive cue. If, for example, all of those opinions were based on the judgment of the "foremost" handicapper, our confidence in them would be lessened. Both in real life and mathematically, independence of predictors is very important because if our predictors come to their conclusion independently, they offer greater predictive value than they would otherwise. On Wall Street, however, the opinions of the "experts" are too often influenced by what their colleagues are thinking. In fact, consistency of opinion on Wall Street about the direction of the stock market is often considered a valuable warning that the opposite outcome will occur (Dreman 1982).

False consistency of experts also occurs when all of the predictors (analysts) are fed the same unreliable data and accept it at face value. Their estimates will then show great consistency but will be wrong. This happens when a dishonest management provides glowing, but false, information that the experts accept as accurate. The experts will therefore recommend a stock highly, but in time the stock will plunge when the actual facts are discovered.

The false consistency of experts is only one of the ways in which consistency of opinion can mislead us and result in poor predictions. Next we will explore how people's need for consistency can produce a variety of investment mistakes.

MINDTRAP #58:
EFFECTS OF GROUP CONSENSUS ON PERCEPTION; OR, "I FEEL COMPLETELY SAFE ABOUT THIS VOYAGE; EVERYONE KNOWS THE *TITANIC* IS UNSINKABLE"

Whenever we are faced with an uncertain situation, such as predicting the market, we tend to be influenced by others. A classic psychological study (Sharif 1935) demonstrates how even our visual perception is affected by others. Sharif presented single persons with a stationary spot of light in a dark room. Without any frame of reference, such a light appears to move around erratically. Some persons report that it moves a few inches, while others report that it moves many yards. After a while each person develops a range within which most of his or her judgments fall. The interesting finding occurs when you put a person in a group with others. In time the estimates converge on a new range on which all of the persons in the group agree. Later, when the person whom you have put in the group is making the judgments by himself, he continues to use the new range.

When predicting the future course of stocks or the market, we can be unconsciously drawn toward group ranges. The judgment of others that the Dow will go to 3,600 or to 5,000 can easily influence our projections. The influence of others can be particularly powerful in the stock market because in the stock market there are no absolute standards and the perceived value of a group of investors directly affects the real price of stocks. There is no assurance, however, that those investors are correct.

All too often, people have followed the "group's judgment," felt quite comfortable and confident in the position they have taken, but then lost considerable amounts of money.

In summary, at the heart of every investment decision is a prediction. The probability-making machine provides you with a technique for specifying precisely your estimates of the future performance of stocks, bonds, or any other investment. You can use this technique to make many different kinds of predictions that have a bearing on your investing – the direction of interest rates, corporate profits, the outlook for the economy, and so on. You should take a number of steps before making your predictions. The information on which you are basing your predictions should be examined closely. You should keep in mind that people are susceptible to wishful thinking and that this causes them to see desired outcomes as more likely than undesired outcomes. The desire of people for consistency can cause them to give unwarranted weight to the opinions of experts and to majority opinions. People tend to overreact to new information and to ignore base rates (the actual probability of events occurring). Unreliable information decreases the predictive power of your decisions. We tend to regard falsely consistent information as reliable and therefore very predictive. Unfortunately, the opposite will often be the case because the rule requiring independence of sources was not met. If you are unsure about the reliability of information, you should act as if you had no information. Before taking action, think of as many of the implications and ramifications of the predictive cues as you can.

Predictive Mindtraps:
or, How Mental Rules of Thumb
Can Mislead Us

I t is Saturday night, your one night out. You have been looking forward to getting out all week, and are eager to see a good movie. Looking through the movie section of the paper, you find that you have already seen some of the movies and that the rest don't appeal to you. However, a new movie, about which you know nothing, is starring one of your favorite actors, and since you really liked his last picture, you decide to see it. After being bored by the movie for two hours, you leave the theater shaking your head and vowing never again to waste your time on a movie without knowing something about it.

What went wrong here? Based on a mental rule of thumb, you assumed that you would enjoy this movie. Since we often associate a movie with its star, it is easy for us to assume (predict) that a new movie starring, say, Tom Hanks, will be similar to the last one. Our assumption is based on similarity, along an important dimension, to something we enjoyed. Sometimes we are right when we do this; sometimes we are wrong. For instance, a "Disney movie" used to mean that we could accurately predict what we would see. Since Walt Disney maintained tight creative control over his studios' products, we could count on consistent products. If our children enjoyed one Disney movie, they would probably enjoy them all. But after Walt Disney's death, the studio began having difficulty in producing Disney movies and the rule of thumb no longer worked.

A commonly used rule of thumb is to regard brand names as representative of product quality. Manufacturers are very aware of this and strive to develop and maintain brand loyalty. This is true whether the products are appliances, automobiles, or hamburgers. General Motors wants us to think that the brand Chevrolet, Buick, or Cadillac means something in terms of product quality and reliability. (A few years ago some GM customers were very upset when they found out that a GM division that made one of the less expensive GM brands had produced the engine in their "more expensive brand" car.)

We use rules of thumb because making decisions is hard. It requires evaluating alternatives, assessing the likelihood of different outcomes, and suffering anxiety about the course we choose. To make the process easier, we apply certain mental rules of thumb. For example, if two products look similar but are priced differently, we might think, "You get what you pay for," and buy the more expensive product. On the other hand, we might think, "Why pay more for the name?" and take the less expensive one. Sometimes we get the best value in this way; sometimes we do not. We are aware of many of the rules of thumb that we use in making decisions, but we also use rules of thumb that *we are not consciously* aware of. We may unconsciously use them to choose cereal at the grocery store, a potential spouse, or an investment. These rules of thumb are usually helpful. Sometimes, however, they result in unwelcome outcomes: an unappetizing breakfast, a divorce, or a financial loss.

The psychologists Daniel Kahneman and Amos Tversky have identified a number of our unconscious rules of thumb. The one presented here, they call *representativeness*. We use the representativeness rule of thumb whenever we predict that something – stock, a movie, or a hamburger – will be like something else because the two are similar along some important dimension. We will next look at how unconscious rules of thumb get us into trouble and how to avoid being trapped by them.

MINDTRAP #59:
REPRESENTATIVENESS; OR, SUBCONSCIOUSLY
JUDGING A BOOK BY ITS COVER

To get a sense of how the representativeness mindtrap can mislead you when you are predicting a stock's performance, you will first make predictions of a different sort-predictions regarding the occupations that people might hold. Let us start off with an easy one. If a man is 6 feet 8 inches tall, athletic, black, and in a high-paying occupation, which is his most likely occupation: (a) a physician, (b) a concert violinist, or (c) a professional basketball player?

If you chose (a), you made the best choice. On the basis of probabilities, the odds greatly favor that choice because there are hundreds of thousands of physicians in the United States but only a few hundred professional basketball players or concert violinists. Since there are so many physicians, many more physicians than basketball players are going to be 6 feet 8 inches tall, athletic, and black. If you chose (c), your choice was based on a "mental model" of what a professional basketball player looks like, and you would have been wrong. Not that your mental model is incorrect: professional basketball players are tall and athletic, and they are more likely to be black than white. What you ignored, however, is the base rate-the number of such individuals compared to the total number of individuals in the population. *The mindtrap is mistaking the likelihood that something is the case with how similar it is to our mental model or stereotype.*

To again see how easy it is to fall into the representativeness mindtrap, consider the following situation. From a list of 100 "biographical" descriptions of men, 70 of whom are lawyers and 30 of whom are engineers, the following description was randomly picked: "Jack is a 45-year-old man. He is generally conservative, careful, and ambitious. He shows no interest in political and social issues and spends most of his free time on his many hobbies, which include home carpentry, sailing, and mathematical puzzles."

What is the probability that Jack is an engineer? Would you change your prediction if 70 percent of the men on the list were engineers and 30 percent were lawyers? If you are like the participants in a research study (Kahneman and Tversky 1973), the proportions of lawyers and engineers would make very little difference to you since Jack fits the stereotype of an engineer. The participants in that study made similar predictions about the likelihood of his being an engineer when 30 out of 100 were engineers as when 70 out of 100 were engineers even though the odds of his being an engineer were much higher when 70 out of 100 were engineers. My guess is that even though you had already seen the example of the tall athletic black physician, most of you probably concluded that Jack was an engineer regardless of the proportion of engineers in the group.

This is the heart of the problem with representativeness. We ignore information about proportions or base rates; we tend to judge primarily by appearances. (Research has shown that this is true even when descriptions do not follow stereotypes.) The injunction not to judge a book by its cover is frequently heard because people so often misuse the representative rule of thumb. Such misuse is typically only mildly detrimental to us; however, it can be quite costly when it occurs in connection with investment decisions. Next we will examine how representativeness is a mindtrap when it is used to make individual predictions about stocks as well as how the field of technical analysis is rife with potential problems that arise from "misrepresentativeness."

MINDTRAP #60:
BASING CONCLUSIONS ON SOME SIMILARITY;
OR, YOU WERE SUCH A BEAUTIFUL BABY-BABY
WHAT HAS HAPPENED TO YOU NOW?

Investors are always faced with making predictions (decisions) about stocks. Is company A a good investment? Has industry B turned around? Stock C is being highly recommended; should you sell stock D to buy it? These are not easy decisions, so it is easy to fall back on a rule of thumb to make them. Let us closely examine the following hypothetical investment recommendation to see how representativeness can mislead us.

ABCD Company is in the middle of today's high-technology explosion. It provides programming systems and computer equipment. Its growth was rapid until a slump occurred last year, but its earnings are on the rebound. The latest quarter shows earnings of $0.26, versus $0.02 in the preceding quarters, and sales gains of 76 percent, versus 33 percent in the preceding quarter. ABCD Company has a high price-earnings ratio, but its expected earnings make that ratio more reasonable. It now controls 60 percent of its niche in the computer field, and its aggressive marketing should enable it to maintain that market share as it expands into new areas. Its management has been able to identify and expand successfully into new areas in the past. Its stock could really break out if it gets beyond its recent high. Now is the time to invest in this company since it seems destined to join IBM and the other computer giants. Remember what a $10,000 investment in IBM 50 years ago would be worth today.

Should we buy ABCD stock? Before we learned about representativeness and base rates, we would have found it easy to think that this stock ought to do very well. But now we will evaluate ABCD Company differently. The first thing we will be cautious about is the comparison with IBM. A company's resemblance to what IBM was like many years ago in no way means that the company will be as successful as IBM. Next we will make our prediction on the basis of base rates, that is, on how well ABCD will do in comparison with all other high-tech companies. To evaluate this company, you need to predict how much the price of its stock will appreciate in comparison with the stock of other companies. Would you predict that this company will be, for example, in the bottom 20 percent of all companies, the top 20 percent of all companies, or somewhere among the remaining three middle 20 percent blocks? When you start thinking in terms of base rates, the question is no longer whether this sounds like a good company but rather how it compares to other companies. You will want to choose companies in the top block. (The Value Line advisory service ranks 1,700 companies this way and has been very successful.)

Almost every company's annual report will make the company sound good and depict its financial position as having great potential for future profits. The question you should be asking yourself is how many companies in the stock market are being depicted in this way. If all companies' futures sound as good as this company's future, then your best guess about it would be that it will be an average performer for the next year. It is not the glowing depiction that is important but what percentage of companies have similar depictions.

MINDTRAP #61:
BLIND TECHNICAL ANALYSIS; OR, SIMILARITY TO THE GOLDEN GOOSE ISN'T A GUARANTEE AGAINST GETTING ROTTEN EGGS

Technical analysis is an approach to understanding the stock market that often makes predictions from graphs showing the daily or weekly fluctuations in the price of stocks. The activity of the entire stock market can also be charted in this way by tracking the Dow Jones Industrial

Average, the S&P 500, or some other broad average. Technical analysis is widely used by both individual investors and large institutions when making decisions about stocks and the overall market. Technicians, as the individuals who employ this approach are called, make predictions based on the formations that emerge on the stock price graphs. Many different formations can occur, and these have such names as "head and shoulders," "head and shoulder bottoms," and "triangles." Aspects of these price formations are referred to by such terms as *support levels, resistance levels, trend lines, tops, double tops, triple tops, and necklines.*

This approach is interesting because the predictions based on it often use the representativeness rule of thumb. If a present formation of a stock is similar to an identified formation, then it is assumed that the stock will perform in the "representative" way. For example, in the head and shoulders formation (see Figure 11-1) technicians explain that the "left shoulder" describes the fact that the price is climbing up to a new high because there are more buyers than sellers. This high is followed by a "normal correction," in which the price declines but then goes up again as buyers are attracted by the lower price. This price rise culminates in a new high – the "head." Then there is another correction followed by another price increase as purchasers are again attracted by the lower price. The demand is not as great this time, so the "right shoulder" does not equal the previous high. A line connecting the lows that occurred during the two corrections is called a *neckline.* This formation indicates that the balance has now shifted to the sellers and the stock is liable to decline significantly. A price below the neckline indicates that purchasers are no longer there to buy the stock, that the stock is on its way down, and that it is time to sell.

This line of reasoning seems sensible and potentially quite useful; however, since technical analysis uses representativeness for making predictions, it would seem worthwhile to evaluate the applicability of the rule of thumb in this instance. A first question to consider is: What are the

FIGURE 11-1

The Head and Shoulders Formation

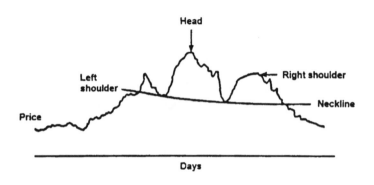

base rates for the different formations – that is, what percentage of the time is a formation followed by the predicted outcome? For example, after breaking below the neckline, what percentage of stocks go down significantly? In the books that I have read, no one has ever given data on the number of times a certain formation resulted in the expected outcome and the number of times it did not. Typically, graphs are shown of historical examples "proving" that the formation predicts a certain outcome. Information is never given on cases in which the price of a stock goes below the neckline but then rebounds.

A head and shoulders formation may be suggestive of a decline in a stock's price, but it is not a completely accurate predictor. The prudent investor needs to ask how likely the predicted outcome is (80 percent? 70 percent? 60 percent?) and what factors might cause the decline, not just whether a head and shoulders formation is occurring. You can keep track of the frequency of successful predictions based on such formations. As long as there is no bias in your selection of instances, you should be able to make a pretty good guess after about 30 formations. Then continue to keep track and refine the percentages as you accumulate more cases.

MINDTRAP #62:
REIFYING TECHNICAL TERMS; OR, HOW CAN THE MARKET GO DOWN? – IT HAS HIT A SUPPORT LEVEL!

The only reason anyone is interested in whether a stock is making a head and shoulders formation is that such a formation is supposed to predict a decrease in demand and therefore a drop in price. The same holds true for all technical indicators – they are all attempts to indicate the workings of some important underlying factor comparable to the decrease in demand in the head and shoulders formation. Sometimes people forget this. They start studying the graphs and formations as if these were the reality, when in fact they reflect reality. As a result of such thinking, there may be more concern over whether a head and shoulders formation has occurred than over whether buying interest has declined.

An example of how this can lead to problems is the concept of "support levels." These refer to the prices at which buyers have previously come in to purchase a stock. The word *support* sounds reassuring. A support level sounds like something you can count on during difficult times – like a good friend that will be there for you when needed. In reality, support levels are merely lines someone drew on a chart; they have no basis in reality. They may indicate levels at which buyers have been interested in a stock in the past, but they are no guarantee that buyers will be interested in that stock today. As conditions change in the world so too do the levels at which there will be buyers for a stock. For example, a stock may have fallen to 100 before buyers rushed in to purchase it and 18 months earlier strong buying may have halted a decline when it was at 80. Does this mean that there will be buyers at 100 and that if the price dips below 100, it will drop to the preceding support level at 80? Of course not. The realities that made the stock attractive at a certain price 6 months ago or 18 months ago may no longer exist. The stock may now be attractive to buyers at 95 or 87 1/2 or 80. But someone who sees graphs as reality may conclude, as I have heard technicians do, that since the next support level is at 80, there is a very good chance that the stock will drop that far.

"Support levels" or "resistance levels" are frequently stated for the entire market (e.g., resistance at 2,680 on the Dow), and the same limitations apply to such predictions. Because buyers rushed in to purchase or sell at those levels in the past is no guarantee that this will happen again. What happens will depend on whether today's reality is fairly similar to the previous reality. If there is a dramatic change in Federal Reserve policy and interest rates shoot up, these facts will produce reactions different from those that previously provided "support." Life changes continually, and what was true yesterday may no longer be true today but could be true again next week. One needs to act as Lord Keynes did: "When the facts change," said Keynes, "I change."

MINDTRAIP #63:
CONFUSING IMAGE FOR SUBSTANCE; OR, DON'T
CONFUSE ME WITH FACTS; MY CHARTS SAY ...

Besides remembering that charts reflect past realities that may or may not predict present realities, it is important to remember that all *"indicators" are ways of representing things of interest and are not the things themselves.* They are merely attempts to identify or measure some economic or psychological reality, such as strength of demand or buyer sentiment (optimism or pessimism). For example, stock market analysts are often interested in knowing what the "small investor" thinks about the market. Since they cannot interview all small investors, they use a stock market indicator that is assumed to be indicative of the small investor's mood. Technicians started keeping track of odd lot purchases and sales (an odd lot is fewer than 100 shares) because they assumed that small investors would be making those purchases and sales. In the often topsyturvy world of stock market prediction, these technicians assumed that the small investor was typically wrong. So if the small investor was pessimistic, as judged by an increased ratio of odd lot *short* sales to total sales, this was seen as indicating that the market was about to turn up (since the "little guy" was assumed to get on the bandwagon just as a major up or down move was ending).

As is true for all indicators, this ratio is *not* measuring a reality; it is measuring only an assumed indicator of a reality. Other factors besides investor sentiment can influence odd lot transactions. For instance, the small investor can now express bearishness through purchases in the options market. Therefore, the odd lot sales ratio may no longer reflect the small investor's sentiment and it would be an error to use it in the same way as it was used 15 years ago.

All indicators are impure measures of whatever they are attempting to assess. Some are more accurate than others, but all have a certain degree of inaccuracy. *It is important for anyone using an indicator to assess how well it measures the factor that it is presumably measuring, not just whether that factor is a valuable predictor.*

MINDTRAP #64:
"UNREPRESENTATIVE" ADVISERS; OR, JUDGING "PROFESSIONALS" BY THEIR COVERS

Professionals, regardless of occupation, are generally concerned with presenting a certain image. They see that image as representing certain things that consumers have very little knowledge about. A lawyer, an accountant, or a financial adviser will usually go to considerable lengths to make the waiting room of his or her office appear to be well furnished. Such an appearance represents success. How would you feel if on your first visit to a financial adviser you stepped into an office with a tom couch and a carpet with holes in it? This would probably impair your confidence in the adviser. But if you stop and think about it, all that the office decor represents is how much money he has decided to spend to gain clients' confidence by meeting what is presumed to be their expectations with regard to a successful financial adviser; it does not tell you how successful his recommendations have been. Yet we are ready to believe on the basis of *representativeness* that an adviser with a sumptuous office has helped others with his financial advice and is likely to help us as well.

Representativeness is a useful rule of thumb, but you have to consider other important factors too. How do his recommendations compare to those of other advisers? If his prior recommendations produced, for example, a 16 percent return on investment, this may sound good until we find out that the national average for all advisers, regardless of the appearance of their offices, is considerably higher.

Prestige and reputation can also be misleading. We assume that if we have heard of persons, firms, or companies, they are successful or reputable. There are many mindtraps here. First, *the success of an adviser or firm in one line of endeavor does not signify that success will also be achieved in other lines.* A brokerage firm's reputation for giving good stock market advice does not qualify it as an expert at putting together real estate limited partnerships. Second, *the appearance of prior success can lead us to mistakenly expect continued success although the circumstances have changed.* For example, a mutual fund may have had spectacular results under a manager who has been replaced, a change of which you are unaware because the name and *record* of the fund have remained unchanged.

MINDTRAP #65:
OVERGENERALIZING FROM A FEW FACTS; OR, ONCE AGAIN, "THE SKY IS FALLING, THE SKY IS FALLING"

"One swallow does not a summer make" is an adage warning us against another rule of thumb that is a potential mindtrap – jumping to conclusions on the basis of a few instances. We are constantly being presented with examples of this mindtrap. For instance, a recent national news story told of a store that had sold a number of winning lottery tickets and was therefore inundated by lottery customers who believed that this store would also sell them a winning ticket. Similarly, *if some "seer" makes a couple of accurate predictions, his or her subsequent predictions will be widely reported by the media.*

Why do people react this way? Because it is easy to believe that the way a small sample of events turn out should be representative of the underlying reality. Historically, if there were all boys or all girls in a family, this was attributed to the husband's virility, or lack of it, but never to chance. (Even today some people will not accept the fact that these events are due to chance.) Since the odds of having a boy are basically 50-50, we tend to believe that every family with two children should have one boy and one girl and that in a family with six children there should be three boys and three girls, or something fairly close to this. If the outcome has been different, we tend to explain it by something other than chance. But the truth of the matter is that as a result of chance alone, some families will have six boys, other families will have six girls, some seer will make a couple of accurate predictions (following years of inaccurate ones), and some store will sell a number of winning lottery tickets. The point is that when we deal with just a few instances, we underestimate the effects of chance and assume that some other factor, such as ability, is operating.

Even experts tend to have difficulty in excluding representativeness and remembering to base conclusions on statistically large samples (base rates). Research has shown that experimental psychologists, who are supposed to know all about drawing conclusions from statistical findings, will overestimate from early trends and assume that findings from small sample studies were representative of powerful factors operating in experiments. If things did not work out, they had a ready "explanation" for why this was so, neglecting to consider that the odds were against them (Tversky and Kahneman 1971).

This sounds similar to what happens to the average stock market player. If a theory or an adviser is initially successful, we are all too ready to assume that this success will be repeated. We base far-reaching conclusions on small incidents or examples. This way of thinking underestimates the difficulty of being consistently successful in predicting stock market action.

Just as experimental psychologists were able to come up with excuses for why their studies did not show results, stock market advisers can come up with excuses for why their predictions aren't going right. It is always easy to find some rationalization: "Some current event got in the way, and the market was too tired to respond, but if these things hadn't happened, the prediction would have worked out." But by doing this, such advisers continue to blind themselves, and us, to the fact that they are overestimating their true ability to pick stocks or trends and that they are using excuses to explain why they are not being as successful as possible. The truth of the matter is that everyone will strike out occasionally. This does not mean that those who do are necessarily bad predictors; it simply emphasizes once again the importance of keeping base rate information and comparing advisers and of doing so over an extended period of time. There are advisory services that do this, and their results are often covered by such journals as *Barron's* and *Money*. Readers should use these resources.

MINDTRAP #66:
DISCOUNTING BASE RATES; OR, I'M NOT LIKE
EVERYBODY ELSE – I'M SPECIAL

Buying options on stocks is very attractive to many investors. Yet 80 percent of all options trades are money losers. Why do people continue to trade options when they know that the odds are against them? One reason is that we tend to ignore the fact that base rate information applies to ourselves. For example, people who smoke often rationalize about why the statistics about smoking won't apply to them: "I exercise. . . . I have good genes. . . . I would be so nervous if I gave up smoking that it would cause more problems than smoking."

When we are dealing with positive outcomes, we also tend to ignore base rates. For example, if you plunk down $1 in a state lottery with a 1 out of 12 million chance to win $10 million, you may rationalize as follows: "I haven't won anything yet, so I am due. . . . Somebody has to win. . . . I feel lucky. . . . I need it" – though none of this affects your minuscule odds of winning. I find it interesting that the same person who does not worry about being killed in a plane crash with hypothetical odds of 1 in 12 million believes that he has a chance of getting a lottery prize with the same odds.

How does the options trader deal with the fact that the odds are greatly against success? It would be hard for most people to admit that their chances are slim – the 20 percent chance that the base rate data imply – and then continue trading.

When investing, as in other aspects of life, we do not accept the figures provided for the general population but instead often come up with some reason why these figures do not apply to ourselves. *We may decide that we will do better than the numbers imply because we are smarter, are harder workers, know someone with inside information, are lucky, or have some special talents that will allow us to do particularly well.* This mindtrap will operate in any kind of investment situation. It is easy to believe, for example, that we will outperform the average gain of the S&P 500 or the leading mutual funds because of some "special" advantage we possess. The danger of this way of thinking is that it causes us to overestimate ourselves and thus run the risk of making poorly thought-out and money-losing decisions.

Assessing base rate information provides the investor with perspective. It provides a context for comparison that can be applied to investors, advisers, mutual funds, and stocks. Base rate information is available on the average performance of the overall market, the performance of different industry groups compared to the overall market, and even special situations, such as how well new issues have performed compared to the market. Base rates provide realistic expectations about what is likely to happen. They are not always accurate, but ignoring them results in an arrogant attitude toward investing. It implies that the present situation or person is unique, so that comparisons with others and the past are meaningless. Experience shows that when it comes to the stock market, arrogance is very short-lived.

AVAILABILITY:
What Comes Easily to Mind
May Lead Us Quickly Astray

C oming home from work. you see a house on fire on the block next to yours. There are fire engines and aid cars in front of the house. Smoke is pouring out of the upstairs windows. While neighbors stand around watching, firemen connect hoses and begin dousing the flames. When you arrive home, the first thing you do is check your smoke detectors (or make arrangements to install smoke detectors). Why do you do this? The chances of a fire at your house are no greater because you saw one on your way home. It is the operation of the mental rule of thumb called *availability* (Tversky and Kahneman 1974) that leads you to alter your prediction about the likelihood of home fires and to take precautionary actions.

The availability rule of thumb produces predictions of the likelihood of something happening that are based on how available information is to us. Availability is often a good predictor because things that are easily brought to mind tend to be likely occurrences (Tversky and Kahneman 1974). However, as will be seen next, the quick availability of information can lead to a variety of incorrect assumptions that can be costly for investors.

MINDTRAP #67:
EMOTIONS AFFECTING PREDICTIONS;
OR, ONCE BITTEN BY WALL STREET, TWICE SHY

If you were at least a teenager when John F. Kennedy was assassinated, you probably remember exactly what you were doing when you heard the news. The powerful emotional impact of this event indelibly stamped that moment into people's minds. Since strong emotional experiences are more readily available to recall, they can alter one's judgment about the likelihood of an event's occurrence. A classic investment example involves people who grew up during the Great Depression. The emotional impact of their experiences altered their investment habits. Frightened by business failures, unemployment, and poverty, they became oriented toward savings (kept in insured bank accounts) and other very safe investments and away from any type of risk. In essence, for more than 40 years they overestimated the chances of another depression and missed out on good investment opportunities because they vividly recalled stocks plummeting, banks failing, and people losing their life savings.

As with the Great Depression, *anytime you lose money, the event is chiseled in your memory and is later readily available to bias your decisions.* For this reason, you may find it difficult to realistically appraise the potential of a stock on which you once lost money. You may think: "I bought that once and lost my shirt.... It's a money loser.... I wouldn't touch it again." Your mind is flooded with recollections of this stock as being a money-losing proposition, and you are therefore likely to overestimate the likelihood of its failure and to underestimate the likelihood of its success.

The success of an investment in the past is also a potential mindtrap. The ready availability of that success to your mind can bias you toward the investment. If ABC Company was a successful investment for you a few years ago and it now appears on a recommended list, you would be tempted to pick it again. You may have heard people make this sort of statement: "I think . . . is a good investment; it's always worked out for me." These people are making decisions based on readily available information rather than on relevant information.

Availability, along with reinforcement and overreaction, causes people to *overestimate and choose previously successful investments and to underestimate and avoid previously unsuccessful ones*. As a result, previously unsuccessful stocks become undervalued because they are excessively avoided, while previously successful stocks become overvalued because they are inordinately desired. This may be one of the reasons that stocks with a low ratio of price-to-earnings produce larger risk-adjusted returns than do high-P-E stocks (Basu 1977).

The undue weight of prior personal experience in our predictions needs to be neutralized. To do this, you might find it helpful to imagine what your opinion about an investment would be if you had not personally experienced the gain or loss on that investment but still knew about it – perhaps from someone else's experience (e.g., "John lost money on this stock a few years ago, but now it is being recommended because the company is a leaner, tightly run operation, aggressively seeking out new markets"). Recognize that a less biased view is possible but that achieving it requires a special effort to go beyond this tendency to base your decisions on what is immediately available to your mind. Therefore, in your investment approach and predictions, compensate for this tendency by searching out and keeping the most recent information and projections available to your mind.

MINDTRAP #68:
FAMILIARITY MAY BREED CONTEMPT, BUT IT ALSO BREEDS INCREASED NAME RECOGNITION, INCREASED SALES, AND OTHER UNEXPECTED RESULTS

Corrupt politicians used to tell reporters: "I don't care what you say about me, as long as you spell my name right." They understood that people often forget the context in which a name appears, recognize it on the ballot, and therefore vote for the candidate. There have been many obnoxious advertising campaigns that grated on people's nerves but produced improved sales because customers recognized the product in stores and bought it. These instances of poor decisions caused by availability are far from isolated. Research (Slovic, Fischhoff, and Lichtenstein 1979) has shown that familiarity with a topic, fact, or name makes it quickly available to one's mind, and then leads to incorrect conclusions. For example, people estimate deaths due to such "familiar" causes as homicide as being much more numerous than they are, and they underestimate the number of deaths due to less dramatic and less familiar causes, such as diabetes.

Investors are often faced with situations in which similar misapplications of the availability rule of thumb can occur. It can occur, for example, in choosing stocks from lists of recommended stocks, such as a list of 15 recommended stocks, a list of the 100 "most timely" stocks, or a list of 4 highly regarded electrical utilities. If one of the names on such a list is more familiar to you (a brand name company, a company in your region, or the maker of your refrigerator), you would often be more likely to choose that stock over the others. But this first, quick choice precludes potentially valuable analysis that might produce a better choice.

In summary, *familiarity with persons, products, companies, or items brings them quickly to mind, and we are then more likely to choose them when we vote, when we buy, or even when we invest.* If you have no reason for choosing among brokerage firms, insurance companies, mutual funds, or stocks, you are likely to pick the first name that comes to mind. Therefore, when making any decision of this kind, ask yourself why this is the best choice and be aware that although the first, familiar name is the one most available to you, it is not necessarily the best choice.

MINDTRAP #69:
ASSOCIATION IMPLYING CAUSATION; OR, WHERE THERE IS SMOKE, THERE MAY NOT BE FIRE, AND WHY WE SHOULD NOT NECESSARILY BE KNOWN BY THE COMPANY WE KEEP

In many situations, when two things are associated with each other, we often assume that there is a causal connection between them: "Where there is smoke, there is fire." This is a reasonable rule of thumb because often there is a causal connection between things that are associated with each other often but not always. If a new president takes over a company and its profits improve dramatically, then we are likely to conclude that the new president caused the turnaround. Similarly, if certain stock market or economic indicators have presaged the last three stock market turns, we are likely to weigh them heavily as predictors and to use them next time. This line of reasoning has many pitfalls.

There is a hemline "theory" that has associated rising hemlines (e.g., in the 1920s and 1960s) with bull markets and falling hemlines with bear markets. This theory implies that you should rush out and buy stocks if miniskirts come back and that you should sell them quickly if maxiskirts become fashionable. The truth of the matter is that the association, or even the statistical correlation, of events does not in any way imply that these events are causally connected. For example, the fact that every drug addict drank milk and chewed bubble gum as a child does not mean that milk and bubble gum are early signs (predictors) of later drug addiction. There is a "theory" that bases predictions of the next year's direction of the stock market on which football conference wins the Superbowl. As with bubble gum and drug addiction, this is merely a correlational oddity, though thus far the victory of a National Conference team has been a 100 percent accurate predictor of bull markets and the victory of an American Conference team has been a 100 percent accurate predictor of bear markets. Stock market prognosticators often present similar statistical correlations. They may say that "80 percent of the time this type of market follows this event and 85 percent of the time the market acts in an opposite fashion following this indicator." When presented with such correlations, it is important to keep the Superbowl "theory" in mind and to remember that *if we look at enough events, something will always be associated with something else, even though there is no causal link between the two.*

Since we know that there can be no causal connection between football games or skirt lengths and the stock market, we dismiss these theories. However, we assume that the new company president caused the improved profits, though in fact he may have benefited from changes that were instituted before he came on board or from entirely unrelated circumstances, such as the price of oil. To evaluate correlational findings, first *try to ferret out any causal connection.* If there seems to be none, then the "85 percent correlation" may be a statistical aberration and meaningless. Second, *even though two events are highly correlated, one may not be predictive of the other because they are both the result of a third phenomenon.* For example, good economic times such as the 1920s and the 1960s may produce both a rising stock market and a freer outlook that leads to more "uplifting" fashions. Thus it is prosperity, not women's legs, that prognosticators should be tracking in order to predict the market.

MINDTRAP #70:
OVERWEIGHING PERSONAL EXPERIENCE; OR, WHY
SEEING LEADS TO BELIEVING

The African famine was a terrible catastrophe. It went "unnoticed" by the public for too long a time, in spite of newspaper articles reporting that massive numbers of people were starving. There was little public response to that catastrophe until pictures of a relatively few starving children were shown on television. Only then were people profoundly affected, and this led to an overwhelming response-extensive fund-raising efforts by many groups, concerts, albums, and so on. As this example illustrates, reading "mere" facts is usually fairly dry and unengrossing, while actually seeing something provides the information with vitality and promotes involvement.

This happens because *"personalized information" is much more available to us than "abstract facts" and influences our decisions much more heavily.* For example, let us say you are planning to buy a new car. You read auto magazines and consumer publications. You pore over sheets of statistics about repair rates, mileage, braking distance, relative safety, and so on. Finally, you decide on a car. You are at a party that night and discuss your choice with a fellow partygoer. He informs you that he just unloaded a car of that kind because it was such a lemon. He quickly lists all of its problems and winds up by saying that he would never own another – even if he got it free. Are you as likely to purchase the car after listening to this fellow? Usually not, yet his is only one case. The consumer reports you read covered thousands of cases. In making your decision about the car, you should add his experience to the thousands of cases covered by the research, and change the research findings by less than 0.1 percent. But *in life, hearing just one person's experience can outweigh accurate statistical summaries covering thousands of contrary cases.*

Madison Avenue is well aware of this fact, which is why every day we run across advertisements that include "testimonials" to the efficacy of some product or service. A fuzzy picture, say of "S.W., from Waco, Texas," accompanies a blurb describing how easy it was for S.W. to make a million dollars in real estate, lose 60 pounds, or become a happier and more successful person. All testimonials are a description of only one case; there may be thousands of people for whom the program advertised was unsuccessful. Yet the personalized story has such a powerful impact that consumers tend not to consider how many others lost money, gained weight, or are just as unhappy now as they were before. In fact, a personal statement makes such a powerful impact that even if base rate information contradicting it is presented simultaneously, the personal statement carries more weight (Nisbett, Borgida, Crandall, and Reed 1976). This may be one reason why despite the printed statements in cigarette ads saying that the surgeon general considers cigarettes dangerous, a picture portraying the joys of smoking can still serve as an overriding inducement to cultivate or maintain the habit.

The next time you hear an ad that uses testimonials, keep in mind that you have no information on how well most clients did, which is what you need to know. The measure of a program's effectiveness is its results for all participants over a period of time, not that "one customer using our recommendations tripled his money in eight days, and another showed a 1,400 percent profit in only six weeks." After you have found out the success rate of an adviser or a mutual fund, you need to compare that result with the results of alternative choices. Financial sources such as *Barron's*, *Forbes*, and *The Wall Street Journal* often provide considerable "dry" statistical information about the success rates of advisory services and mutual funds. But this useful information will typically not have as much impact as seeing someone spiritedly touting a company, a mutual fund, gold, or his or her personal services.

MINDTRAP #71:
BELIEVING THAT YOU HAVE SINGULAR KNOWLEDGE; OR, THIS GREAT RECOMMENDATION WAS GIVEN TO JUST ME AND LOUIS RUKEYSER

You should also remember that when you are reading something, or even seeing it on television, it seems very personal and is therefore readily available. Because you are reading by yourself or watching TV alone in your living room, you may feel that the information is being presented just to you. You may think of yourself as an "insider" receiving privileged information, when in fact the book has sold a million copies. "Wall Street Week" is seen by millions of viewers, and brokers from your firm are giving the same information out to thousands of clients throughout the country. It is not unusual for stocks to go up the day after they have been recommended on a national TV show or by a brokerage firm-since many individuals act in concert on this "special" information. This should not be taken to imply that the information is not useful or that it would result in a poor investment; the point is simply that you should not base your actions on the assumption that you are the only one who is privy to that information.

MINDTRAP #72:
LAST IS CERTAINLY NOT LEAST, AND OTHER FACTORS THAT INFLUENCE RECALL AND AVAILABILITY

As you have seen, emotional experiences and personalized contacts have a strong impact on us and are readily accessed from memory. Since such events are available to us, they have an inordinate effect on our judgment. Such factors as novelty, uniqueness, contrast, and recency affect us similarly. *Things that are unique, different, or novel are more easily recalled.* Actors and actresses assume distinctive stage names so that they will be noticed and remembered. Memory experts tell us to make up an unusual mental image involving the elements of a person's name so that we will remember it in the future. Some advisers and economists are very dynamic speakers or just colorful individuals, and we are therefore more likely to remember them and their predictions, but these persons may not be particularly good at what they do. Fame and competence are not synonymous.

Information that is presented first or last has a disproportionate influence on us. We tend to give greater weight to items or facts that appear early or late. (That is why it is best to be either first or last when interviewing for a job or giving a presentation.) This bias can also influence us when we are investing. Would you be as likely to purchase a stock if you read a glowing report about a company just a few minutes before your broker called as you would if you had read the report last week? Probably not. Similarly, if you decide that you want to invest in the market today, are you more likely to choose a stock that was just recommended or one that was touted last week? Obviously, the recent recommendations or ideas are not necessarily better than previous ones. It may be beneficial to keep a list of recommendations as part of your system, to rate recommendations for potential appreciation when you receive them, and sometime later to rate them again as part of a general, constant review of your entire list of potential purchases. In this way you will base your choices on predictions of success, not on the happenstance of recency.

MINDTRAP #73:
STOCK MARKET TRENDS; OR, SOMETIMES THE TREND IS NOT YOUR FRIEND

When looking at trends in the market, keep in mind that the most recent actions in the stock market are often the most available information that you use to predict the future of the market. For instance, imagine your prediction about the stock market's potential for further gains if the DJIA went up 34 points yesterday versus your prediction if it went down 1 point. Even though the long-term direction of the market may be unchanged, a recent surge in the market's strength is what will be most available to your mind and most likely to produce predictions of continued growth (or vice versa in a down market). This could be one reason why markets on a strong roll may continue to move in the same direction beyond seeming reasonableness. Movement in one direction leads to predictions of continued expansion in that direction, and these self-fulfilling prophecies sustain the existing trend.

MINDTRAP #74:
CONFUSING PERSONAL EXPERIENCE WITH GENERAL TRENDS; OR, IT BEATS ME WHY IT WAS A FLOP; I LOVED MY NEHRU JACKET

As we have seen, the mind accesses information—relevant instances, prior examples, stored facts, and personal experiences—for use in the decision-making process. Recall of information, however, can be biased by such factors as recency, emotional connotations, and personal presentations. Yet another type of incorrect prediction is based on availability of information: overgeneralizing from personal experience. For example, you are thinking about buying stock in XYZ Company because it has introduced a new product. You want to assess whether this will be a hot new item for the company. You ask around, and everyone you know is using it. Since the product is "obviously" very popular, you decide that it will be a big money-maker for XYZ and you buy the stock. The question to be asked of course is why you and your friends are the bellwethers of popular acceptance. I recently overheard a woman telling the manager of a grocery store that he should stock "health foods for pets." They would be a big seller since she would buy them, and she was sure that most of the people she knew would do so as well. I don't know whether there is a large market for "organic" pet foods, but I do know that each of us is just a small sample of the population. We may be representative of future trends, but it is also possible that we do not have our fingers on the pulse of the nation.

Availability misleads us not only because we may conclude that something is popular simply because we like it, but also because our personal dislikes may dissuade us from investing in profitable companies with great growth prospects. Obnoxious ads may turn you off, but the profit margins of the advertiser may turn you on. Moreover, you do not have to enjoy Big Macs to like McDonald's stock. Keep in mind what you are interested in predicting – future profits and a stock's price appreciation.

MINDTRAP #75:
MORE CONFUSING OF THE PERSONAL AND THE
GENERAL; OR, WHITE KNUCKLERS ON WALL STREET

Drawing on our own experience can lead us to some other interesting but incorrect conclusions. For example, people who are afraid of flying often report that they would not be anxious if they were piloting the plane. Since everyone else would be terrified if that were the case, this is clearly an odd belief. Airline pilots have undergone intensive screening, have had extensive training, and have accumulated years of experience. A white-knuckled passenger would be inferior to such a pilot in every area. We may therefore ask why fearful passengers believe that they would be safer if they were piloting the plane.

The answer is that people are used to "being in control" in their everyday lives and that since their everyday lives are typically free from harm, they conclude that being in control leads to safe outcomes. To some degree all of us are susceptible to such mistaken assumptions. For instance, if you asked your friends whether they regard themselves as above-average drivers, they would all probably say yes (as with Garrison Keillor's Lake Wobegon, where all the children are above average in intelligence). Since only half the population can be above-average drivers, why do most people believe that they are above average? Probably because they have driven many years and thousands of miles with few, if any, accidents. Since what is most available to them is their history of "successful" driving, they assume that they are better than average. They could make a truer appraisal of their driving ability by comparing their history of accidents to that of the general population – a base rate.

In financial affairs an investor who has had a successful financial history (some good gains with only a few costly "accidents") could easily develop an inflated opinion of his or her abilities. This could lead to money-losing decisions because the investor might then decide to maintain control over stock selection rather than handing it over to others, such as mutual funds, trust accounts, or financial advisers, based on the belief that he or she is a better-than-average stock picker. This can be a poor decision when investors do not attempt to compare their own success against different base rates, such as the S&P's 500 or the success rates of various mutual funds. It may turn out that the investor is indeed much better than average, and therefore deserves to be in control, or the investor may find out that it is advantageous to let someone else manage his or her portfolio. Whatever the decision, it will then be based, not just on what is available to the investor's mind, such as remembered successes, but on a comparison with other standards that are investment options.

MINDTRAP #76:
GOOD SALESMANSHIP OVERRIDING THOUGHTFUL ANALYSIS; OR, 101 REASONS WHY THIS IS A GREAT STOCK

You hear a presentation about a new company with a very interesting and unique product, "brilliant" inventors, and enthusiastic young managers. If the presenter is an effective salesman, he will try to fill your mind with as many positive facts and potential opportunities for the company as he can muster, because whether you decide to invest in the company depends on the factors that you are weighing in your mind. If the information available to your mind consists of a long list of rosy scenarios, you feel positive, predict success, and rush in to buy. On the other hand, if that information is negative, or if you are just cynical and only think about potential pitfalls, you feel pessimistic about the company's chances and keep away.

As Kahneman and Tversky (1973) state, "The plausibility of the scenarios that come to mind, or the difficulty of producing them, then serves as a clue to the likelihood of the event. If no reasonable scenario comes to mind, the event is deemed impossible or highly unlikely. If many scenarios come to mind, or if the one scenario that is constructed is particularly compelling, the event in question appears probable." The ability to develop numerous or convincing economic projections, marketing strategies, or financial scenarios can be very misleading. In football, every play is designed to be a touchdown, but some teams never score. On paper the play is flawless, but in reality the opposition may overpower a team, the quarterback may break his leg, or it may rain. By definition, all stock recommendations are based on rosy scenarios, but many are wrong. Similarly, one's projection of a stock's performance can easily be derailed by changing energy prices, unexpected competition, political instability, changes in the value of the dollar, and so on. Thus it is easy to feel more certain of a prediction than is warranted and some increased caution may be beneficial. There will always be unexpected economic changes, regulatory delays, production bottlenecks' problems with suppliers, and new competitors. *Time and effort are well spent in attempting to envision potential problems, but this does not come naturally to people.*

That is why people are too often conned by examples of "unlimited potential" and why the need to consider potential problems cannot be emphasized enough.

MINDTRAP #77:
UNDERESTIMATING POTENTIAL PROBLEMS; OR, WHY MURPHY WAS AN OPTIMIST

The same human tendency to feel more certain of a prediction than is warranted operates when people repeatedly underestimate the time required to complete projects. Even when asked to give themselves a larger-than-needed cushion, people still underestimate. The underlying reason for this is that *the scenarios we plan in our minds are simplified schematic steps that flow easily into each other but that this is not the way the world works.* Here is an everyday example. You are on a tight schedule heading home after work, and you need a quart of milk. You decide to stop at the store because it should only take a minute. In your mind's eye you pull right into the front of the store, get out of your car, get the milk, and zip through the checkout line. In actuality, the only parking place you find is in the back of the lot; milk is always in the back of the store; as you walk through the store, you grab some other items you need and of course there is a long line at the "quick" checkout counter. It takes three times as long as you anticipated, throwing your whole schedule off for the evening and resulting in more problems and stress for you later on. *Learning to be more realistic in one's expectations about problems is an important stress management technique* that I always emphasize to my clients. I recommend that when facing any new project, you make your best estimate and then multiply that by pi (i.e., 3.14) – and don't be surprised if you still come up short.

MINDTRAP #78:
EGOCENTRIC BIAS; OR, "THE OTHER GUY"
ALWAYS HAS IT EASIER

If one follows sports, an interesting view repeatedly appears in after-the-fact analyses by participants. If a team wins, it is because the team gave 110 percent, worked hard in practice, or had a good game plan. If a team loses, it is never because the other team was simply better; it is because of the team's own mental errors, lapses in concentration, failure to give 110 percent effort. Both teams believe that they alone cause the game's outcome – it is their fault if they lose, and it is due to their effort if they win. Even when there are problems in relationships, people tend to assume a greater share of the responsibility: "I'm to blame.... I should have done more.... I was gone too much...." (Ross and Sicoly 1979). Why do people put so much emphasis on their own contributions and ignore the contributions of others? Since we are most familiar with our own experiences actions, and thoughts, this is the information that is most available to us, and we therefore base our assessments and predictions on it. This leads to a *systematic bias that overweighs our influence and contributions and downplays the influence and contributions of others.* We are more aware of our contributions to projects than of those made by others because we know how much time, effort, and suffering we have undergone. This is why people frequently complain about how hard they work, how difficult their job is, and how easy others have it. Misunderstandings of this kind produce a great deal of resentment and conflict in work environments, voluntary organizations, and, what I see clinically, marriages. This is also why good communication and a willingness to open up and understand other people's situations produce happier and better-functioning relationships.

In summary, it is important to be aware that our assessments of reality and our predictions of the future are biased. The information accessed by our minds is distorted by such factors as emotional connotations, associations between events, the recency of events, and whether something has been personally experienced or read about. Our predictions are based on such factors as our ability to develop scenarios, which may be independent of whether something is or is not likely. We tend to overdraw on our own experiences, to overgeneralize from them, and to exaggerate our contribution. We need to focus more on "dry" facts and to be more skeptical about our own views and more accepting of contrary views. A helpful technique for counteracting our biases is to take a position opposite to our own and then to assess the situation from that perspective.

ASSESSING RISK AND REWARD:
or, Everyone Wants to Go to Heaven, but Nobody Wants to Die

Your granduncle Ralph recently passed away, leaving you $100,000. Being a prudent individual, you want to invest this money wisely, so you discuss alternatives with an adviser. After ascertaining your needs and goals, she explains that whenever one is making an investment, there is always a trade-off between risk and return. She suggests that you invest your money either in a certificate of deposit earning $8,000 a year interest or in a mutual bond fund, where it could earn $10,000 a year, but with some risk involved. Your adviser believes that with the mutual fund there is a 15 percent chance that you would earn nothing (because of falling bond prices due to rising interest rates) but an 85 percent chance that interest rates will remain the same, so that you would earn $10,000. (For the sake of argument, assume that the adviser's predictions are accurate and that there is no chance of appreciation.) Thus you face a choice between (1) a 100 percent chance of earning $8,000 and (2) an 85 percent chance of earning $10,000 but a 15 percent chance of earning $0. What would you do?

When presented with a guaranteed gain or a gamble producing a higher return, *most people prefer the sure thing*. Mathematically, this preference is illogical because the "monetary expectation" or value of the gamble, determined by multiplying the probability (85 percent) by its outcome ($10,000) is equal to $8,500, and this is greater than the $8,000 value of the sure thing (100% x $8,000 = $8,000). This human tendency to value certainty and find risk or uncertainty aversive, called *risk aversion,* was first identified by the mathematician Daniel Bernoulli in 1738.

You might argue that although risk aversion is illogical if the gamble is repeated many times, it makes sense this one time to go for the sure thing. But let me present another investment problem to you.

You take your $100,000 and on the recommendation of your astute adviser you buy 1,000 shares of stock at $100 a share. One month later the stock sits at $92 a share and you stand to lose $8,000. Being reasonably concerned, you discuss the situation with your adviser. Her outlook now is that there is a 15 percent chance that the stock will go back to $100 a share and an 85 percent chance that it will drop to $90 a share. Would you take your present loss or take a chance and hold on to the stock?

When faced with similar choices, most people choose the gamble over the sure loss. You argue that this is reasonable because you have a chance to make your money back and because you do not stand to lose too much more if the stock goes down to $90. This argument certainly makes sense; however, let us examine the two situations closely.

In the second situation you have a choice between (1) a 100 percent chance of losing $8,000 and (2) an 85 percent chance of losing $10,000 but a 15 percent chance of losing nothing. Notice that except for the fact that you are dealing with losses rather than gains, the second situation is identical to the first situation. In both situations there is a choice between a sure thing, a loss or gain of $8,000, and a risky option with a monetary expectation of a loss or gain of $8,500. Ironically, the typical choice that people make in both situations is to their disadvantage. *When facing a loss, we become gamblers, are "risk seeking," and choose the risky option over the sure thing even though in the long run it will produce a greater loss—$8,500 rather than $8,000. But when dealing with a potential gain, we become quite cautious, are risk aversive, and take the "sure thing" even though its monetary value is less than that of the risky option—$8,000 versus $8,500.*

Why are people risk seeking in the second situation and risk aversive in the first? One answer is that in both situations people want to avoid "being a loser" – this is the stock market attitude "I cannot sell a stock for less than I paid." A more proper way of putting this is that people are particularly sensitive to loss. Therefore, they tend to be too cautious when dealing with potential gains, because occasionally they may come out "losers," while in the opposite situation they are likely to incur greater losses by taking extra chances in an effort to avoid "losing." To avoid taking a loss, people "may sell winners too early and ride losers too long" (Shefrin and Statman 1985).

In summary, risk aversion makes conservative investment options more appealing than their profit potential warrants, while the fear of suffering a loss leads people to choose unnecessarily risky options in order to avoid losing money and having the horrific label "loser" applied to them. When making financial decisions, an investor will always benefit from identifying the degree of risk and the amount of potential return that are involved. But typically this is very difficult to do; therefore, a mathematical way of clarifying risk and return using the "prediction-making machine" is presented after the next section.

MINDTRAP #79:
BETTING ON THE EXTREMES; OR, WHY PEOPLE PAY PREMIUMS FOR SURE THINGS AND THE LONGEST OF LONG SHOTS

A brand-new sports car is the prize in a raffle. Through a series of circumstances best left unreported, you have acquired 90 percent of the raffle tickets for considerably less than the price of the car. If you could buy the remaining 10 percent for $500, would you do it? Now imagine that this time you have 40 percent of the tickets. Would you be as willing to pay as much money – $500 – to increase your chances from 40 percent to

50 percent as you would to increase them from 90 percent to 100 percent? If you are like most people, your answer would be no. But why? In both cases you are paying for a 10 percent increase in your chances of winning the prize. A 90 percent chance of winning the car means that you are very, very likely to drive it home, while a 50 percent chance of winning means that you are as likely to win as not. The answer to this inconsistency is that we desire certainty – the absence of risk – and are willing to pay a premium for it.

People's desire for certainty can make a choice with the "appearance" of certainty seem more attractive than it really is. Kahneman and Tversky provide the example of an insurance policy that covers fire but not flood. People would be more likely to purchase such a policy when it is presented as full protection against fire rather than as partial protection against overall loss. *Since people overvalue certainty, this causes them to undervalue moderate and high probabilities when investing, and therefore to miss out on higher returns.*

For example, the closest thing to certainty is a U.S. government bond, and people are willing to accept a significantly lower interest rate on such bonds than on other sound bonds. At the time this chapter is being written, bonds issued by my home state, Washington, earn 8 percent tax free (which is equivalent to more than a taxable 10 percent), while taxable U.S. government bonds are paying 7.1 percent. The question an investor needs to ask is whether the risk of an investment is "really" equal to the reward it provides, or is other peoples' desire for certainty and risk aversion producing an attractive opportunity for you? What is your estimate of the odds that the state of Washington would default on a bond as compared with the odds of the United States defaulting? If your answer is that the odds of both are infinitesimally small (hypothetically 1/100,000 and 1/1,000,000), does it make sense to lose 3 percent in interest (a premium of 40 percent) on the U.S. bond for a 0.00009 improvement in the probability of safety? This same evaluation can be applied to "junk bond" mutual funds (junk bonds are low-rated, higher-interest-paying corporate bonds). These are seen as riskier investments than they are, and they are often avoided by conservative investors, even though their return can be twice that of government bonds and their net return has been superior even with some default.

Besides undervaluing moderate and high probabilities people are also poor judges of unlikely events. Any chance is perceived as some chance, so people tend to overvalue low probabilities. Lotteries are successful moneymaking enterprises because people optimistically overestimate their chances of winning and keep buying those tickets.

Recently the enormous potential profits from an AIDS vaccine or treatment have caused investors to vastly inflate the price of companies that have only the slightest connection with AIDS or even the remotest possibility of developing a successful product. Penny stocks have always been attractive because people overestimate their chances of success: "I can buy 1,000 shares for $100, and if they go to $1 a share, I'll make a lot of money, and if they don't move, all I'm out is one hundred bucks." No estimate is made of probability in any of these situations: for example, a 1,000,000 to 1 chance that this investment may be successful with only a return of 100 to 1. Typically, very slight chances are overestimated because people have difficulty in comprehending very low probabilities, so very unlikely outcomes, such as 1,000,000 to 1, are seen as "some chance" and lumped together with understandable outcomes, such as 1,000 to 1.

In summary, *our perceptions do not accurately reflect the true probabilities of success.* We are risk aversive and pay excessive premiums for certainty with highly probable events, and we overestimate our chances for success in situations involving highly unlikely occurrences and therefore consistently lose our investments in such situations.

ASSESSING RISK

The trade-offs between risk and reward are rarely consciously considered by investors. Instead, they are usually dealt with in a vague way: "This seems like a pretty safe investment, and it has good potential." One way to deal more precisely with the trade-offs between risk and reward is to use the probability-making machine described in Chapter 10. This can provide you with a relatively simple tool for assessing some aspects of the risks and rewards involved in an investment decision. This will not be a complete assessment, which is a very complicated task; however, specifying any aspects of the risks and rewards involved is certainly preferable to diffuse impressions.

As we have seen, *people are risk aversive and will pay a price to avoid risk.* Usually the "premium" people pay is never considered or calculated; people just decide subconsciously what trade-off they are willing to make. For example, when people were given a choice between a guaranteed amount of money and a gamble involving a 50-50 chance of making either $100 or nothing, people considered $35 equal to the gamble – the point of indifference between the two options (Kahneman and Tversky 1982). The gamble has a monetary expectation of $50 (0.5 x $100 = $50), so they are paying a 30 percent premium to be risk aversive since they are accepting $15 less than the monetary expectation (15 ÷ 50 = 30%). No guaranteed option is available in the stock market, but as presented next, investors can develop a more objective way of analyzing the risks and returns of potential investments.

One way to begin assessing the risk and return involved in an investment decision is by stating the return you wish to make. (You may have already set this figure with the goals you identified in the Goals and Plans chapter.) If you are interested in making a 25 percent annual return on your stocks, then calculate your subjective probability of the investment-stock, bond, or mutual fund-increasing by 25 percent within the next year. For example, if you are considering purchasing a stock costing $10, what is the probability that it will be worth $12.50 within the next year? (You could determine this in a variety of ways, such as predicting increased earnings, increased price-earnings multiples, lower interest rates, or an improved economy.) You decide on the probability by setting your probability-making machine to the figure that makes you indifferent between having the stock go up to $12.50 and having the machine set to some probability figure that would produce a dire consequence for you – say losing your home. When the machine is set at 90 percent (90 white balls and 10 black balls in the machine) in favor of keeping your home, you choose the machine, and you do the same when it is set at 80 percent and 70 percent. At 60 percent you prefer the chances of the stock going up to $12.50; therefore, our best estimate of the stock going up to $12.50 is somewhere between 60 percent and 70 percent. You narrow the figure down to 65 percent, and at this amount it makes no difference whether you choose the machine or the stock going up; therefore, 65 percent is your probability estimate that the stock will go up to $12.50. The monetary expectation of the gain is 0.65 x $2.50 = $1.625.

Assessing the probability of rewards is only half of the equation. You will also need to assess the chances of the stock going down. There are many different values that you could choose; for this example, however, let us use a 10 percent loss. This is a figure commonly used in setting stop-loss orders for stocks. Also, risk aversion leads people to want a substantial return if they face a possible loss (you might turn down a 50 percent chance of losing $100 unless it is paired with an equal chance of winning $200 or more). In this case we are comparing a loss of 10 percent with a potential gain 2 1/2 times as great (25 percent), which makes it an attractive proposition. Now using the probability-making machine, specify the odds of the stock going down 10 percent in price – let us say that you come up

with a 25 percent probability. The monetary expectation of this loss is −
$1 (10 percent of $10) x 0.25 = - $0.25

Clearly, you are very positive about the potential for this stock and you
should purchase it since you feel that the rewards greatly outweigh the
risks. The ratio of gains to losses is $1.625 to -$0.25. This is certainly a
conservative, risk-aversive investment that almost anyone would make.
The question is not whether you should buy this stock but how often you
will be able to find an opportunity this good. If there are none, will you
take a guaranteed return through CDs or money markets, or a riskier
investment where, for example, there may be a 40 percent chance that a
stock will appreciate 25 percent and a 35 percent chance that it will
depreciate 10 percent? A 40 percent chance of a $2.50 gain is 0.4 x $2.50 =
$1.00, and a 35 percent chance of a $1 loss is 0.35 x $1.00 = − $0.35. This
may be very acceptable to some investors but no longer to others. Finally,
if there were a 20 percent chance that a stock will go up $2.50 but a 35
percent chance that it will go down $1, would you feel comfortable with
the investment (an upside monetary expectation of $0.50 and a downside
one of − $0.35)? Your answer would of course depend on your expectations
of risk and reward not only for this investment but also for others that you
might be considering.

We would all like stocks with fantastic upside potential and no risk;
however, since such stocks are not always available, we have to make other
investment choices. The method of assessing risk outlined above is a way
to help the investor analyze such situations. It is not meant to be the
complete answer; it is merely a simple tool to give the investor some
structured approach to assessing risk and return as the basis for a somewhat
reasonably thought-out decision.

MINDTRAP #80:
CONFUSING RELATIVE AND ABSOLUTE VALUES;
OR, "EVERYTHING WAS 50 PERCENT OFF, SO I
MADE YOU A FORTUNE BY SHOPPING TODAY"

There is an anecdote about a congressman discussing budget cuts. His view was: "You cut a billion dollars here, a billion there, and soon you are talking real money." This anecdote points out how easy it is to lose perspective on the absolute value of money. Many of our daily life experiences prove this fact. We are much happier purchasing a $20 item that is on sale for $10 than a $100 item that is on sale for $90. A raise in salary from $10,000 to $20,000 will make us happier than a raise to $50,000 from $40,000.

The context against which gains and losses are compared makes a great difference in people's perceptions of money. These shifting perceptions are a cause of illogical and inconsistent financial decisions. This can be seen from a study by Kahneman and Tversky (1982), who have extensively studied this phenomenon. In one study they asked one group of participants to imagine going to a store to buy two items: a jacket for $125 and a calculator for $15. The salesman tells you that the calculator you want is on sale for $10 at another branch of the store, a 20-minute drive away. Would you make the trip? A majority of the people answering the question said that they would drive to the other store.

Another group of participants were presented with a similar question, but this time the cost of the jacket was $15 and that of the calculator was $125. The calculator was again on sale at the other branch, at a sales price of $120. Would you make the trip? This time a majority said that they would not make the trip.

The two situations are of course identical. The total purchase price of both items is $140, and the buyer has to decide whether a 20-minute drive is worth $5. But in relative terms the savings of $5 appear to be much greater on a $15 purchase than on a $125 purchase. Clearly, people's perception of the value of money is different in the two situations, leading to different conclusions and different actions.

We are susceptible to the same mindtrap when investing. For example, you own 100 shares of two stocks: Alpha Company and Beta Company. Alpha has gone from $100 to $110, while Beta has gone from $10 to $20. Will your perception and evaluation of these two stocks be the same? First, you will probably be much happier about the stock that doubled in price – even though it hasn't made you any richer than the other stock. Second, it is easy to place a higher value on Beta's stock because it has shown a much larger percentage increase. Since Alpha has not done as well proportionally, you may not appreciate the $10 gain it has made. You may not monitor Alpha's activity as closely or contemplate its future growth, even though you have five times as much money invested in Alpha, making it the one to watch more closely.

Your perception and subsequent reaction to a major drop in price, let us say a $5 per share decline, may also be quite different. You may be more risk aversive and more disturbed as a result of a $5 decrease in Alpha's price as you see your "little bit of profit" shrinking than as a result of this same change in Beta because with Beta you may think, "What the heck; I'm up a lot anyway." Even though you may perceive and react to these two stocks quite differently, a $1 drop in either stock is still $100 out of your pocket. We need to be concerned with absolute value and not relative value when we "evaluate" a situation.

Costly shifts in perception also occur in situations where we have already sustained losses. For instance, imagine that you have been at the race track all day and are down $80 with one race remaining. You have $20 left in your pocket. After losing $80, most of us value that $20 differently than we would if we were even for the day. A horse that you think has some possibilities is going off at odds of 6 to 1, and you are very tempted to bet the whole bundle, your biggest bet of the day, on it. You think, "If it wins, I go home ahead, and if it loses, I'm down only another $20." *When losing, people may be more risk seeking because they value money less and they wish to avoid becoming that "loser" again.*

The same mindtrap can operate in the stock market. When you have sustained a major loss in a stock – let us say that it has gone from $15 to $5. More bad news about the company becomes public, causing a further drop, to $3. Compare your reaction if you had just bought the stock for $5 with your reaction if you had originally purchased it for $15. The loss from $5 to $3 does not seem as bad if we bought the stock for $15 as it does if we bought the stock for $5. Once again, too many of us would take a "what the hell" attitude toward the stock, be willing to take more risk than usual, and ride the stock down in price rather than selling and recouping whatever money we could. This attitude toward severe losses is another reason why people wind up holding losing stocks for so long rather than taking their losses and investing the money they still have in more promising companies.

Losing can make you more risk seeking and a more reckless bettor on a horse or a more reckless investor in stocks. We value money less when we are losing at the track or in the market. So it is not surprising that once people are losing, they are willing to take more risks, thereby making losses more likely, and that this can easily snowball into greater and greater losses. This holds true when we are gambling, and it can happen in the market when we buy riskier stocks, buy on margin, or invest in very risky options or future contracts.

MINDTRAP #81:
DECREASING RELATIVE VALUE OF
INCREMENTAL GAINS OR LOSSES; OR,
THE CAR IS ALREADY COSTING YOU A FORTUNE
– WHY NOT GET THE LEATHER INTERIOR?

After months and months of looking, you have finally found your dream house. Of course, it wound up costing you more than you expected. You went through a fair amount of emotional turmoil during the negotiations, and it was a bit hard to swallow the final price, but you love the house. There are some repairs and minor remodeling you want done, so you get estimates from a roofer and a contractor. These seem reasonable, and you immediately tell them to go ahead. You also need to buy some furnishings for the house. You do not bat an eye at the prices, and order what you want without thinking about the cost. You, who spent three months getting the best buy on a stereo and compare the prices of peach brands at the grocery store, are now spending money as if it were going out of style. What is happening here? Why are you so free with your money when you just spent more than anticipated on a house and should be saving money? Interestingly, in a short while you will revert to your usual style and demand three different estimates for every repair job and comparison-shop for everything.

The reason for this unusual behavior is that, as we have seen, people's perception of value is influenced by the relative amount of gain or loss (not its absolute amount) and, further, that each extra dollar of gain or loss is valued less than the preceding one. Going from no bonus to a $100 bonus makes us happier than does getting a $1,100 bonus rather than a $1,000 one, and this increase in turn makes us happier than does getting a $10,100 bonus rather than a $10,000 one.

You are spending money freely on the house because you value each incremental dollar less when it is added on to the money you have already spent on the house. This is why consumers of big-ticket items are so willing to purchase additional options. It is what makes you susceptible to the car salesman who points out that "for only a few more dollars you can get these luxury options," so you buy a more expensive sound system, a sun roof, or extra undercoating for your car. For this reason you may also buy extras for a house – perhaps a patio, a hot tub, or life insurance in the amount of your mortgage. Appliance manufacturers are aware of this tendency and try to get you to buy extended warranties on a new refrigerator, a freezer, a washing machine, or even a lawn mower.

The same tendency can operate on people when they are investing in the stock market. For example, you have made a killing in the market – you bought just as a major bull market started, and now you have exceptionally nice gains. Now you are rich, as well as smart and good-looking, and you are considering buying some new stocks. You could buy stocks that are projected to have nice but not spectacular gains or riskier over-the-counter stocks that could really take off in price. In your present situation the riskier stocks may look a lot more appealing than they would otherwise. Your attitude might be something like this: "Why should I even bother with the stock for a piddling few dollars? It has to make some real money for me to put my time and money into it." This attitude occurs because you value each incremental dollar less and less, so in order to derive the same amount of satisfaction you have to make more money than would have been the case if you had been less successful. On the other hand, any loss of funds is of less concern to you because of the spectacular gains you have made. Your attitude might be something like this: "What if I lose a few dollars? I have made so much, it is no big deal." So you want more speculative stocks because your gains have to be substantial to be "satisfying," and you feel little distress about any losses. A good formula for losing money.

The fact that incremental gains are valued less and less may also help explain the greed and actions of those convicted in the Wall Street insider scandals. Their profits from insider trading were so great, and so far beyond those possible from normal trading, that they may have seen normal profits as almost valueless. They would not stop, despite the vast amounts they had accumulated, because in order to continue to derive "satisfaction" from their investments, they had to continue to engage in insider trading, since this was the only way to achieve phenomenal gains.

We often hear stories about the tightfisted ways of some very rich people – oil billionaire J. Paul Getty, for example, had a pay phone installed in his home for guests to use. We wonder why someone with so much money would care about a few extra dollars, and we tend to view this as "unnecessary thriftiness" because we perceive the amount saved in such ways as infinitesimal relative to the persons' total worth – we think that they should see the few dollars saved as having almost no value. The answer to why the frugal rich act like this may also be the answer to how they became so rich. They continue to see added dollars in constant rather than relative terms. For them, a dollar is still a dollar and each additional dollar needs to be earned and protected as if it were the first. It is interesting that heirs to fortunes often value their fortunes less than do those who accumulate them, and are therefore more likely to squander them in a variety of ways-including foolish investments. The expression "shirtsleeves to shirtsleeves in three generations" refers to this fact.

I am not suggesting that we become miserly but that it would probably be beneficial for us to develop a mixed perspective on our investments. This would mean trying to *see each extra dollar as constant and important and to react to dollars earned later as if they were the first ones earned.* This would make us more appreciative, more focused, and less careless about investments and would help avoid profligate attitudes and excessive risk taking.

Although this approach is helpful initially, it can also produce too narrow a perspective. To provide some balance, particularly regarding losses, one should also evaluate investments in terms of our total wealth rather than in terms of our gains or losses from each individual stock market trade. This provides a constant yardstick for measuring all of our stock selections. It can also provide us with some perspective on individual gains or losses. For example, we will feel much less upset over losing 25 percent on a stock and have a better understanding of the situation if we perceive the loss as less than one tenth of 1 percent of our total wealth. To summarize, we should always value money, but we should also keep in mind that it is only money.

MINDTRAP #82:
FRAMING; OR, A ROSE IS A ROSE IS A ROSE, BUT, DEPENDING ON HOW IT IS CATEGORIZED, A DOLLAR MAY OR MAY NOT BE A DOLLAR

You are given a gift certificate for two dinners at the nicest restaurant in town. The gift certificate does not include wine or drinks. You have eaten at the restaurant before, and the food is superb. When you order the wine and pay the tip, are you more likely to order a costlier wine and to give a more generous tip than you would have if you had purchased the meal yourself? Probably. Would you have been as extravagant if you had received an unexpected tax refund or a yearly raise equal to the price of the dinner? Probably not.

The perspective that people take on a situation greatly influences their reactions to it. According to the economist Richard Thaler (1985), people have "mental accounts" by which they categorize their money. They perceive and label the gift dinners as a "windfall," so they are likely to view them differently than they would if these were labeled "dinner out." They place the wine and tip in the mental account "dinner out" and are therefore more extravagant in this situation, but they would not make a larger-than-usual donation to a charity because they had received the gift certificate. Such labeling is not particularly dangerous, and it may help a struggling waiter, but listen to this message touting speculation in stock futures or options: "If you have a few thousand dollars lying around that you do not need, and would not miss if it were lost, buying a September ... contract could double your money in a week." Here money is being categorized as "lying around" and "unneeded," which can lead people to lose perspective on its value and to take risks that they would not take ordinarily. After all, you should "use" something that is just "lying around," and if you do not need it, then you won't miss it if it is lost.

The fact that people make distinctions among situations based on how they label them and on the mental accounts that they use to separate different categories of funds is but one example of how "framing" makes a difference. The separation of funds into different accounts leads to some illogical decisions. For example, Mr. and Mrs. Jones have wanted a vacation home on the lake for years. They have saved $20,000 toward this purchase, and it is in a savings account earning 7.5 percent interest. They hope to buy the home in five years. Their old car has finally given out, so they are buying a new one for $15,000, which they are financing with a three-year, 15 percent loan at the bank in which they have their savings account (Thaler 1985).

To paraphrase Gertrude Stein, a dollar is a dollar is a dollar. Except for tax purposes, all money is the same and should be valued the same. The Joneses are being charged 7.5 percent by the bank to use their own money – not too bad a deal for the bank. This is happening because they have two mental accounts: "vacation home" and "car." They treat these accounts differently because in their minds "you finance your car and pay for it out of earnings – you do not dip into capital for this type of purchase." (The Joneses may also have some concerns about self-control. They know that they have to pay the bank loan off but may be afraid that if they pay cash for the car, they may squander the money instead of putting it back into savings.)

Categorizing or labeling money causes people to perceive it differently in different circumstances, to act illogically and inconsistently in using it, and then to rationalize poor money management. When people lose money gambling, for example, they may label this outlay as "entertainment." Rationalizing the loss as entertainment makes it easier to accept psychologically. Dividing money into different categories can also lead investors to take unnecessary risks. For example, people who categorize some money as "profits" and other money as "capital" might then decide to invest their profits in "risky" stocks but to keep their capital in "conservative" investments, and thus they might buy riskier stocks than they would buy otherwise. But it is illogical to place money in different mental accounts and then to be unnecessarily risk seeking with some of those accounts. To paraphrase Gertrude Stein again, a dollar is a dollar is a dollar, and an investment should be a good investment, and under no circumstances should any "category" of money be placed in any other kind of investment.

MINDTRAP #83:
SEGREGATING GAINS AND INTEGRATING LOSSES; OR, WHY CHILDREN LIKE MANY SMALL PRESENTS RATHER THAN ONE BIG ONE AND WHY IT IS BETTER TO BE DISPATCHED QUICKLY RATHER THAN LEFT SLOWLY TWISTING IN THE WIND

As has already been pointed out many times, people place different values on equivalent gains and losses. They give losses greater weight than gains and go to considerable lengths to avoid them. They value later gains and losses less than earlier ones. These different reactions to equal gains and losses allow people to be emotionally manipulated by the way situations are presented – that is, the happiness or distress that people feel about situations is distinctly influenced by the way in which those situations are "framed." For example, ask a child, or the child in you, whether it is better to receive one big present or many smaller ones whose total worth is equal to that of the big present. Most children, and adults, would rather receive many smaller presents. There is more happiness when presents are distinct and separate. On the other hand, people prefer to lump losses together and suffer one big hit rather than be tortured by having them strung out separately. Thaler (1985) summarizes these positions with the rule that *for maximum happiness people should segregate gains and integrate losses.*

This technique is used by salespeople who are trying to get you to buy something. Aficionados of late night television may remember the pitch for the Vegematic: "It dices, it slices, it makes julienne fries [whatever the hell those are] in minutes. Also, you will receive all of these extra attachments free. And if you order right now, this incredible set of knives will also be yours. All of these items for the low price of …" This pitch is trying to convince you that you are receiving many items that have many uses and that you are paying one low price for them: "Thousands of the … have been sold for …. but you can get this entire package of items for less than half that price if you call right now." More sophisticated marketing approaches may also try to lure you to join or buy something because of all the services and amenities that are provided for a single "low" price. It is of course incumbent on us as consumers to investigate whether the price is indeed low and to consider how often we will use the services.

We are happier if we can appreciate each of our individual gains; we are also less unhappy if we can lump all of our losses together. This can be seen from a simple example (Thaler 1985). Which would make you more unhappy: receiving a letter from the IRS saying that you had made a minor arithmetic mistake on your tax return and owed $100 and on the same day receiving a letter from your state income tax office saying that you owed $50, or just receiving a letter from the IRS saying that you owed $150? The vast majority of people queried said that receiving the two letters would make them more unhappy. As vigilant consumers, we need to be wary of being presented with a large lump-sum expense – such as a large bill or a large financial loss – precisely because getting a large total bill upsets us less than receiving a number of smaller bills that add up to the same amount. It is for this reason that anyone who is trying to gouge the consumer would rather present a total amount than break down a bill or estimate into itemized charges.

If one has had a large gain and a small loss, then the least painful experience is to integrate the loss with the gain. The government uses this approach in tax-withholding plans. We feel the pinch of taxes much less because they are integrated with our gains – our salaries. This makes us more accepting of our taxes than we would be if we had to write out a check regularly to pay them. For your own peace of mind, if you have lost small amounts on a few stocks and have made large gains on others, you will want to compute your total profits for the year. If you have had a great year and have achieved nothing but a string of stock market successes, you will want to savor each of those successes separately. If you have had a bad year in the market, you will want to integrate your losses for that year with your gains in previous years or to lump your losses together with your yearly salary. It is beneficial for you to do this for yourself, but be wary of others who do this for you as a way of making you less aware of their costly actions or bad advice.

The last kind of situation to be aware of in connection with this mindtrap is one with a silver lining. In such situations a small gain is presented along with a large loss. This is what gambling houses do when they provide complimentary rooms and meals to big rollers. The losses at the table are offset by the silver lining of the freebies. The silver lining technique is used in the sale of any large item where something extra is thrown in—such as "free" car mats when buying a new car. This extra makes the purchaser more willing to accept a higher price for the big-ticket item. Needless to say, the consumer needs to be cautious anytime something is provided "free." As we were all taught in Economics 1, there is no such thing as a free lunch.

In summary, our emotional reactions to gains and losses make us risk aversive when we deal with gains and risk seeking when we deal with losses. As we accumulate gains or losses, our perceptions of them shift, so that we value each successive amount less and less. This leads us to take more risks with our investments. Our perceptions also do not reflect the true probabilities of success. We undervalue moderately and highly probable situations, and we overvalue certain and highly improbable situations. *We therefore pay a premium for certainty and miss out on higher returns from less certain investments.* The way situations are framed can affect our emotional reactions. Segregating gains increases our happiness, and integrating losses diminishes our unhappiness. The probability-making machine is a way to get an objective handle on the risks and rewards involved in investments.

HINDSIGHT AND OVERCONFIDENCE:
or, If We Are So Smart, Why Aren't We Rich?

When people first start to invest in the stock market, they usually believe that they will do well. Many popular stock market books and advisers reinforce this belief. It is easy for us to fantasize the quick multiplication of our money, so that in a few years we are rich enough to retire and live in luxury. Since the performance of professionals shows that it is not simple to make money in the market (Dreman 1982), how is it that we are sure we will be successful? The answer is that in retrospect we have no trouble knowing how to get rich. You and I should have foreseen the energy crisis years ago and invested in oil stocks before they doubled or tripled in price. Of course, our investments should then have gone into real estate as inflation spurted ahead. Then, in the summer of 1982, the move to make was clearly into the stock market, as the greatest bull market in history took off. We are also capable of such perspicacity with regard to individual stocks. For example, we have all said or thought things like this: "You know, I should have bought Chrysler at 3. I knew it was going to bounce back. That Lee Iacocca is really something, isn't he?" Since all of this appears to have been so simple, it is very reasonable to ask why we did not do these things. Obviously, because our perception of the situation at those times was not as clear as it is now.

"Knowing" about Chrysler's revival exemplifies the mindtrap of hindsight, which is a more complicated and insidious process than it appears to be at first. We know for a fact that Chrysler rose from 3 to the 90s, and hindsight causes us to *forget* the great uncertainty that existed when its price was 3. At that time, if you bought Chrysler, there was a good chance that you would lose your entire investment. The company had no money, Japanese imports were taking over large segments of the American auto market, and the economy was in terrible shape. If you wanted to risk your money under those conditions, you deserve the gains you made. Notice the insidiousness of hindsight in the statement "I should have bought Chrysler at 3." This was the absolute bottom. Why not at 4, 5, 8, 12, 15, or even 30? Any of these prices would have produced exceptional returns.

To obtain a "feel" for how insidiously hindsight operates on one's perception, think about some everyday stock market examples that you may have experienced. On a day that the Dow Jones average goes up 50 points, it is not uncommon for people to think: "I knew that was going to happen . . . I should have bought." This is a sincere statement. We really believe we "knew" it because our minds operate in such a way that we tend to "make sense" out of outcomes by immediately "causally" connecting them to some previous facts. You might tie this market behavior to an expert's prediction of a "major rise in the market," to some current political event, or to an "oversold" market. In your mind, though, you will tie it to an "obvious" fact that predicted this "inevitable" rise. At the same time, however, other facts that led to a contrary conclusion disappear from your consciousness. If the market reverses itself the next day and drops by 45 points, we make a mental shift that allows the cause of this up-and-down pattern to seem obvious. The fact that was the obvious cause of a rise in the market is now relegated to obscurity, together with the other predictive facts that never came to fruition. Today's obvious (hindsight) predictor is the one foretelling a choppy market.

To experience how hindsight unknowingly affects our perceptions and judgments, read the stock market analysis taken from *The Wall Street Journal* during the week this chapter was written (see Figure 14-1).

FIGURE 14-1

Stocks May Face Tough Hurdle In Institutions' Low Cash Position

By PAMELA SEBASTIAN

The stock market has been Idling on back roads lately. and some experts think money managers may have let the "cash tank" run too low to fuel any rally attempts soon.

It takes cash to buy stocks, and it takes institutional buying to lift the market. At the end of April, cash accounted for 6.1% of institutional portfolios. compared with 6.3% the previous month and 7.6% at yearend, according to Indata, a Southport, Conn., portfolio-evaluation service.

Indata says its April measure of stockbuying power is near the 5.4% recorded in September 1976, the lowest point since it began tracking cash in 1973. The top level measured by Indata was 16.9% in August 1982, at the very kickoff of the bull market.

"Low cash is typically something you see at market tops" says Philip Erlanger, chief technical analyst at Advest Inc. in Hartford, Conn.

Of course, investors have lots of other questions to ponder before reaching for their wallets: Is a recession around the corner? Will interest rates rise sky-high again? Will corporate profits continue to be anemic?

"In conjunction with everything else you think about, a very low cash position across the board by all money managers would certainly imply the market would have to overcome" that hurdle "before a meaningful rally," says James N. von Germeten, president and chief investment officer of Boston Co., a unit of Shearson Lehman Brothers.

Mr. von Germeten, who manages some $7 billion, says his portfolios' cash position is running around 10% or a little less.

Most money managers may be closer to the 10% level than 6%, asserts John A. Mendelson, a senior vice president at Dean Witter and a critic of cash-monitoring services.

Mr. Mendelson says that based on his own conversations with money managers, he believes "a lot of people have 10% cash."

He contends that Indata's numbers are off because it counts funds as cash only if they are in instruments maturing within one year. Mr. Mendelson says that many money managers have parked some money in fixed-rate investments of longer maturities to take advantage of higher yields, and that this money could be switched into equities.

Indata responds that "we don't look at maturity. If (a money manager) calls it cash, we do too." Indata says Its figures are based on more than 600 money managers who oversee more than $200 billion.

Whatever the case may be, nobody considers even a 10% cash level as particularly bullish. But Mr. Mendelson thinks more cash than meets the eye is on hand, or at least at hand, for deployment in the stock market. He notes some $93.8 billion in broker-dealer money market funds and some $52.8 billion in institutional money market funds. Even if only 30% or so of those funds flowed into stocks, the market impact would be significant, he says. However, he concedes there isn't a guarantee that any of this money will find its way into stocks.

Of course. institutions don't provide the only firepower for stock market surges. Individual and foreign Investors are the other big stock-buying groups, but they aren't likely to get the market started on a climb; they traditionally lag the institutions in jumping aboard a market rally. And, on any given day on Wall Street, institutions account for better than 80% of stock trading.

Meanwhile, retirement-account statistics indicate that individual investors continue favoring fixed-rate investments, such as bonds. Final numbers aren't available yet, but the biggest portion of individual retirement account investments through the just-ended tax season again was in the fixed-income category, according to W. Wesley Howard, editor of the IRA Reporter, a Cleveland-based industry newsletter. But when the market was rallying in January and February, there were big increases in contributions to equity IRA investments, he said.

A month later the Dow Jones Industrial Average had dropped over 89 points (this was a more significant move at that time than it would be now). After reading the article, check off your estimate of how probable this outcome would have been if you had not known what was going to happen.

Probability market up:

90%	60%	30%
80%	50%	20%
70%	40%	10%

At this point I have to confess that I was not totally honest with you, as some of you may have suspected. The Dow Jones Industrial Average was up 68 points a month later. Now that you know this, reread the article and see how your predictions and your judgments of the relevance of the different facts have been altered by this new "truth." It is now obvious that the amount of cash available was greater than was suspected and that money from bonds could easily have been switched into stocks if money managers saw a very good opportunity in stocks. We now "know" that it would be stupid for money managers not to do this if the conditions called for it.

Hindsight does not occur just in evaluations of the stock market – it is a general tendency that people manifest in many kinds of situations. Evidence that people alter their perceptions of a situation after receiving information that describes the outcome has been reported in a number of studies by the research psychologist Baruch Fischhoff. Just as your explanations of the stock market outcome were influenced by knowing what it was, so too were the explanations of historical outcomes by the people in those studies. They judged historical outcomes as being more probable and the facts supporting them as more important and relevant after being told what the outcomes were. As will be shown next, this tendency has important consequences when people put their judgments on the line and invest.

MINDTRAP #84:
HINDSIGHT SIMPLIFIES A COMPLEX WORLD; OR, "ONLY BUY STOCKS THAT WILL GO UP; IF THEY WON'T GO UP, DON'T BUY THEM" (WILL ROGERS)

Hindsight produces a distorted view of the past that is very misleading. Looking at the past, people perceive a world that has obvious, and often simple, cause and effect relationships. Since we can identify obvious patterns in the past, we assume that we will be able to pick out similar patterns in the future. Looking back, we all know precisely when we should have bought a stock and when we should have sold it – you buy a stock when the price is low and sell it when it is high. Why those dummies on Wall Street haven't figured this out yet is incomprehensible to some beginning investors. They really believe that they will easily predict the future courses of the market and make money very quickly.

Such groundless confidence is one reason novices lose an unfortunate amount of money when investing. They can take heart though: even an experienced investor can be unknowingly influenced by hindsight. This can be seen from an interview (*Barron's*, September 17, 1984) in which a very successful stock trader was asked about one of his successes.

Q: And made another killing?

A: I didn't really know anything about the bond market, but I heard Henry Kaufman saying that interest rates were going to go to 15 percent or 16 percent. Bonds were trading around 90. Again, there was line formation on the chart. So what I did was shorted some bonds, a pretty big position for myself, at 90; and watched the charts, and listened to Kaufman, and rode the bonds futures all the way down to about 65. Thank you, Henry Kaufman.

Here is the case of a successful stock trader falling into the hindsight mindtrap. In retrospect it all sounds so obvious and easy. Anyone can get rich this way and still have plenty of spare time to pursue other interests. But this stock trader's next answer, regarding retiring, suggests a much more accurate picture. "On my 40th birthday," he says "I retired. I was only 40, but on the inside I felt like 96." You don't feel like 96 if trading stocks and bonds is that easy and simple.

Hindsight not only causes distortions in our perception of how the world operates. As will be shown next, it also produces an exaggerated opinion of our abilities to make predictions and it leads us to denigrate the abilities of others.

MINDTRAP #85:
OVERCONFIDENCE; OR, WHY MONDAY MORNING QUARTERBACKS FUMBLE ON WALL STREET

It is Sunday afternoon, and your local football team is engaged in a tough game against a bitter rival. Your team is trailing by three points in the fourth quarter. It has put together a long drive that results in a first and goal on the opponent's eight-yard line. After three running plays, it is fourth and goal from the one-yard line. The coach decides to try a field goal rather than going for the touchdown, but the kicker misses. Your team loses the game. The next day everyone agrees that the team should have gone for the touchdown. It had been moving the ball well on the ground throughout the drive, and it could have scored easily on a running play. The coach is fainthearted, doesn't know anything, and should be fired.

Monday morning quarterbacking is all too familiar and usually harmless; when it involves investing, however, it can result in costly fumbles.

Hindsight makes those against whom we are comparing ourselves appear less competent than they are. Once we know the result, what should have been done seems obvious – everybody is a great Monday morning quarterback. Once we know that the field goal kicker missed, it is clear that the coach should have gone for the touchdown and that he is always too cautious. Many sports fans whose only exposure to football is watching it on television actually believe that they know more about the game than the coach, who has spent years in the game and often devotes 18 hours a day to it. This is why it is hard for political or corporate leaders to look good. If a decision doesn't work out, they made a stupid mistake that anyone could have foreseen; if it does work out, it was the obvious thing to do. Hindsight makes it obvious that we should have been better prepared for Pearl Harbor and that we should have listened to those who warned us against sending up the space shuttle *Challenger*. Since the errors of the past seem obvious, it is easy to believe that we would have made better decisions than those individuals who had to act in the face of unknown outcomes. *With hindsight knowledge we discount the judgment, wisdom, and abilities of those who had to make the difficult foresight decisions.*

Discounting the intelligence and ability of others can breed dangerous overconfidence in novice investors. Until people are actually faced with a dilemma, it is hard for them to comprehend the difficulty in making decisions when there is significant doubt about the future. This was shown in another of Fischhoff's studies (Fischhoff 1975). He asked people with hindsight knowledge to make predictions as if they did not know the outcome. They were not able to do this. They could not place themselves in the uncomfortable shoes of someone who is faced with making a difficult decision involving uncertain outcomes. They believed that they would have the same perspective beforehand that they had after the fact. This led them to become overconfident in their abilities: "I would have known what to do, while they didn't." Difficult as it may be to believe, even though we all know about hindsight, that knowledge does not stop the process from distorting our perception of our ability to predict the future.

That misperception produces not only overconfidence but arrogance as well. Beginning investors do not respect the abilities of other investors, the "competition" – for the stock market is a competitive game. Because they lack the experience of making decisions in the face of stock market uncertainty, beginning investors underestimate the difficult task and achievements of longtime investors. Yes, the market is down, but will it go down even further? Are you better off investing in the market or in some other type of investment? Your stock has appreciated in price – should you sell, or will it go higher? If you sell, where should you then invest? Making these foresight decisions is hard, but because of hindsight we may assume that we are better able to make them than is actually the case. The trader quoted earlier offers an excellent warning against overconfidence. He states: "Trading . . . is very difficult . . . A doctor or lawyer goes to school for seven or eight years to learn his profession and then makes a little money and comes into the market expecting to win right away. Remember, trading is by far the toughest game in the world, because you're competing against the keenest minds in the world."

MINDTRAP #86:
BELIEVING SELECTED MEMORIES; OR, I WAS SO MUCH SMARTER THEN; I'M OLDER THAN THAT NOW

As we have seen, through hindsight we deprecate the abilities of others and we think it much easier to predict the future than is actually the case. It also turns out that hindsight produces another source of mistaken overconfidence. It causes people to remember themselves as having been smarter and cleverer than they really were. This was shown in an experiment (Fischhoff and Beyth 1975) in which people were asked to make predictions about the likelihood of major events. Then, after the major events had taken place, these same people were asked what their predictions had been. In hindsight they remembered themselves as having more accurately predicted the outcomes than they actually had. Overconfidence that results from overestimating our own abilities, underestimating those of others, and believing that the world operates in simple, obvious, and easily predictable ways is usually costly only to people's pride. But *when you invest, thinking that you are competing against pussycats in a simple game will cause you to be eaten alive by tigers who are experienced at playing a game in which no sympathy is shown and no handicap is provided.*

MINDTRAP #87:
INVESTING IS EASY; STOCK MARKET SECRETS WORTH MILLIONS FOR ONLY $2.98 – VISA AND MASTERCARD ACCEPTED

Hindsight makes it seem possible to get rich quick without too much work (which is the basic pitch of all hucksters). While this desire is understandable, it is not very realistic. Yet many how-to books, investment pitches, and financial advisers present plans that make it seem possible. These sources rely on our susceptibility to hindsight's functioning by using simple and obvious cause and effect relationships from the past to "prove" how their system works: "If you had followed our recommendation and in May invested $1,000 in a futures contract, it would be worth $12 million today." Of course, if you had bought it in May and sold it last month, you would have $12 left, and if you hold on until next month, you may owe $1,000.

The approach used always makes it seem very easy to make money. You only have to do the same thing that the authors or promoters showed you how to do. But what happens when you try? First, before the fact there are never the clear-cut, obvious signs that there were in the book – these only emerge after the fact. Second, even if you actually identify the necessary "signals" and do exactly what is recommended, you may still be wrong and lose money. In such how-to books the authors tend not to mention situations that, though identical to their successful examples, never panned out. They make it sound as if their "theories" will produce 100 percent success, while in actuality this is not the case. Their methods are undoubtedly successful some of the time, but the real question is: How often do they work? Is it 25 percent, 50 percent, or 75 percent of the time?

MINDTRAP #88:
MORE OVERCONFIDENCE; OR, PRIDE GOETH
BEFORE THE FINANCIAL FALL

A friend of mine invested in a stock after it had been exceptionally well recommended by an analyst in whom he had great confidence. The stock dropped from a high of 36 to 17 1/2, then bounced around from 17 1/2 to 19 and back to 17 1/2. My friend was convinced that it couldn't go below 17 1/2, so he invested the rest of his money, a considerable amount, in the stock. He was 100 percent certain in his judgment, and he put his money where his judgment was. Unfortunately, the stock is now selling for 11 1/4. (My friend wasn't the only one to invest in it, so I am well aware of its price!) This example is unfortunately not an isolated case. What caused my friend to take such risks and lose all that money?

Intuition suggests that people would be cautious and conservative when facing uncertain situations, such as the stock market, and not, like my friend, overestimate the likelihood of being right. However, psychological research indicates that this type of overconfidence is unfortunately too typical when difficult, important decisions are being made. Studies have repeatedly shown that people overestimate the probability of their being correct. For example, research (Lichtenstein and

Fischhoff 1977) has shown that when people, like my friend, were 100 percent certain about the accuracy of an answer, they were wrong roughly 20 percent of the time. Even when people report that they are not completely certain, they still tend to be overconfident. For instance, when people think they are right 75 percent of the time, they are actually right 60 percent of the time. Moreover, research has shown that wagering money on their judgment does not stop people from being overconfident. (This probably comes as no surprise to America's bookies.)

Choosing stocks that will appreciate in value is a very hard job – which is one reason why money managers and stock market analysts get paid six-figure salaries. We might think that people who find themselves dealing with a difficult task would recognize that fact and show some caution. But research (Lichtenstein and Fischhoff 1977) shows that the tendency to be overconfident does not diminish as tasks become more difficult. Interestingly, however, as people receive training in making difficult judgments, they get *better at the task and their overconfidence decreases.*

Does facing an important decision deter overconfidence? It would seem reasonable to expect people to become more cautious and less confident as a task becomes more important. Yet some research (Sieber 1974) has shown that when a task means more to people, their overconfidence *increases* (as with my friend who invested all of his money in a stock because he was convinced that it would go up).

If the threat of losing money is not enough to keep you from becoming overconfident, awareness of the tendency may help curb it. Overconfidence undermines optimum decision making because it makes decisions seem simple and thus results in snap judgments rather than quests for information and thoughtful evaluation of alternatives. In fact, feeling very confident may be a danger sign for the novice investor. The need to climb the "wall of worry" when making an investment has already been discussed. If there is no wall to climb – be careful. This is a sign that you should be seeking out information and evaluating your move rather than rushing into this seemingly wonderful and safe opportunity.

BREAKING OUT OF THE HINDSIGHT MINDTRAPS

To break out of the hindsight mindtraps, it is necessary to break away from the focus on the past and begin the harder job of predicting the future. As suggested earlier, write down a list of the factors that you think are influencing the stock market right now and include them in your "system." If you have not already done so, take a few minutes to develop a list of your own.

_____

_____

_____

_____

_____

_____

_____

After you have identified the factors that are influencing the market at present, it makes sense to review the past and see what lessons you can glean from it. Knowing that hindsight produces distortions does not mean that we stop examining the past but that we recognize the need to study it carefully. History provides us with cumulative experiences and with insights about possible future patterns of action. If you think that declining interest rates and presidential elections have important effects on stock prices, obtain information on those factors and then apply that information if you consider it relevant.

A point already mentioned that is especially pertinent to the problems of hindsight is the need to write down your predictions. One reason for writing them down is that you are likely to have many thoughts each day about different investments – thoughts like these: "GE might be a good stock to buy"; "IBM seems like a bargain at $163 – maybe I should buy it"; "It looks like the market may go down – maybe I should sell my GM shares." Three weeks later, when one of your predictions is fulfilled, you may feel that you are a genius, forgetting that four other predictions didn't work out, so that you would be losing a considerable amount of money if you had acted on all of them.

There seems to be a human tendency to remember the positive and to forget or minimize the negative. The "good old days" actually included plenty of hard times when you were going through them. This tendency is also manifested in the stock market: people tend to remember the predictions that worked out and to forget the ones that didn't. It is very helpful to begin keeping records of your thoughts and predictions before you invest your money. (Don't worry. The market will always be around, so you don't have to jump in tomorrow.) By keeping such records, you will be able to learn about your abilities without actually losing money.

By keeping track of your thoughts and predictions, you calibrate yourself and get feedback on your abilities. You may find out that you tend to overestimate or underestimate how well stocks will do. You may find out that you expect results too fast (a fairly typical tendency) and then impatiently sell too soon. You may find out that you are very good with one type of investment, instrument, or group of stocks but atrocious with others. Learning this, you may decide to specialize in that one type. Few people are good at everything they do. *Learning to recognize and accept your strengths and limitations is vital in the stock market as well as in life.*

By keeping track of your thoughts and predictions, you also get feedback on errors that are easy to overlook – as when you are wrong in your judgment but still do well. For example, you may have bought an airline stock because you thought that new management would turn the airline around. It then turns out that the new management is as inept as the previous one, but oil prices plummet and the stock becomes a takeover candidate for reasons you were completely unaware of. Although your judgment was in error, you make money. In such a situation it is valuable to go back and figure out why you were wrong. In order to learn and develop foresight, the trader previously quoted recommended, "Always analyze your mistakes and everyone else's. I never look at my big wins, but I always try to analyze my losses." There is a stock market adage that says, "Don't confuse brains and a bull market," and there is another that says, "A rising tide lifts all ships." In your retrospective analysis, work on identifying what the operative factors were, because next time you may not be so lucky.

Research (Koriatt, Lichtenstein, and Fischhoff 1980; Slovic and Fischhoff 1977) has shown that one way of overcoming hindsight bias is to have people develop arguments for why their predicted outcome should not have happened and why other outcomes could have happened. This approach can be used to analyze and evaluate any simple hindsight-based techniques that are being presented to you. Identify the underlying premises and develop arguments against them. Ask yourself a few questions, such as: "Why does it have to come out that way? ... What events could change the result? .... Why is today *not* like 1929, 1974, 1982, and so on? .... Would it happen if_____ occurred? ... What can derail this market? ... Why might gold not skyrocket?" This should not take much time, but it could save you considerable money.

In summary, overconfidence in our knowledge and abilities leads us to see tasks as easier than they are and to overestimate our chances of being right when we feel certain about a choice. Paradoxically, people are more overconfident when tasks are hard or important. Hindsight makes a complicated multifaceted world appear to operate on the basis of simple, easily discernible cause and effect relationships. Unconsciously, hindsight produces overconfidence by making it appear easier to predict outcomes than is actually the case and by making us believe that we are more competent than we are and that others are less competent than they are.

Successful experienced investors don't expect to be right all the time. In fact, they protect themselves against the mistakes they know they will make. They do this by placing stop-loss orders, which result in an immediate sale if a stock hits a preset price (usually a certain percentage below the purchase price or the current price). Experienced investors, along with mutual funds, banks, and corporations, also hedge their positions by buying or selling futures contracts or options as insurance against being wrong. If people whose job is to "know" the market are aware that they will be wrong in some of their predictions, doesn't it make sense for the average investor to have the same humility and to exercise some caution?

Mastering the Enemy Within

The Introduction to this book begins with a quote from Walt Kelly's Pogo, "We have met the enemy and he is us." Throughout this book we have seen how formidable an enemy we are. By nature people are emotionally, attitudinally, and cognitively ill equipped to combat the market. Mastering this enemy is a true challenge for all stock market investors.

Reading this book provides knowledge of investor psychology and the market, but years of clinical experience have shown that more than knowledge is required to overcome troublesome emotions, attitudes, and actions. Changing established habits and cognitive strategies most often requires using different psychological techniques for establishing new ways of acting. As a first step, I urge you to do the assignments in this book, but more is required.

The tasks ahead involve developing your goals, plans, and individual system for investing. Some specific recommendations are given in the appendix. Whatever your goals and plans, you will find it invaluable to develop a systematic, regimented, and habitual approach toward the market. You have seen how hindsight and overconfidence make investors believe that they are more competent, capable, and smarter than is the case. This leads them to employ passive, slipshod, and vague systems and predictions. Instead, use the full power of your mind to derive what you believe is important. Prepare lists of important cues and describe their meaning and consequences so that you can assess and react quickly to them when they occur. Give the most important factors weights based on your estimate of their impact; decide whether any of these factors are interrelated and give the interrelations weights; and then put it all together in your system. You do not have to reinvent the wheel every time something happens; it is best to prepare your moves in a relaxed atmosphere and not under the pressure of a swiftly shifting market. When changes occur, plug them into your system. This mechanical approach is recommended because people are good at figuring things out but not good at systematically and repeatedly putting information together. (We have been blessed with computerization and robotics to help us overcome this deficiency.) In addition, Dr. Van K. Tharp (1989) has modeled successful investors and traders and developed a very useful model which helps eliminate mistakes.

Within your system the probability-making machine allows you to specify your judgment about any or all aspects of the market. This technique will always produce precise numbers that represent your best guesses about the market. You can then use those values anywhere they are appropriate within your system.

You have seen how fallible people's memory and impressions can be, so an important part of your system is the keeping of good records. These will provide a realistic picture of your ability, feedback about your decisions, and the opportunity to learn from your mistakes and to hone your skills. Before refining your personal systems and plans, it would be advisable to reread Chapter 8, "Goals and Plans"; Chapter 9, "Information Processing"; and Chapter 10, "Predictions."

People are emotionally volatile and often go to excesses – strangely enough, just like the stock market. It is essential to learn how to act contrary to your gut reactions (feelings) when your mind or system calls for it. As you have seen, this is very difficult to do. An approach that can be helpful involves preparing for the real thing by imagining different problematic situations and then picturing yourself coping with them.

Such athletes as Jack Nicklaus and Jean-Claude Killy have reported doing this on their own, and recently psychologists have used this approach with Olympic athletes and professional sports stars to enhance their performance in the toughest and most tension-filled competitions in the world (Suinn 1983). If this approach helps beat the best athletes in the world, it could also help you beat the market. Jot down as many aspects of the different scenes as you can. Describe what the market is doing, how you are reacting, and where you are likely to be when you are grappling with the decision. Imagine as detailed and realistic a picture as possible. The usual approach has the individual relax, imagine the scene, and then picture himself or herself as actually coping with it. A very quick relaxation technique is provided in Chapter 1, "Fear on Wall Street." If you do not find this technique sufficient, then you might consult some of the numerous books on relaxation that are available in the psychology section of public libraries or bookstores.

For example, to practice controlling fear, imagine situations where the market is falling and there are many predictions of worse times ahead. See yourself as wanting to buy stocks but as being afraid that you will lose your money very quickly. Feel the fear. Picture yourself as facing that wall of worry – all of the reasons to be fearful. Next picture yourself as coping by using the four steps for controlling disturbing emotions:

1. Write down a description of the situation.

2. Identify the facts of the situation, and divide them into lists of positives and negatives.

3. Get perspective on the situation.

4. Based on the information now available, develop different outcomes or scenarios for the future.

We need to understand that our attitudes and our perceptions of situations are a constant source of bias. None of us see reality; what we see is only our own version of reality. However, our version must not be so far removed from the market's reality that it is costly to us. Investors must understand that they are never impartial judges of information and neutral predictors of the future. Our need for consistency is a pervasive mindtrap. It biases us toward maintaining present positions and attitudes. Once we are committed in one direction, it is very difficult for us to change our market positions. Practice imagining that you hold a position opposite to your current one, and become aware of how your feelings, thoughts, and predictions change when you do this. Also practice changing positions when you believe that the weight of evidence has shifted. We accept confirming information but are skeptical of contradictory facts. It requires practice and great effort to keep an open mind to discomforting news. For example, imagine feeling worried about a stock that you own because it has just taken a big hit in price, and then studying, not just reading, a newspaper article that is very negative about the company.

As was discussed in Chapter 10, "Predictions," the market is 100 percent predictable, but we are never aware of all the factors that are influencing it. A major factor that confuses novice investors is that the market anticipates future events, whereas people are designed to react to present events. This means that the market leads the general economy by six to nine months, so when we are seeing an economic boom, the market may already be anticipating bust, and when the bad economic news is appearing, the market may already be anticipating better times ahead. We will always be confused and months behind the general market if we do not keep this fact in mind. It requires experience and practice to focus on leading indicators and tune in to the factors that are moving the market.

The importance of regularly devoting a specified amount of time to investment planning has been stressed repeatedly. But the necessary habits are difficult to establish. First, you want to make the physical environment as comfortable and pleasurable as possible. The advantage of starting small and associating the new habits with an already established habit was presented earlier. People who are already well organized and highly motivated will require nothing else to establish good investment planning habits. But for the vast majority of readers, more will be needed. So once you decide when and where your investment planning will be done, reinforce or reward yourself for actually doing it. Since establishing a new productive habit is very difficult to do, you deserve some reward for doing it. As discussed earlier, what one person finds rewarding may not be rewarding for another person, so the rewards you give yourself must be rewards that appeal to you. For some people, checking off a completed assignment on a list or a calendar is enough of a reward. Other people reward themselves by engaging in some very pleasant activity – reading the paper, watching a football game. Still others treat themselves to something special – a dessert, a snack, or a small purchase. Some people imagine getting money or give themselves play money for doing their investment planning. A similar approach is to give yourself points for each completed assignment and then to give yourself some very special large prize when you have earned enough points. Think about how you might reward yourself to establish good investment habits. Although the ideas suggested may seem simplistic, if you want to establish good investment habits, you will find that some type of self-reward system will make doing this easier.

Repetition is the basic requirement for developing any new habit. An old story will highlight this point. A young boy in New York was to be picked up by his father near Carnegie Hall following his violin lesson. He lost his way, so he asked a passerby, "Excuse me, sir, but how do you get to Carnegie Hall?" The man looked down at the boy clutching his violin case and patiently answered, "Practice, my son, practice." Those words are the key to overcoming the well-established but inappropriate habits and mindtraps described in this book, so "practice, my friends, practice."

Finally, I would advise you not to take all of this too seriously. Remember that what we are talking about is only money and that the market will continually be a challenge because you will never totally master it – so have fun along the way.

NEW IDEAS AND FINAL THOUGHTS:
or, The Continuing Challenges of Investing

In this concluding chapter to the second edition of *Mindtraps*, I want to re-emphasize three challenges constantly facing investors: 1) The necessity of committing sufficient time, thought and energy to your investing 2) Overcoming unproductive investment approaches and 3) Making decisions in the face of uncertainty, and confronting any losses head on. I also want to present a new way of overcoming emotions that hinder financial success.

Many novice investors quickly learn a surprising lesson. *It is easier to earn money than to keep it.* There are a number of reasons it is so hard to keep our money. Investing is the most consistently competitive game in the world, significantly more competitive than one's daily occupation. Therefore, you have to stay on your toes because the financial world is often a zero sum game where there is a losing side for every winning transaction. This means there are professionals, people who invest for a living, constantly working to get your money. Further, as was discussed throughout *Mindtraps,* the rules and actions of investing are often quite different from those that produce success in other spheres of our lives. This is why it is so important to be aware of our approach to investing and overcome our mindtraps – because the competition already has done so.

People have different levels of involvement in their approach to investing. It may range from monthly purchases of a favorite mutual fund to daily trading and constant monitoring of the stock market. Successful investing requires a commitment of time, thought and energy commensurate to your level of involvement, not just a willingness to play the game. It is easy for novices to start investing and then become complacent about their purchases and pay sporadic attention to the market. They may soon suffer significant losses because they forget that others are playing the game at a different level. Those investors are constantly involved, intense and with an eye to the jugular.

For most investors it is harder to change old unproductive investment styles than they anticipate. One's current investment predilections reflect the sum total of *all* one's life experiences. Our present approach is our *best* effort – given the totality of a person's knowledge, experience, personality and emotional makeup. Change is difficult because when all pluses and minuses are weighed, those decisions are our optimum approach not some slap dash acts. This is why so many investors do not "learn" from their mistakes and continue to repeat the same errors. A chilling example is financial scam artists using telephone lists of investors who have lost money in previous fraudulent schemes to sign up prospects for new scams. One definition of insanity is doing the same things over and over and expecting a different outcome. If you were a football coach and your team was losing 21-0 at half time, would you keep the same game plan or change it? If you feel that you are losing in the investment game then it is time to alter your *investment* game plan.

If you have been investing unsuccessfully for a while, realize that your results are not due to chance, bad luck, or bad advice, but reflect who you are as an investor. To begin turning things around review your actions and strategies. One repeats the same unsuccessful approach because *more productive ways are too emotionally painful or troublesome* (and even generally poor approaches do occasionally succeed). So just thinking, "I'll do better next time" is not enough. Hold a mirror up to yourself and find your problem areas. Are you systematic in your approach? Have you set up goals and standards? Do you follow good investment habits? Do you lack confidence and fear "pulling the trigger"? Are you tossed about in your investment choices by whatever emotional currents are carrying you that day? For most investors, *emotions* control their investment decisions – *greed drives them to buy and fear drives them to sell*. We feel greedy when the market has been shooting up, (and is therefore open to a correction) and we are fearful when the market has fallen (and is now ready to bounce back). When emotions control our actions, instead of realistic assessments of risk and return, poor results are sure to follow.

Once you have identified your issues, develop your personal plan for correcting them. Problem areas and ways of overcoming them are covered in great detail in the book; however, you need to marshal significant effort in order to undo your unproductive habits. Change is always discomforting. It requires a willingness to experience unpleasant emotions, a commitment to overcome well-established habits, and having new and well-defined alternatives to use in their stead.

The defining tasks of investing are to make decisions in the face of uncertainty and to deal with the consequences of wrong choices. This is why the most troublesome emotions for investors to cope with center around *losses*. It is impossible to know where any stock, bond, mutual fund, option or futures contract will be tomorrow, a month from now or a year from now. Because all investments are unpredictable, by definition active investing means you will make wrong choices and lose money. All professional investors accept this fact, take their losses, and move on. In your mind you think "of course – that's obvious," but investors' hearts often do not accept this fact and stubbornly resist taking a loss. The non-acceptance of this *reality*, just like the non-acceptance of other realities, is what causes psychological, emotional and financial problems. Emotional problems in life derive from not accepting realities, whether it is the aging process, that "life is not fair", or your stock's price is sinking like a stone.

A cardinal rule of investing is *cut your losses and let your profits run*. This is simple, straightforward and easy to comprehend. A ten year-old child could do it. I am willing to bet that even though you have known this axiom there have been instances where you did not follow it. Coming to grips with losses and being able to control them may be the most important lesson any investor learns. While this concept is covered in the book a number of times, I want to present an additional way to deal with it.

When people lose money they can feel fear, anxiety, embarrassment, sadness, sense of failure or low self worth. These emotions are painful. We defend against the pain through diversions, wishful thinking or denial. People may drink or take drugs, bury their heads in the sand, or pick a fight with their spouses to avoid those "bad" feelings. Not being willing to accept the emotions resulting from making a wrong decision can cause small losses to become major losses. Even nest eggs can disappear as people continue to avoid bad news or take unwarranted risks – remember that people are risk aversive when it comes to gains, but risk seeking when dealing with losses. Once a stock is down it is easier to accept greater risks and think "maybe it *will* go down few more points, but there is still a chance it will go back to its purchase price." We repeat these same hopeful thoughts as our stock sinks further and further.

In order to be successful in the market you need to accept the reality that you are dealing with an unpredictable entity and therefore you *will* lose money. Investors are typically not that affected by the *actual monetary loss*, but they have difficulty tolerating the *feeling* associated with the loss. An investor must be willing to feel those painful emotions rather than "run" from them. Years of clinical and personal experience attest to the fact that this is easier said than done. It takes a leap of faith for people to believe that in the long run it will be easier and less disturbing to just feel the bad feeling rather than "run" from it. When you allow yourself to feel "bad" then you can transcend the feeling and overcome the fears and problems. Let me share a personal experience about pain as an example of what happens when one is willing to feel bad, rather than "running" from the painful feeling.

When I was in graduate school I was playing a pick up basketball game and, although I did not know it at the time, tore the ligaments in my ankle. I went to the student health service, and with the typical interest and expertise that university health service doctors are famous for, my ankle went unexamined and I was handed an Ace bandage. So I was in pain for about a week until I went to the hospital where it was examined, X-rayed and casted. During that week I discovered that when I would not accept the pain because I "had to" study or go somewhere, the pain was excruciating and I "could not stand it." I wanted it just to be "taken" away. But when I was willing to accept being in pain and was not fighting against it, it became tolerable. I was able to live with it and work around it.

I would argue that investors need to be willing to feel the pain of a loss – not fight, deny or run from it. You have to be willing to be "wrong", feel that you made a "bad" choice and accept the fact that you *lost* money. A constant theme of *Mindtraps* is that we make our best decisions when we have the clearest view of the financial environment. Running from our emotions means turning away from reality. So we want to be aware of what we are feeling, try to diffuse it or transcend it, because only then can we accurately perceive the situation.

Acting rationally means *always* preparing for losses by establishing reasonable stop loss points. Does this mean that the stock will not then turn around and skyrocket to new highs? No, this can absolutely happen. The market is not completely predictable. You will be wrong some of the time with stop loss decisions; however, you will be successful over time if you cut your losses and let your profits run. If you hold on to your losers in fear that the day after you sell it will go back up, you will lose money in the market. Like death and taxes, losses will always be with us. Prepare for losses and have the courage to face and deal with them. Make them learning experiences – the only benefit of losing money.

The best investment you can make is to become a better investor. It is easier to earn money than to keep it, so prepare yourself for the world of investing. Take what you have learned about the psychology of investing, pitfalls to avoid and ways of overcoming troublesome emotions and habits; then apply it to yourself. Next provide the most important ingredients – *the commitment of time and energy* – to learn and hone your skills This will make you more successful and better able to reach your investment goals.

If you'd like to pursue the journey into peak performance investing and trading, Dr. Van K. Tharp's home study course is an excellent first step. Information is contained on the last page of this book. In addition, you may receive a free report on dealing with emotions just by sending in the card or calling the International Institute of Trading, Inc. at (919) 362-5591.

BIBLIOGRAPHY

Asch, S. E. "Opinions and Social Pressure." *Scientific American 193* (1955), pp. 31-35.

Basu, S. "Investment Performance of Common Stocks in Relation to Their Price-Earnings Ratios: A Test of the Efficient Market Hypothesis." *Journal of Finance 32* (1977), pp. 663-82.

Behn, R., and J. Vaupel. *Quick Analysis for Busy Decision Makers.* NY: Basic Books, 1982.

DeBondt, W. F. M., and R. Thaler. "Does the Stock Market Overreact?" *Journal of Finance 40* (1985), pp. 793-807.

Dreman, D. *The New Contrarian Investment Strategy.* NY: Random House, 1982.

Festinger, L. A. *Theory of Cognitive Dissonance.* Stanford, CA: Stanford University Press, 1957.

Festinger, L., and J. M. Carlsmith. "Cognitive Consequences of Forced Compliance." *Journal of Abnormal and Social Psychology 58* (1959), pp. 203-10.

Fischhoff, B. "Hindsight = Foresight: The Effect of Outcome Knowledge on Judgment under Uncertainty." *Journal of Experimental Psychology. Human Perception and Performance 1* (1975), pp. 288-99.

Fischhoff, B., and R. Beyth. "'I Knew It Would Happen'-Remembered Probabilities of Once-Future Things." *Organizational Behavior and Human Performance 13* (1975), pp. 1-16.

Grant, J. *Bernard Baruch: The Adventures of a Wall Street Legend.* NY: Simon & Schuster, 1984.

Heider, F. "Attitudes and Cognitive Organization." *Journal of Psychology* 21 (1946), pp. 107-12.

Kahneman, D., and A. Tversky. "On the Psychology of Prediction." *Psychological Review 80* (1973), pp. 237-51. "The Psychology of Preferences." *Scientific American 246* (1982), pp. 160-73.

Koriatt, A., S. Lichtenstein, and B. Fischhoff. "Reasons for Confidence." *Journal of Experimental Psychology: Human Learning and Memo 6*, 1980.

Lefevre, E. *Reminiscences of a Stock Operator.* New York: George H. Doran, 1923.

Lichtenstein, S., and B. Fischhoffi. "Do Those Who Know More Also Know More about How Much They Know? The Calibration of Probability Judgments." *Organizational Behavior and Human Performance 20* (1977), 159-83.

Lord, C., M. R. Lepper, and L. Ross. "Biased Assimilation and Attitude Polarization: The Effects of Prior Theories on Subsequently Considered Evidence." *Journal of Personality and Social Psychology 37* (1970), 2098-110.

McGuire, W. J. "Cognitive Consistency and Attitude Change." *Journal of Abnormal and Social Psychology 60* (1960), pp. 354-58.

Nisbett, R. E., E. Borgida, R. Crandall, and H. Reed. "Popular Inductions: Information Is Not Necessarily Informative." In J. S. Carroll and J. W. Payne, eds. *Cognition and Social Behavior.* Hillsdale, NJ: Erlbaum, 1976.

Oskamp, S. "Overconfidence in Case-Study Judgments." *Journal of Consulting Psychology 29* (1965), 261-65.

Ross, M., and F. Sicoly. "Egocentric Biases in Availability and Attribution." *Journal of Personality and Social Psychology 37* (1979), pp. 322-36.

Sharif, M. "A Study of Some Social Factors in Perception." *Archives of Psychology* 27 (1935), no. 187.

Shefrin, H., and M. Statman. "The Disposition to Sell Winners Too Early and Ride Losers Too Long: Theory and Evidence." *Journal of Finance 55* (1985), pp. 777-91.

Sieber, J. "Effects of Decision Importance on Ability to Generate Warranted Subjective Uncertainty." *Journal of Personality and Social Psychology* 30 (1974), pp. 688-94.

Slovic, P. "Analyzing the Expert Judge: A Descriptive Study of a Stockbroker's Decision Processes." *Journal of Applied Psychology 53* (1969), pp. 255-63.

Slovic, P., and B. Fischhoff. "On the Psychology of Experimental Surprises." *Journal of Experimental Psychology: Human Perception and Performance 3* (1977), pp. 544-51.

Slovic, P., B. Fischhoff, and S. Lichtenstein. "Behavioral Decision Theory." *Annual Review of Psychology 28* (1977), pp. 1-39.

Slovic, P., D. Fleissner, and W. S. Bauman. "Analyzing the Use of Information in Investment Decision Making: A Methodological Proposal." *Journal of Business 45* (1972), pp. 283-301.

Slovic, P., and S. Lichtenstein. "Comparison of Bayesian and Regression Approaches to the Study of Information Processing in Judgment." *Organizational Behavior and Human Performance 6*(1971), pp.649-744.

Smith, A. *The Money Game*, NY: Random House, 1968.

Suinn, R. "Imagery and Sports." In A. Sheikh, ed. *Imagery: Current Theory, Research, and Application.* NY: John Wiley & Sons, 1983.

Thaler, R. "Mental Accounting and Consumer Choice." *Marketing Science* 4(1985), pp. 199-214.

Tharp, Van K. "The Peak Performance Course for Investors and Traders." Raleigh, NC: Van K. Tharp Associates

Tversky, A., and D. Kahneman. "The Belief in the 'Law of Small Numbers.'" *Psychological Bulletin* 76 (1971), pp. 105-10.

- - - . "Judgment Under Uncertainty: Heuristics and Biases." *Science 185* (1974), pp. 1124-31.

- - - . "Availability: A Heuristic for Judging Frequency and Probability." In D. Kahneman, P. Slovic, and A. Tversky, eds. *Judgment under Uncertainty: Heuristics and Biases.* NY: Cambridge University Press, 1982.

APPENDIX

Get a Free Report, Newsletter, and Audio Cassette

The free report contains 24 proven money-making secrets from Dr. Van K. Tharp that you can put to use right now! It includes information on the following:
- Building self-confidence while learning discipline and emotional control in your investing/trading.
- Learning how to assess your risk tolerance and devising methods that are right for you.
- Dealing with trading mistakes immediately so you don't repeat them.
- And much, much more!

The newsletter is a 12-page insightful interview with peak performance coach Dr. Van K. Tharp. Dr. Tharp candidly answers the most commonly asked questions about what makes people successful at trading and investing.

The audio cassette was recorded during one of Dr. Tharp's seminars and features Dr. Tharp presenting an introduction and overview on his model for trading success.

Information Request Form

Name _____

Address _____

City _____ State _____ Zip _____

Country _____

Phone _____ Fax _____

I'm interested in (check one or more):

☐ Free report on 24 Proven Money-Making Secrets.
☐ Free newsletter interview with Dr. Van K. Tharp.
☐ Free audio cassettee (please enclose $3 to cover postage/handling in USA & Canada; $6 for all other countries).
☐ Send me more information on your products and services.

Please mail this card with appropriate handling charges, if necessary, to:
International Institute of Trading Mastery, Inc.
8303 Belgium Street — Raleigh, NC 27606
(919) 362-5591 — (919) 362-6020